The Political Economy of

Human Service Programs

**CONTEMPORARY STUDIES IN
APPLIED BEHAVIORAL SCIENCE, VOLUME 5**

Editor: Louis A. Zurcher, *Ashbel Smith Professor of Social Work and Sociology
School of Social Work, The University of Texas at Austin*

CONTEMPORARY STUDIES IN APPLIED BEHAVIORAL SCIENCE

Series Editor: Louis A. Zurcher
School of Social Work,
University of Texas at Austin

IN MEMORIAM

Louis A. Zurcher, Ashbel Smith Professor of Social
Work and Sociology, The University of Texas at Austin.

1936 - 1988

The Political Economy of Human Service Programs

by DAVID M. AUSTIN
School of Social Work
The University of Texas
at Austin

 JAI PRESS INC.

Greenwich, Connecticut   *London, England*

Library of Congress Cataloging-in-Publication Data
Austin, David M.
  The political economy of human service programs / by David M. Austin.
  p. cm.—(Contemporary studies in applied behavioral science: v.5)
  Bibliography: p.
  Includes index.
  ISBN 0-89232-958-0
  1. Human services—Economic aspects—United States. 2. Public welfare—Economic
aspects—United States. 3. Voluntarism—Economic aspects—United States. 4. United States—
Social policy.
  I. Title. II. Series
HV91.A.92 1988
361.6′1′0973—dc19

                                                                    88-9043

Copyright © 1988 by JAI PRESS INC.
55 Old Post Road, No. 2
Greenwich, Connecticut 06836

JAI PRESS INC.
3 Henrietta Street
London WC2E 8LU
England

ISBN: 0-89232-958-0

Library of Congress Catalog Number: 88-9043

Manufactured in the United States of America

CONTENTS

Acknowledgments

The beginning of the ideas on which this book is based go back some two decades to my experiences as a student, and then faculty member, at the Florence Heller Graduate School for Advanced Studies in Social Welfare at Brandeis University. But the most important influence in developing the focus of this book on the distinctive political economy of human services was my participation in the Conference on Human Service Organizations and Organizational Theory, organized by Dr. Herman Stein of Case Western Reserve University, held at the Center for Advanced Study in the Behavioral Sciences at Palo Alto in 1979.

The development of a paper for that conference, which was supported by the Lois and Samuel Silberman Fund, on "The Political Economy of Social Benefit Organizations" resulted in support by the Fund for the early stages of preparing this book. Dr. Stein's encouragement and suggestions were most important in the original planning of this book. My colleague, and editor of this series, the late Dr. Louis A. Zurcher, provided decisive assistance in the final completion of the manuscript. Throughout the extended process of writing, and re-writing, my wife Zuria Farmer Austin, classmate and graduate of the School of Applied Social Sciences, Western Reserve University, social worker and volunteer advocate for community services, provided critical commentary and assistance. Full responsibility for the final version of this book, however, is mine.

Introduction

Human service industries are a major part of the rapidly growing services sector of the American economy. The quality of life in the United States is directly affected by the quality of services produced by education, health care and social service organizations. To an increasing degree the future of American society is tied to the quality of educational services, the quality of health and personal care services, and the adequacy of social support services for individuals in their 70s and 80s, and for young families with children. Yet the administration of these service production organizations has received only casual attention from academic theorists dealing with organizational and administrative theory.

The nonprofit and governmental organizations which are the major producers of human services are viewed by economists as a marketplace anomaly, and dismissed by business management theorists as being an amateurish activity that does not involve a standard profit and loss balance sheet. The central argument of this book is that human service industries constitute a major force in the political economy of American society and have distinctive characteristics that affect the nature of both administration and program policymaking.

This volume addresses critical policy issues for administrators and policy-makers in voluntary nonprofit and governmental service organizations in social services, health care, education, mental health, developmental disabilities and other related human service fields. It also provides an analytic framework for students who are preparing to work in administration and program policy design in human service programs. But this is not a book about the techniques of organizational management. It deals, rather, with the political economy context of administration and policymaking in human service industries in postindustrial United States, a distinctive context which has important consequences for the nature of human services administration.

This volume is analytic, rather than prescriptive. It is an attempt to describe the actual pattern of rapidly changing political and economic forces which are shaping the environment within which human service programs are developed and administered, for example, the impact of changes in the traditional pattern of college-educated women being available to serve as low-cost front-line service workers, or volunteers, in social services, education, and health care organizations. This is not an effort to describe an ideal organizational pattern for human services. It does not attempt to fit current reality into a single ideological model. It does not assume that there is a single model of effective administration, nor a single correct answer to the public policy issues involved in the future development of human service programs. It does assume that understanding the political and economic dynamics which actually impact human service programs is essential for the design of effective program policy initiatives and for the administrative implementation of such policies.

This volume assumes that understanding the political economy of human service programs requires an analytic framework that deals with specific types of service programs with attention to their variety and distinctiveness, rather than a global category of "human services." I have given particular attention to social service programs, reflecting my own experiences as a social work practitioner and educator. But a fundamental premise of the book is that the political economy context of human service programs in the United States has a high degree of commonality across such fields as elementary and secondary education, health care, mental health services, child welfare, developmental disability services and gerontological services. The understanding of this context is of critical importance to administrators and policymakers in all of these fields.

Most forms of collectively sponsored human service programs, both voluntary nonprofit and governmental, were originally initiated to provide services to low-income households. Today, however, such programs, including education, health care and social services, serve individuals and families from a wide variety of economic backgrounds, including, but not limited to, low-income households. Indeed, one of the characteristics of human service industries is the increasing commercialization of nonprofit and governmental organizations, and the rapid expansion of for-profit firms, as the potential market for such services expands to include the total society. This expansion of human service programs, however, has not altered the distinctive characteristics that affect the nature of administrative practice.

Human service programs have *moral* consequences. Policy choices and program administration decisions involve moral choices as well as technical and operational choices. Human service programs affect the lives of particular individuals in fundamental ways—through educational opportunities; through the treatment of illnesses; through the resolution of family conflicts; through the rehabilitation of adults with physical injuries; through personal counseling which enables individuals to cope with injury and loss, to understand themselves, and to participate in the choices and decisions which shape their lives; through the rebuilding of the economic and social structure of urban neighborhoods; through the redistribution of economic resources involved in the provision of financial assistance that prevents long-term effects of poor nutrition and inadequate health care; through the provision of personal care for children without families and for older adults with serious disabilities living alone; through "consciousness-raising" and "mobilization" services that enable groups of individuals to support each other in efforts to realign basic cultural patterns in the society.

Human service programs are highly dependent on their environments. Human service executives must give as much attention to the political economy of the organizational environment as they give to internal production technologies. Human service programs involve multiple "stakeholder" constituencies. There are service users, advocacy organizations, organized professions, funding sources, policy boards and legislative bodies. Each group has a distinct set of concerns, objectives and standards of accountability. The service production technologies are "soft," primarily involving person-to-person interaction, and "co-production," that is the active participation of the service user in the actual production of the service. The evaluation of the effectiveness of a particular service is generally very imprecise.

Human service programs are labor-intensive, and locality specific, and expensive. The unit costs of human services cannot be dramatically reduced by substituting machines for people in the production of services. For example, the skill of the surgeon in the operating room cannot be replaced by technical equipment, and computers in the classroom cannot replace the motivational impact of a superior teacher. Nor can a child protective service agency be relocated to the Far East or Central America to take advantage of lower personnel costs. A major part of the costs involves the professional specialists who make critical judgements and decisions under conditions of uncertainty—in the classroom, the operating room, the psychiatric counselor's office, or in a family investigation where child abuse is suspected. These professional specialists are not only part of the service organization, they are also members of a separate organized profession to which they are accountable.

These distinctive aspects of human service industries are critical elements in shaping the external political economy that is the primary focus of this book. There are other important aspects of the internal political economy of human service industries which this book does not address. These include the role related dynamics which shape the behavior of staff members, policymakers and service users, the functions of the human service executive, the role of organized professions, the nature of production technologies in human service programs, the relationship between human service organizations and communities, and the nature of interorganizational processes involved in complex service delivery systems.

The first five chapters of this book examine the current societal political economy context of human service programs. Chapter 1 deals with the nature of human service programs and with varying interpretations of the role of human services in postindustrial society. Chapter 2 deals with three traditional ideological perspectives on human service programs. These are socialism, capitalism and welfare capitalism. Chapter 3 deals with changes in social and economic patterns in the United States that contradict many of the traditional assumptions in both socialism and capitalism ideologies. Chapter 4 examines current political economy issues in income transfers, in particular, differences between the issues involved in labor force related transfers for able-bodied adults, and categorical transfers for children, individuals with disabilities and individuals beyond the retirement age. Chapter 5 examines issues involved in the quality and effectiveness of human service production, in particular, issues related to the impact of large scale organizations and the centralization of authority.

Chapters 6 and 7 deal with the impact of the distinctive institutional history of voluntary nonprofit and governmental service organizations on the current political economy context of human service programs. Chapter 6 deals with the parallel development of voluntary nonprofit service organizations and governmental service orgainzations from the mid-1800s through the 1930s. Chapter 7 deals with the increasing convergence of the voluntary nonprofit service system and the governmental service system from the 1940s to the mid-1980s.

Chapters 8, 9 and 10 set forth two analytic frameworks for the identification of similarities and differences among human service organizations and programs which have consequences for political economy dynamics. Chapter 8 deals with similarities and differences which are related to organizational sponsorship and funding, and also includes an analysis of the role of for-profit firms in human service industries. Chapters 9 and 10 deal with similarities and differences in the societal functions of human service programs. Chapter 11 is a summary and an exploration of the implications of the analysis presented in this book for research and for administrative practice in human service programs.

Chapter 1

The Societal Framework
of Human Services

Fundamental to an understanding of human service programs and human service industries, is an understanding of their relation to the total society and of the political and economic forces which shape that relationship. The analysis of the relationships of human service programs to the social order is, however, more philosophical than scientific. The historical processes through which human service programs have developed are open to a variety of interpretations. The contemporary relation of such programs to other parts of the society is similarly subject to differing interpretations. This chapter explores alternative views of the societal function of human service programs.

THE HUMAN SERVICES

The concept of human services, as discussed in this volume includes:

- education and socialization of children and youth
- care and treatment of individuals who are sick, including mental illness
- care and treatment of individuals with disabilities
- care and protection of dependent persons
- mutual assistance in emergencies and catastrophes
- control of dangerous or deviant individual behavior
- development of work skills
- recreation and social activities
- the organization of problem solving groups
- transfer of economic resources, or the direct provision of food, shelter, and medical care to individuals and households without such resources
- advice and counseling for individuals with personal psychological problems

- development of social interaction skills involved in group participation and in collective decisionmaking

THE FOUR DOMAINS OF COLLECTIVE ACTION

The role of human service programs in the social order must be examined in the context of the total pattern of collective, or cooperative, action involved in the production of goods and services. Bell (1974) identified three domains of "economic activity."

> In a classical tradition of economic activity there are two realms of economic activity. There is the domestic household, including farms, whose products are not valued (a housewife is not paid; the produce consumed on the farm is not always measured in GNP) because they are not exchanged in the market, and there is the market economy in which the value of goods and services is measured by relative prices registered in the exchange of money. But there is also now ... a third sector which has come to the fore in the last twenty-five years, and which in the next twenty-five will play an even more crucial role, the public household.

Weisbrod (1977), in a different approach often used in public administration theory, defines three domains involved in the production of goods and services as: (1) private market, (2) public or governmental, and (3) voluntary nonprofit. A combination of these two approaches leads to an inclusive model of the production and distribution of all goods and services, including "human services," consisting of four domains of collective action: (1) the household (family) and other primary, or communal, groupings; (2) the marketplace and for-profit organizations; (3) governmental organizations, including both policymaking or rulemaking governance components and governmental production components; and (4) voluntary, nongovernmental, nonprofit production organizations. Any particular form of goods or service may, in principle, be produced within the framework of any one of these four domains.[1]

All of the activities which are involved in the production of human services within any of these four domains originated first within the household as services produced by household members for the benefit of other household members. In every society it is still the household that continues to produce the largest proportion of all types of person-to-person human services.

Moreover, the basic technical activities involved in the production of any one type of human service are similar in all four domains. Teaching children to read or to do arithmetic is essentially the same, whether it is done by a parent within the home, by a private tutor employed through the marketplace, by a teacher in a nonprofit or nongovernmental classroom, or a teacher in a public school. The fundamental processes involved in the care of a severely handicapped child, or in counseling individuals with personal problems, are similar whether carried out by another member of the family, by a private specialist employed through the marketplace, or by a staff person employed by either a governmental or a nonprofit service organization.

The production of human services is part of every society; and it has been part of every society from the beginning of organized societies. Important differences do exist, however, among societies in the pattern of human service production. These differences are not a result of differences in the total level of "need" for services. The total "need" for these human services is essentially a constant in any given society. The need for nuturing, care and socialization of children or for care of infirm older persons varies only in terms of the absolute number of the persons in such category within the society. Every child, and every infirm older person, needs some form of care and protection; every person who is seriously ill needs nursing, every child needs to learn a language.

The significant differences that do exist among societies are in the patterns of production and distribution of these services across the four domains of collective action. A particular society may be characterized at a given time by the relative importance of each of these four domains. Moreover, many of the important public policy issues in every society involve the interrelationships among these four domains in the production, and in the distribution, of human services. Differences among societies in these patterns of production have far-reaching consequences, since the pattern of power and authority, and of social roles, is different within each domain.

In the United States (which serves as the primary context for this book) and other postindustrial[2] societies the production of human services takes place simultaneously within all four domains—within the household and other communal units, through marketplace, for-profit organizations, through governmental organizations, and through voluntary nonprofit organizations.

Given the production of similiar services in all four domains there is a high degree of potential substitutability. That is, there are nearly always opportunities to substitute one form of service production for another. Children may be educated in the home, or through a private school, if parents decide that public school education is unsatisfactory. Adolescents may learn entry level job skills through work with other household members, through employment directly as an apprentice in an on-going business, or through technical training in for-profit, or nonprofit, or governmentally administered schools or training programs.

Substitutablity is a significant factor in the difficulty of defining the level of "demand" for any particular type of *organizationally produced* human service at any given time, or in anticipating the potential level of utilization for any such service at some future time. The specific characteristics of a service provided by a particular organization, and the conditions under which it is available, are more significant in determining the utilization of that service than any absolute level of need within a given population group. That is, there may be a high level of need for health care but a low level of utilization of a specific organizational health service.

Public policy enactments may have both intended, and unintended, consequences for the pattern of substitution in a given society, and, in turn, for the general structure of human service provision within that society. For example, in the United States in the 1980s, there has been a substantial change in federal policies dealing with the role of federal funding, and with governmental production, in general, of human services. These policies, in turn, have had consequences for family, nonprofit, and for-profit production of human services (Bendick 1985; Gilbert 1983; Kramer 1985).

THE SOCIETAL FUNCTION OF HUMAN SERVICE INDUSTRIES

Postindustrial societies have been characterized by an elaborate development of governmental and nonprofit organizations for the production of human services, as well as by the large-scale production of similar services through the marketplace. This has been accompanied by occupational specialization and professionalization among those persons directly involved in the production of human services.

As the scale of human service production through organizations has increased, the pattern of organizational activities has taken on all of the characteristics of an *industry*, or series of industries (Zald 1978). For example, it is possible to identify a health care industry, an education industry, an income-transfer industry, a child care industry, and a mental health industry. Within each of these industry groupings there are rules, procedures, and technical terminology that are recognized as common to all service producing organizations. There are also a variety of interorganizational structures, such as training institutions, research centers, standard setting bodies, industry-wide conferences, technical journals, professional associations, and trade associations. These industry level organizations have been created to deal with common operational issues within the industry and to deal with relations between the industry and the larger society (Benson 1981; Milward and Francisco 1983).

These human service industries include for-profit firms, as well as governmental and voluntary nonprofit organizations (Gilbert 1983). For example, for-profit, voluntary nonprofit and governmental organizations providing similar health care services, are all eligible for third party financial reimbursement from insurance systems. This mix of for-profit, governmental and voluntary nonprofit organizations is increasingly characteristic of the "mixed economy" of postindustrial societies. However, in most human services industries the key policymaking, regulatory and financing institutions, that is the institutions responsible for service *provision* arrangements, as well as most of the actual service *producers* (Ostrom and Ostrom 1978), are governmental or voluntary nonprofit organizations because these industries are involved simultaneously in the production of both public goods and private goods (Austin 1981).

Human service industries are, in general, shaped primarily by nonmarket-place processes even when they include marketplace producers. In part this is because for-profit marketplace production organizations are freer to enter, or to leave, any specific service industry, or any specific sector of the market within an industry, depending on perceptions of profitability. They, therefore, have fewer incentives for long-range investment in the development of the total industry. Moreover, the developmental and network coordination costs in complex human service industries cannot, in general, be financed through marketplace processes.

The societal function of human service industries, and in particular the governmental and voluntary nonprofit segments of these industries, can be analyzed from a number of different perspectives. One of the complexities in the production of human services is the mixture of perspectives about societal function which exists within any one human service industry, and indeed often within a single organization. The distinctions among these perspectives are, therefore, primarily philosophical rather than technical. Each perspective involves in varying degrees both *analytic elements*, that is particular ways of describing what exists, and *normative elements,* that is particular views of the preferred or desired pattern of service provision and production. Each perspective has different implications for evaluating industry-wide policies, for defining the social goals of particular service organizations, and for the analysis of administrative practice.

The Communal Perspective

The communal perspective is based on a belief that organized human service activities, in particular governmental and voluntary nonprofit service organizations, are an expression of, and an integral part of, the communal fabric of society, and should be linked as closely as possible to other communal structures (Hillery 1968). From this perspective human service production organizations should have as a major goal the support of social solidarity within specific communities, and within the total society (Gottschalk 1975; Hadley and Hatch 1981; Novak 1982).

This communal perspective assumes that membership in a communal group is an essential element of personal identity, and that participation in the processes of communal interaction is of central importance for the social development of all human beings. The "need" of any individual for any specific service can only be analyzed within a particular community context with its distinctive culture. The primary criteria for measuring the societal value of any formally organized service production activity is the contribution of that activity to the strengthening of communal linkages and in turn to the maintenance of *gemeinschaft* values within the society.

From the communal perspective an important aspect of any specific service program is its function as a "mediating structure," that is, its contribution to community development, to the strengthening of community decision processes, to extending the involvement of community members as policymakers and service volunteers and to its compatability with and reinforcement of community norms (Berger and Neuhaus 1977; Glazer 1983; Novak 1982). Tradition is more important than innovation in the shaping of service programs. Consensus negotiation based on common acceptance of communal norms is the preferred approach to program policy decisionmaking.

A combination of volunteers and employed personnel, who are "locals" and "generalists," is viewed as the preferred staffing pattern for service production activities. Highly developed occupational specializations which highlight status distinctions between "professionals," and "nonprofessionals" or "lay persons," are to be avoided. The criteria for selecting service personnel emphasize commitment to communal norms over technical competence. Organizational activities supportive of self-help and self-care programs are viewed as preferable to highly structured professionalized services (Brewer and Lait 1980; Glazer 1983).

One implication of this communal perspective is that large-scale "industry" characteristics in human service production are to be minimized. Community created and controlled services are preferred to large-scale programs controlled by administrative units outside the local community (Barclay 1982; Hadley and Hatch 1981). Proposals for dismantling comprehensive nation-wide governmental service programs are based on the argument that "local control" of such activities has positive consequences for both the service and the community (Barclay 1982). Even social change efforts are viewed as preferably developing from a "grass roots" base with more attention given to changing individual attitudes within the community than to changing social and legal structures from the societal level (Illich 1970).

Within this perspective many important societal values, such as social solidarity, are linked to a vision of the past as a time when stable, long-term social relationships were prevalent. The past is also viewed as a time when there were high levels of consensus on community norms, spontaneous cooperative responses to the needs of individuals and households rather than large-scale bureaucratic organizations, and extensive involvement of community members in collective decisions (Bellah, Madsen, Swidler, Sullivan and Tipton 1985). In many of the discussions of this perspective there is a harking back to the image of a self-governing participating society identified with Athenian Greece (Sullivan 1982).

For some advocates of this perspective the preferred goal for the future is the re-creation of a society around these principles, even, if necessary, at the expense of improvements in the material standard of living. For others, the reestablishment of consensual communal norms even at the expense of individual autonomy, and control of service programs by the local community, are viewed as ways of controlling disruptive changes in social norms and social relationships which are felt to be a result of uncontrolled technological development and "mass society."

The Universal Value Perspective

The universal value perspective is based on the belief that human service activities should be an institutional embodiment of universal human values applied to the total society (Harrington 1968; Rochefort 1981). Human service programs from this perspective are often described in the United States as being an operational expression of Judeo-Christian religious values, with specific reference, for example, to the moral teachings of the Old Testament prophets and to the Golden Rule and Sermon on the Mount in the New Testament (Klien 1968; Rauschenbusch 1912). The Roman Catholic theological concept of "natural law" also assumes the existence of fundamental moral values which are independent of community and cultural variations.

From the universal value perspective medical care programs and medical research are viewed not as applications of technology but as expressions of a fundamental belief in the importance of protecting and preserving human life. Other service activities are grounded in other universal humanitarian societal values—justice, brotherhood and sisterhood, charity. Human service programs are viewed as instruments for achieving the "good society," a society characterized by "freedom," "social justice," "equality," "peace and universal brotherhood," "the elimination of poverty, racism and sexism." Historically, this universal value perspective has been particularly prominent in the United States during periods of "social progress" such as the Age of Enlightenment (1820s), the Progressive Era at the turn of the century, and the 1960s. These have also been periods in which the "social gospel" has been prominent in organized religion (Hutchinson 1968).

This perspective is embedded in normative social policy statements such as the Declaration of Independence, the Charter of the United Nations, the March on Washington speech of Martin Luther King, Jr., Papal Encyclicals such as *Rerum Novarum* (1891), and the Conference of Catholic Bishops' *Pastoral Letter on Catholic Social Teaching and the U.S. Economy* (1986). Supporters of this perspective often give limited consideration to the complexities involved in implementing such broad policy statements.

Policy decisionmaking is often viewed as an on-going contest between persons who are committed to universal values and those who are opposed to the implementation of such values, either because of self-interest, or because of a commitment to traditional cultural attitudes and practices which are inconsistent with universal values. From this perspective all individuals are viewed, in principle, as fundamentally "moral," as responsive to ethical standards and to opportunities to contribute voluntarily to the good society. Actual human behavior in a given context, however, may be viewed as threatening basic values. Moreover, at any one time, there may be severe conflicts among persons who support the concept of universal values as to which values should take precedence in formulating public policy.

The criteria for public policy choices are viewed as ethical rather than as economic, political or technical (Rawls 1971; Titmuss 1975). Consensus decision making in developing social policies may be viewed as leading to compromises of fundamental principles. The enactment of ethically correct policies, even if such policies are opposed by the majority of citizens, is an appropriate political objective. The use of political power and governmental authority, as well as moral persuasion, to overcome opposition to normatively-oriented changes in the social order is viewed as appropriate, on the assumption that changes in attitudes will follow from changes in behavior, even if the initial behavior changes are, in part, coerced. The history of civil rights and affirmative action in the 1960s and 1970s reflects a pattern of social policy action consistent with these assumptions of the universal value perspective (Schwarz 1983; Warner 1977). The "liberation theology" movement within the Roman Catholic church in Central and South America, rooted in concepts of "natural law," is another contemporary expression of the universal value perspective.

This perspective often includes an emphasis on individualism, that is on the unique significance of every human being, on the equality of social worth of all human beings, on the "rights" of every individual, and on the perfectability of human society. The national society as a whole, or preferably the world society, rather than the local community, is viewed as the relevant context for human service programs. The moral commitment of service personnel, both volunteer and employed, to these values may be viewed as more important than technical competence, although professional skills combined with moral commitment are highly valued. Research to develop innovative technologies consistent with universal values is supported.

Tradition is often viewed as a poor source of guidance in developing human service programs since programs of the past have not, in general, been effective in achieving the full implementation of universal values. The development of centrally controlled, large-scale, complex interorganizational or industry-wide systems in human service programs may be viewed as desirable if they lead to comprehensive and uniform implementation of policies and programs that are congruent with universal values.

From this perspective human history is a record of the struggle to improve human society, a record of human "progress." Human service programs, when administered in ways that are consistent with fundamental human values, are viewed as major elements in the achievement of social progress. The future, rather than the past, is viewed as holding the greatest promise for the realization of the good society.

The Instrumental Perspective

A third perspective is that human service production activities are primarily instrumental. They are discrete, technically specialized, problem-solving activities designed to fulfill discrete "needs" of particular individuals, or to deal with specific societal problem conditions that cannot be dealt with through marketplace processes (Olson 1965). From this perspective much of the emphasis in evaluating service programs is on effectiveness and efficiency in the achievement of specific program objectives, rather than on the relation of such programs to any single pattern of societal values (Cyert 1975). The normative framework is pragmatic and relative rather than ideological and absolute. Science and logical empiricism are viewed as the primary sources of relevant knowledge (Cohen 1931). Professional specialization, the use of scientific technology and the development of large-scale bureaucratic administrative organizations are all desirable if they contribute to operational effectiveness and efficiency. Service specialists are expected to be selected on the basis of credentials and evidence of technical competence, rather than on the basis of personal beliefs or commitment.

Rational planning, needs assessment, policy analysis, cost-benefit analysis, information systems, operations research and program evaluation are viewed as important policymaking and implementation tools (Cyert 1975; Kahn 1969; Mayer and Greenwood 1980; Wholey 1983). Scientific management, which is the preferred administrative orientation, may include the use of organizationally controlled "human relations" participatory procedures, such as "quality circles." It is assumed that the choice of the administrative auspice for service production should be based on considerations of competence and efficiency. Competitive bidding among service producers using technical criteria alone is thus the preferred approach for implementing public service programs.

The preferred model of policymaking involves the use of cost-benefit oriented policy analyses to select the most effective and efficient alternative (Morris and Ozawa 1985). Policy decisionmaking by technical and professional specialists is viewed as more relevant than decisionmaking by "lay" citizens without technical knowledge. Volunteers are valued primarily for their contribution to efficiency in the specific production of services.

This instrumental perspective is consistent with a view that human beings are autonomous individuals motivated primarily by economic self-interest calculations, including the possibilities of both rewards and losses or punishments, rather than by either ethical belief systems or communal loyalties. The pursuit of economic interests is viewed as the dominant dynamic in the social order. The good society provides the greatest opportunity for individuals to meet their self-defined "needs" at as low a cost as possible, as well as an opportunity to satisfy their economic "wants" as fully as possible.

Marketplace processes are preferred on the basis that they encourage efficiency in the use of limited resources and provide autonomy for the individual in selecting a preferred service producer (Friedman 1962; Gilder 1981). Little attention is to be given to secondary consequences, or "externalities," for individuals, communities, or the society as a whole, which might result from particular forms of service production. Prominence of the instrumental perspective in the United States has been particularly associated with periods of institutional consolidation such as the 1920s and the 1970s.

From this perspective the relevant value context is the present rather than either the past or the future. Progress, except in quantitative economic terms, is essentially a meaningless term. Current public opinion provides the normative criteria for decisionmaking. As conditions in society change, norms change, and the relevance of particular forms of organizationally produced human services may be expected to change. Therefore, deliberate efforts to use "social engineering" to shape the future development of society in terms of current social values is both inappropriate and wasteful (Glazer 1984).

The Political Economy Perspective

The three preceding perspectives assume that human service programs and, indeed, human service industries, should be regarded as internally consistent systems with distinctive goals and organizational structures. These perspectives also combine an analytic framework and a distinctive normative orientation so that the analysis of any given human service industry focuses as much on its congruence with specific normative criteria as on the characteristics of its performance.

An alternative approach to the analysis of the societal function of human service programs is the political economy perspective. The political economy perspective, which is primarily analytic, views human service industries as a particular type of societal structure which has developed in a pattern which is highly interrelated with all of the other elements of the larger society (Gough 1979; Walmsley and Zald 1973). The performance of these industries, and their constituent organizational units, is viewed as being shaped by the political and economic structures of the society in which they are embedded (Milward and Francisco 1983; Zald 1978). In turn, it is assumed that the performance of human service industries can be most appropriately assessed in terms of their actual impact on other elements within the society and on the structure of the society as a whole.

This analytic political economy perspective focuses on both the external societal forces, and the intra-industry factors affected by such forces, which control the processes of organizational legitimation and shape the flow of resources to individual organizations, and thus control the continuity of existence of human service producing organizations. From this perspective it is this pattern of legitimation and resources which determine the actual characteristics of the human service production activity (Benson 1975).

This use of the political economy perspective is an extension of its original development in the eighteenth and nineteenth centuries as a framework for examining the relation between the political systems of nation-states and the economy dynamics of marketplace capitalism. The use of this perspective to examine contemporary human service industries, however, is particularly relevant, given the significance of such industries, in the mixed economy structure of postindustrial societies.

The political economy perspective rests on a view of human behavior as being fundamentally motivated by personal perceptions of self-interest. That is, every individual views every choice, or decision, from a unique personal concept of what is valued, and what is not valued, within a given social and cultural context. Moreover, individuals use their particular personal value perspective in all areas of decisionmaking, including both economic marketplace decisions and political collective action decisionmaking (Buchanan and Tullock 1962). However, this definition of personal self-interest includes not only economic self-interest, but also social identity self-interest. Social identity is related to the particular pattern of roles through which each individual participates in a complex network of social relationships.

Many political economy analyses adopt a narrow economic self-interest model of individual behavior (Downs 1957). In part, economic self-interest assumptions have been used because it is easier to model human behavior if all elements of the model can be defined by a single criteria, that is monetary value. But such assumptions are also used because they are particularly relevant when the total process of social interaction among human beings is viewed as being dominated by economic exchanges through the marketplace, that is, those exchanges which are central to the "economic standard of living" of the individual. Individuals either directly produce products, such as farm produced food products, which are exchanged for other products, or they exchange their labor (muscles and time) through the labor market for such products. The economic organization of industrial societies developed around such exchanges, and the behavior of individuals is viewed as being primarily shaped by the terms of such exchanges. Moreover, economic self-interest models include the self-interest of all family members under the economic self-interest definition of the "head-of-household," or primary earner, assuming that decisions consistent with the self-interest of the primary earner advance the self-interests of all other household members. "Public choice" theories of political behavior assume similar economic self-interest motivations as an explanation of the behaviors of individuals in political contexts, both as voters and as public officals (Ostrom V. and Ostrom E. 1978; Tullock 1965).

However, a purely economic definition of self-interest ignores the other major arena of human interaction, that is, the family, and other communal relationships, in which relationships are not mediated by economic exchanges. While there are distributions of economic resources within families these distributions are determined by role definitions rather than by marketplace processes, for example, whether one is defined as a parent or as a child. Moreover, the pattern of relationships involved in exchanges of love, and affection, and in the nuturing and socialization of children, are largely independent of the level of economic resources available to a family except, perhaps, at the extremes. They are also relatively independent of the pattern of distribution of economic resources within the family. Moreover, since there is no marketplace equivalent for such interpersonal exchanges among persons who define themselves as a family, that is as a unique and persistent social unit, there is no way of assigning a monetary value to such exchanges for purposes of analysis.

Interactions within the family are shaped by social identity definitions, rather than by economic processes, and such definitions always involve expectations about nonmonetary reciprocal interactions with other family members. That is, the behavior of a mother, or a father, towards children, is shaped primarily by self-perceptions of the requirements of maintaining the identity of being a parent, which include expectations about nonmonetary interactions between the adult and the child. The behavior choices available in interactions within the family between adults and children are viewed by the adults as either potentially enhancing, or demeaning, their social identity associated with the role of parent. Similarily, choices available in the interactions between two parents are viewed as enhancing, or demeaning, the social identity associated with the role of either husband or wife.

Even the distribution of financial resources within the family is viewed primarily in terms of its meaning for the interaction among family members, and, in turn, for social identity. Such distributions are viewed only secondarily in terms of their specific economic value to a particular individual. The provision of a personal allowance to a child is a confirmation of an important change in the child's identity within the family, quite independent of the amount of the allowance. In many instances, individual members of a family will explicitly sacrifice economic benefits, or take on additional economic burdens, because of self-perception of the expectations of maintaining a valued identity as parent, marriage partner, daughter or son. Moreover, life-risking actions by one family member on behalf of another are not guided by the income-producing potential of either the individual in danger, or the individual taking a risk.

While social identity is rooted first, and foremost, in the pattern of relationships within the family, other identity elements are critical parts of the self-interest definition of particular individuals. These may include identities rooted in nationality, religion, gender, language, or political party, to name a few. The dynamics of identity self-interest rooted in these identities may be similar to the dynamics of family role identity; individuals may make decisions based on identity protection or enhancement which run contrary to economic self-interest. Moreover, the dynamics of identity self-interest are distinct for each individual; the head of the household definition of identity self-interest does not include the definition of identity self-interest for other household members, as it does in analyses based on definitions of economic self-interest.

The political economy perspective assumes that all individuals, at all times, seek through their choices and their actions to protect, or enhance, personal economic resources and benefits, *and* that they also seek to protect, or enhance, self-perceived social identity status. In many instances the enhancement of, or defense of, an identity status may be a more important source of motivation for the actions of a particular individual than an opportunity to obtain specific economic benefits. Active and committed participants in a social movement in which particular social values are highly salient are more likely to respond to opportunities to exemplify those values in their own behavior, including the risk of death, than to economic opportunities which contradict those values (Zurcher and Snow 1981). Other individuals may forego economic benefits in favor of maintaining a valued identity status within a local community. Individuals avoid law-violating behavior as much, or more, because of the perceived risks to identity status, than because of the fear of economic consequences. These social identity dynamics, rooted in family and communal relationships more than in marketplace dynamics, are particularly important in the political economy of human service programs. Social identity dynamics are more significant in the arena of political, or collective, action than in the marketplace; human service programs are primarily shaped by political, or collective, processes, although economic processes are of substantial importance. Indeed, it is the dynamics of social identity self-interest, rooted in familial and other communal roles, rather than economic self-interest, that explain the existence of those voluntary and governmental human service programs that do not represent a "pure" public good, and which, therefore, are not explained by economic theory (Olson 1965). (see Chapter 9)

From the political economy perspective each individual is viewed as participating in a variety of formal and informal activities with the objective of the shaping of the processes of social decisionmaking, which in turn shape the network of social roles in which the individual is a participant, and ultimately the general social order. Such activities may include a wide variety of individual actions such as boycotting imported products, participating in coffee-break gossip, or a bar-room argument, about the private life of an elected official, contributing to the support of a political candidate, writing a letter to a Congressman, serving as a political party official, or running for public office. Such activities may also include the use of resources which the individual controls as a consequence of the social role which she or he occupies, for example as president of a corporation, or of a labor union, in an effort to influence collective action.

While some of these "political" activities may have a very short time span, others may persist over many years. The objective of all such activities is to increase the probabilities for the individual of achieving that combination of both economic benefits and social identity benefits that constitute the individual's unique definition of self-interest. The sum total of all of these efforts to shape the social order, by all of the members of the society, many of which involve acting through a group or organization, creates the pattern of political and economic dynamics that determine the responses of the society to critical societal issues, including those issues involved in the future development of human service programs.

From this political economy analytic perspective *communal, universal value*, and *instrumental* perspectives represent three competing normative interpretations of the potential function of human service programs within the society. The relative influence of each of these perspectives on the actual development of human service programs in a given society is determined, not by its philosophical "correctness," but by its relation to sources of significant power, and by the political and economic dynamics within the total society (Berger and Luckman 1966). In a given society different perspectives may be dominant in human services policymaking at different times under different political economy conditions.

This volume was written from the political economy perspective, rather than from a communal, universal value, or instrumental perspective. It is an effort to explore the societal political economy dynamics that shape human service industries in the United States. The chapters which follow deal with the political and economic dynamics of the larger society in which human service industries are embedded, the political economy dynamics of the institutional development of human service programs in the United States, and the differential characteristics of human service programs and human service production organizations which shape their adaptation to the political economy dynamics of this society.

NOTES

1. There are also a variety of mixed-type settings. These include: families and communes that are also business organizations; cooperatives that combine nonprofit and marketplace characteristics; governmental organizations organized as free-standing nonprofit corporations; and nonprofit organizations which are subsidiaries of for-profit organizations. (See Chapter 8)

2. "Postindustrial" is used to refer to the contemporary national societies of Europe and North America, and societies in other regions which have a similar pattern of economic and social development (Bell 1973).

Chapter 2

Human Service
Policy Issues and
Political Economy Paradigms

HUMAN SERVICE POLICY ISSUES

In postindustrial societies the *scope, structure and financing of human service programs* have become one of the three most critical societal concerns. The other two concerns are the choice between world-wide war and a peaceful international order, and the determination of the most effective form of relationship between political decision processes and marketplace decision processes in managing the economic system. Each of these issues has a distinctive set of political and economic dynamics. They are also interrelated in complex ways with which this volume does not deal.

As the scale of organizational production of human services has increased, societal decisions about such issues as: the financing of social insurance; access to education; the nature of the educational system and the relation of education to economic productivity; the impact of organizational service programs on communal structures such as the family and the locality community; economic provision for the able-bodied unemployed; the organization of a health care system; and the organization of services for individuals with disabilities, including the mentally ill, have become critical personal issues for large numbers of individuals.

There has been an extension of adolesence and the period of formal education, and, in turn, the extension of economic dependency, as well as the institutionalization of retirement as a standard part of the life cycle. This means that there are two very large population groups, at either end of the age distribution, for whom collectively established social policies and service programs are the most significant elements in their lives outside of their immediate family (Preston 1984). Collectively established social policies, including tax policies, and the characteristics of human service programs are more important factors in the realization of immediate personal self-interest objectives for most adolescents and for most retired persons than their participation in marketplace economic processes. Personal opportunities for entrepreneurship have little direct relevance for elementary and high school students, or for persons who are dependent on Social Security retirement benefits.

Individuals with temporary or permanent disabilities which effectively exclude them from the labor force are another significant group within the population for whom the achievement of personal objectives is largely determined by social policies and the characteristics of human service programs. Particularly during times of economic recession unemployed workers and their families are directly affected by both social policies and human service programs. Individuals employed in human service organizations are also directly affected by societal decisions about the scope, structure, and financing of human service programs.

Moreover, nearly every household in the society has some degree of economic or social responsibility for children, or elderly parents or relatives, or for a disabled family member. These households are, at least indirectly, affected by the strengths and weaknesses of collective programs and policies intended to meet the needs of such persons. Moreover, those households in which there are employed adults are the immediate source of the economic resources which provide the financial support for human service programs through tax payments, insurance premiums, contributions, and fees for service. Every household in the society has some form of important self-interest involvement in the collective decisions that are made about the legitimation of human service programs and about the allocation of economic resources to such activities.

Since the policy issues involved in the development of human service programs have become critical issues for the entire society, the outcome of those issues is, in general, not shaped by individual judgements about the importance of a specific problem with which a particular human service program is intended to deal, or about the technical effectiveness of a particular service technology. The policy outcomes are primarily shaped, rather, by the connections that individuals make between particular program issues and their self-interest (social identity and economic) based beliefs about fundamental political and economic issues within the society as a whole. For example, the outcomes on policy decisions related to family planning are determined not so much by specific programmatic issues but primarily by the linkage of such issues to the conflicts perceived by individuals between traditional religious belief systems and the individualistic, relativistic philosophical perspective which is sometimes identified as "secular humanism."

There are two key issues in particular which are central to public policy debates about the scope, structure and financing of human service programs in postindustrial societies. The first, the *redistributional income transfer* issue, involves the role of income transfer policies and programs, and the direct provision of basic necessities to individuals, in the organization of the national economic system. The second issue involves the *effectiveness and efficiency of the production of personal services by governmental and voluntary nonprofit human service organizations.*

The *redistributional income transfer issue*, and the *quality of service issue*, are both linked to the issue of the future scope, structure and financing of human services in postindustrial societies, that is to the "future of the welfare state," although it is the income transfer issue which is most often argued in discussions of "the welfare state." This issue, the future of the welfare state, has, in turn, become closely linked to the credibility and stability of political parties, of governments, and the democratic political process in general.

For some one hundred and fifty years this issue has been viewed primarily from the perspective of a fundamental conflict between a free-market capitalism political economy paradigm, or world view, and a socialism political economy paradigm. Most of the current arguments about redistributive income transfer systems and many of the issues involved in the development of equitable, effective, and efficient personal service programs involve different fundamental assumptions about the nature of society, based on these two paradigms.

The Redistributional Income Transfer Issue

The nature of income transfer policies affects all human service programs in several ways. First, the pattern of income distribution directly affects the relations within the society between family, marketplace, governmental or voluntary nonprofit provision as a response to the needs and wants with which human service programs deal. Second, the expenditures involved in income transfer programs are often viewed, in the public mind, as being linked with expenditures involved in *personal service programs*, that is human service programs other than those that deal with income and basic needs provision. The political economy dynamics of income transfer programs often shape the political economy dynamics of personal service programs. "Welfare state" arguments often make no distinction between income transfers, and the publicly subsidized provision, for example, of job training services, or day care services, to adults who receive AFDC payments. Third, the actual provision of a particular type of human service often involves a policy choice between an unrestricted income transfer (Supplemental Security Income payments), a limited purpose voucher (food stamps), or direct provision in the form of a personal services program (Meals on Wheels).

The income transfer issue encompasses a wide range of public policy areas. These include taxation systems (earned income tax credit), income maintenance systems (unemployment compensation), and systems of direct provision (public housing) all of which may be used to transfer, or "redistribute," income or equivalent economic benefits (Medicaid) to households in which the income from labor force participation is inadequate to meet basic costs of day-to-day living. (While there are persons who argue that the objective of income redistribution should be to achieve actual income and wealth *equality* throughout the society, such an objective is not a significant part of the debates about the welfare state in the 1980s (Hochschild 1981).

The income transfer issue also includes the use of antidiscrimination and "affirmative action" policies to redistribute access to economic opportunities and benefits. The income transfer issue includes as well consideration of the role of those public policies, such as income tax deduction policies, which result in positive distribution, that is that add to the level of economic benefits which a household, whose income is above the median, obtains directly from marketplace activities.

The production and distribution of *personal services* by *public service organizations*, both governmental and voluntary nonprofit organizations, are, to a substantial degree, part of the pattern of economic redistribution within a given society. The users of services produced by such organizations are either totally, or in substantial part, individuals who do not have the economic resources to obtain these services through the marketplace. In large part this is a function of inadequate household income, but it may also be a function of the high costs of services associated with some relatively infrequent occurrences such as the premature birth of a child or the birth of a multi-handicapped child, a disabling accident such as a spinal cord injury, or a prolonged terminal illness, such as cancer. The choice between income transfers to cover the costs of personal services (Medicare) or the direct provision of such services by governmental or voluntary nonprofit organizations (state psychiatric hospital) is one of the important policy choices within the broader area of income redistribution.

The availability and quality of organizationally produced personal services has become a major factor in the extent of real redistribution which takes place in a given society. The existence of, and access to, particular types of human service programs (quality education at the elementary level, physical rehabilitation services, daycare services) may be directly linked to the equality of access to employment, and, in turn, to the likelihood of an adequate level of household income without direct income transfer.

Advocates for expanding income transfer programs and redistributional personal service programs argue that existing programs fail to assure an adequate standard of living for many households, and that both the scope of coverage and the level of income transfer benefits should be increased

(Galbraith 1958; Harrington 1968). Critics of current income transfers argue that these programs are already too large as a proportion of the total economy, and that they discourage labor force participation on the part of many of those eligible for transfers (Friedman 1962; Gilder 1981; Murray 1983). They also argue that the rate of taxation and/or contributions required to maintain current transfer programs results in a reduction of work effort incentives for those who are employed. In turn, it is argued, this results in a reduction in the total amount of goods and services produced in the society and available for distribution, and therefore a reduction in the general standard of living (Friedman 1962).

The Quality of Service Issue

The second key issue in the debates about the scope, structure and financing of human service programs concerns the *effectiveness and efficiency of organizationally produced human services*, that is the quality of the personal services produced by governmental and voluntary nonprofit organizations. This includes public education, health care services and a wide variety of social service programs. Among the criticisms of these human service programs are that they provide inadequate, inappropriate and ineffective services, that they are insensitive to the personal preferences of service users and that in some instances such programs result in the abuse and neglect of service users. It is also charged that they are not cost efficient, are over-professionalized, are primarily remedial rather than preventive, and involve inflexible and excessive red-tape in a complicated and uncoordinated service delivery system that is slow to accommodate to new knowledge or to adapt to new conditions.

Many of the criticisms of personal service organizations attribute the problems to the chaotic pattern of human service industries and a failure to apply contemporary managerial technology through centralized administration (Hagebak 1979). On the other hand other critics attribute the problems to the bureaucratic structure of many service organizations, that is to "bureaupathology" and "bureausis" (Neugeboren 1985). But the solutions to these problems, and the solutions to the policy issues involved in redistributional income transfer programs, are most often argued in the context of the larger societal conflicts between the *socialism paradigm,* the *free-market capitalism paradigm* and a twentieth century version of the capitalism paradigm, the *welfare capitalism paradigm.*

ALTERNATIVE POLITICAL ECONOMY PARADIGMS

Since the beginnings of the Industrial Revolution arguments have raged about the appropriate allocation of economic benefits from the total production of goods and services in a society as between the owners of wealth, in particular the owners of investment capital, and those persons who provide the labor input for such production. Karl Marx is generally viewed as having set forth the central issue in the argument, that is the issue of the legitimate pattern for the distribution of economic "surplus value profits," resulting from industrial and commercial activities in an economically expanding society (Marx 1968). *Surplus value profits* represent the difference between the total income realized from the sale of the goods and services which have been produced and all the direct costs of production including wages, rents, interest on money borrowed to finance buildings, machinery and current production of products which cannot be sold until some future time, and taxes to pay for "national defense" and for essential infrastructures such as roads and a common currency.

During the eighteenth and nineteenth centuries as industrial production and distribution replaced agriculture and commerce as the major form of economic activity, two distinctive perspectives emerged about the appropriate principles for the distribution of surplus value profits. These two political economy paradigms, *free-market capitalism* and *socialism,* are often perceived as polar opposites. The international social order during the twentieth century has been viewed by citizens of industrialized societies as being primarily organized around these polar opposites. Political party alignments within nation-states are defined as the political "right" and the political "left" in relation to these two paradigms.

Each paradigm in its simplest form involves a distinctly different set of theories and assumptions about the organization of both political and economic systems within the nation-state, about the appropriate relationships between the two, and about the appropriate principles for the distribution of the goods and services produced through the economy, including income transfers.

The importance of income transfers in the economy, and in political economy theories, has increased along with the elaboration of the total economic system in postindustrial societies because of: (1) an increase in the proportion of households in which there is no adult household member regularly employed, primarily because of age, disability condition, or structural unemployment, and (2) the existence of large numbers of households in which employment earnings are insufficient to meet the monetary costs of basic necessities because of currency inflation, low wages, irregular employment, temporary unemployment, or family size.

One characteristic of each of these two paradigms is the assumption of the existence of continuous class conflict within capitalist societies. The nature of the conflict is viewed differently in each paradigm. But each views the conflict as resulting from the "exploitation" of workers through their exclusion from the distribution of surplus value profits (Marx 1968). The identification of this issue as the source of class conflict appears not only in the writings of Karl Marx, but in the writings of the such free-market theorists as Malthus, Ricardo, and Adam Smith (Malthus 1951; Ricardo 1971; Smith 1937).

Among the assumptions that are associated with the concept of class conflict are those dealing with the role of the "welfare state" in capitalist societies, and in particular with the role of income transfers and other redistributional programs. The implications of class conflict theories for redistributional policies have become significant issues in the current, highly polarized debates about the scope, structure and financing of human service industries (Adams 1985; Gough 1979). The following sections examine traditional *capitalism* and *socialism* paradigms, as well as the *welfare capitalism* paradigm, and their implications for the policies of the welfare state.

The Free-market, Capitalism Paradigm

The traditional capitalism paradigm (particularly as this has been understood in the United States and Great Britain), is based on the economic "self-interest" perspective of the owners of investment capital (Smith 1937). From this perspective surplus value profits are considered to be an economic return for entrepreneurial skill and a form of compensation for investment risk. Surplus value profits are viewed, therefore, as belonging to successful business executives and to those who have assumed a capital investment risk through the purchase of "shares" in the business firm.

To the extent that there is a surplus value profit it is assumed that it should be distributed to entrepreneurial executives in the form of bonuses and other forms of salary enhancement, and to shareholders either in the form of enhanced "dividends" from their investment, or as an increase in the value of their "share" of the ownership of the firm. If the firm fails to achieve such a surplus value profit, these individuals, in principle, may suffer economic losses. However, the capitalism paradigm basically assumes a continuously expanding economy in which the opportunities to obtain such surplus value profits far outweigh the probabilities of losses.

From this perspective it is assumed that the reinvestment of surplus value profits by shareholders and corporate executives, as well as the investment of other capital funds, should be determined to the greatest degree possible by "natural" marketplace processes. Through market processes capital resources are invested in the development of the most economically effective firms, that is the most "profitable." As a result the total stock of goods and services that can be produced with a given set of resources is maximized and the general standard of living in society is increased. The allocation of such investments through incremental decisions by large numbers of individuals utilizing stock markets, bond markets, and banks as mechanisms for investment is viewed as the best procedure for dealing with the uncertain balance between financial risk and profit making potential in individual business situations.

This capitalism paradigm gives priority to individual freedom, or *liberty*, in particular the right of each individual to own and to use private economic resources with the least amount of collective, or governmental, restriction (Friedman 1962; Smith 1937). Economic freedom and the ownership of private property are viewed as desirable in and of themselves, and also as essential for civil and political freedom. Indeed, within this paradigm the protection of individual political rights cannot be legitimately asserted as grounds for the destruction of individual economic rights. An important element in the historical development of societies under capitalism is the legal definition of corporations as having a status under the law which is similar to the status of individuals, and therefore as having comparable constitutional "rights" to own and use property, and to be protected against the arbitrary seizure, or "taking," of such property by governmental bodies.

It is accepted within this capitalism paradigm that economic freedom will result in an unequal distribution of economic resources and benefits among the participants in a society. In part this is viewed as being a result of differences in initial personal resources, and in access to opportunities, because of accidents of birth and of fortune, or "luck"; in part it is viewed as being a result of differences in outcomes that reflect differences in economically relevant abilities and in individual initiative and effort (Sowell 1983).

The capitalism paradigm assumes that the exclusion of workers from direct participation in the distribution of surplus value profits is both legitimate, and essential, in a world of limited resources if there is to be adequate encouragement of entrepreneurship and sufficient investment capital to support continued economic growth and development. Workers, it is assumed, will ultimately benefit from the long-range increase in economic production. However, it is recognized that in the short run the exclusion from such economic benefits may be viewed as a form of exploitation which can lead to a pattern of class conflict.

In the capitalism paradigm the police powers of the state are legitimately used to control class conflict and to protect "private property," that is to protect the owners of capital from efforts by others to gain control of their financial resources, efforts which may range from illegal strikes and boycotts to robbery and guerilla warefare. Moreover, the owners of capital are assumed to have a social responsibility to use the economic resources under their control to prevent the more numerous "workers" from gaining political control of the government. Political control by workers, or by the "proletariat," and in turn the use of political authority to control economic processes in favor of workers, could be expected to disrupt the effective functioning of the economic system by imposing higher taxes on the owners of capital, and by imposing disruptive regulations on the functioning of corporate firms. Under the capitalism paradigm it is assumed that the result of direct worker political control would be decreased economic production to the disadvantage of all members of the society.

Under the capitalism paradigm those individuals who participate in the economic system primarily through the sale of their labor services in return for wage or salary payments are expected to divide their income between current consumption and savings. The savings function as a protection for members of the household against economic uncertainty, unusual expenses, and the effects of the loss of employment through disability or old age. Adequate individual savings would make it unnecessary to provide any universal form of social insurance. Such savings for future personal use also serve as a current source of funds for capital investment. However, it is assumed that the savings of any single worker are too small to have any significant impact on the policy governance of the businesses in which they are invested. Thus, it is only the owners of a substantial portion of the shares of the firm, or their agents, together with the executives of the firm, who are expected to have a significant role in the governance of the firm.

Under this free-market capitalism paradigm there is always a degree of tension for the individual between the allocation of personal income for current consumption which stimulates the economy by creating a demand for the goods and services which are currently available, and the allocation of such income to savings which makes possible the creation of the investment resources required for increased future production, an increase which is required, in part, because of the continued increase in human population (Malthus 1958). This tension is resolved through marketplace processes. Small but frequent variations in the values of corporate stocks and in the interest rates paid on savings and charged for loans, reflect the cumulative effect of constantly changing judgements of a large number of individuals about their preferences as between the potential for increased future economic benefits resulting from investment, and the personal benefits of current consumption.

From the perspective of this paradigm the fundamental responsibility of government is the defense of the territory of the nation-state, and of the economic interests of citizens of the state, together with the maintenance of internal law and order to facilitate economic production activities. Government is also viewed as having an important, but limited, role in maintaining those infrastructure elements essential for economic activity, such as a universal currency and a system of civil courts.

Taxation, at any level above the lowest level required for the minimal essential, or "core," elements of government required to protect and support the economic system, is viewed as a loss of funds for the individual who might either use those funds for personal consumption or for savings and investment (Friedman 1962). Fundamentally, taxes, regardless of their immediate purpose, are viewed as a disruption of market processes. It is assumed that any allocation of funds by governmental bodies, above the absolute minimum required for core functions, is by definition less efficient than choices made by individuals either directly, or through their agents, operating in the financial marketplace. This is, in part, because inefficient "system maintenance," or "political," considerations enter into governmental expenditure decisions, as well as economic efficiency considerations (Tullock 1965).

Any interference with marketplace processes through governmental regulation is viewed as a cause of extra production costs which in turn creates distortions in marketplace processes and reduces the overall economic efficiency of the economy. From the perspective of this traditional capitalism paradigm business monopolies or cartels which result from profit maximizing strategies may have similar negative consequences by restricting the total amount of production in order to protect prices and profit levels. But the risk of such an outcome can be viewed as, in general, preferable to governmental regulatory interference to prevent such occurances, since such regulations may impose substantial costs on the entire economy in an effort to prevent occasional distortions in the marketplace processes involving a limited number of firms.

From the perspective of this traditional capitalism paradigm such social policies as the forty-hour week, universal public education, workmen's compensation, public assistance and social insurance, as well as the establishment of voluntary service organizations such as nonprofit community hospitals and voluntary child welfare agencies, are the result of the public leadership, generosity and personal commitment to humanitarian values, of business leaders and the "well-to-do." These persons are viewed as motivated by religious beliefs, or by "enlightened self-interest," as well as by the communal tradition of "voluntarism." These motivations are expressed through financial contributions to voluntary nonprofit organizations to help meet "residual" social welfare needs (Wilensky and Lebeaux 1965). The development of voluntary community fundraising organizations such as the United Way and the establishment of community and corporate charitable foundations are viewed as key elements in this personal response to human need.

It is assumed that the existence of these institutions, both governmental and voluntary nonprofit, reflects the willingness of business leaders and other well-to-do individuals to share some part of their income with lower-income households. The expectation is that such charitable generosity will be acknowledged with gratitude by the beneficiaries of such policies and services, and a recognition that the policy control of such programs should rest in the hands of those who provide the financing, just as the control of for-profit corporations rests, in principle, in the hands of those who have provided the capital investments. In turn, both the specific benefits provided by human service programs, and gratitude on the part of those who are benefitted by such programs, are viewed as contributing to social solidarity and the creation of a positive "community climate" for economic activities.

As the complexity of the industrial economy increased over the past one hundred years, elaborate "welfare state" income transfer provisions have been established in capitalist societies, regardless of the contradictions between such provisions and the assumptions of the traditional capitalism paradigm. These income transfer provisions have come primarily as responses to the periodic recessions, or "depressions," which are endemic in a capitalist economy, and which result in sudden increases in the level of unemployment among normally employed workers (Piven and Cloward 1971), and as a response to the realities of age and disability.

The supporters of a free-market capitalism ideology primarily support those income transfer policies which reward entrepreneurial initiative and individual work effort. These include contributory social insurance programs with benefits related to past levels of earnings (Plattner 1979). They also include taxation policies which result in positive distributions, that is an increase in the relative economic position of individuals and households with high levels of earned income and wealth, in order to encourage risk-taking investment and entrepreneurial effort (Gilder 1981). Such policies, in turn, allow for substantial economic inequality even at the risk of economic hardship for some households.

Preferred income transfer policies are those which provide minimal "safety-net" or residual protection for the "worthy needy," while also encouraging individual voluntary acts of charity, rather than redistributional policies requiring broad-scale governmental action (Gilder 1981; Sowell 1983; Tocqueville 1968). This philosophy also calls for consistent governmental action, for example through the tax system, which will encourage the production of personal services either through voluntary nonprofit organizations or through marketplace, for-profit organizations, rather than through governmental agencies.

From a traditional capitalism perspective government administered human service programs are viewed as often becoming indiscriminate forms of public subsidy to individuals in return for political support, and as sources of political patronage employment (Janowitz 1978). The tax costs of such programs, which are generally assumed to be inefficiently administered (Tullock 1965), are viewed as a disincentive to entrepreneurial effort. On the other hand, voluntarily supported services are viewed as being inherently more efficient, run by professionally qualified personnel under the policy guidance of businessmen with "practical" management experience who serve as volunteer board members (Starr 1985).

The Socialism Paradigm

The socialism paradigm, which is often identified as the "working-class" paradigm, argues that the capture of surplus value profits by entrepreneurial executives and the owners of capital, who constitute only a small group in the total population, is not a "natural" result of economic processes (Marx 1972). Rather, this outcome is viewed as being the consequence of an interlocking pattern of illegitimate control by "capitalists" over the power and authority of government, including the police, the courts and the military. Capitalists are also viewed as controlling other major institutions in the society including the communication media and educational institutions (Gough 1979). These societal institutions are viewed as shaping public opinion through the "social construction of reality" (Berger and Luckman 1966) to the extent that many of the workers and small businessmen who are "exploited" in the sense that they do not receive an appropriate share of surplus value profits, are among the strongest defenders of the economic system that exploits them.

From the perspective of this paradigm a crucial factor in the ability of a small group of "capitalists" to maintain control of the economic system is the existence of a "surplus labor pool" of unemployed workers which assures competition for employment opportunities. A large surplus labor pool, it is argued, depresses industrial wage rates and assures the availability of seasonal and part-time workers at a minimal wage level (Galper 1975; Piven and Cloward 1971). In turn this labor surplus serves to control demands for increased wages, or for a share of the surplus value profits, and undercuts efforts to organize workers into unions and to create a workers political movement (Piven and Cloward 1982).

The analysis of the capitalist economy from a socialist perspective suggests, for example, that it is only when the availability of men within a society decreases in proportion to the need for workers that women are encouraged to enter the labor market in increasing numbers to maintain the surplus labor pool. The immigration of workers from other societies, both legally and illegally, is also encouraged by capitalists with the objective of increasing the size of the available labor force, and thus the surplus labor pool, regardless of the actual provisions of immigration legislation.

From the perspective of the socialist paradigm the objective of a workers movement is to educate and "raise the consciousness" of all members of the working class, and to bring into existence, through either political action or revolution, a society in which the surplus value profits will be used for the collective benefit of all members of the society (Gil 1976; Gough 1979). In such a society control of the political system by the working-class would be used to control the economic system in order to assure such an outcome. Political decisions, rather than marketplace decisions, would determine the allocation of surplus value profits, and other investment resources, between current consumption and investment, and would determine the choices among alternative investment opportunities.

Workers and their families, being more numerous than business executives and the owners of capital, would collectively receive a greater portion of the benefits from such a distribution of surplus value profits. Under this paradigm economic security and the degree of equality in the distribution of economic benefits, rather than the total amount of production, are viewed as the critical criteria for evaluating the success of the economic system. Economic and social equality, assured through universal participation in public policy decisions is more important than individual freedom. Some loss of freedom in the use of private property is accepted as necessary to achieve economic equality.

All human service programs should be administered directly by governmental agencies so that they are democratically accountable to all members of the society, with the cost, in turn, being shared by all members of the society. Voluntary nonprofit human service organizations, regardless of the quality of their operation, are viewed with suspicion on the grounds that they are generally controlled by, and dependent on, wealthy individuals and therefore always represent capitalist class interests (Gough 1979).

Economic security and equality are viewed as contributing to the development of an inclusive sense of social solidarity and mutual assistance among all members of society. Social solidarity, rather than private property, becomes the source of protection for civil and political liberty. Ultimately, under the assumptions of the socialist paradigm, the development of social solidarity could make it unnecessary to maintain the governmental law and order control functions which are needed in a capitalist society to protect the power and position of the wealthy from attacks by the nonwealthy. Following this theory the development of collective socialist societies in all nations replacing competitive capitalist societies should make it possible to eliminate military expenditures.

There are two views incorporated in the socialist paradigm about welfare state provisions in capitalist societies (Gough 1979; Piven and Cloward 1982; Taylor-Gooby and Dale 1981). This can lead to contradictory positions on particular policy issues. One socialist or "working-class" perspective on welfare state provisions in capitalist societies is that social policies such as the eighthour day and forty-hour week, workmen's compensation laws, and social insurance constitute a form of "social wage" or collective "fringe benefit" for all workers (Adams 1985).

It is assumed that these collective benefits have been established primarily as a result of organized pressure by workers through a combination of union bargaining and political action, and the implicit threat of more violent methods, over persistent opposition of "capitalists." The expansion of welfare state benefits can thus be viewed as a method for securing some part of the surplus value profits as a benefit to workers under capitalism. Such benefits, however, should be noncontributory and should be redistributional, offsetting economic inequalities resulting from the labor market.

Such social wage benefits are viewed as a integral part of the basic wage bargain between workers and business owners, along with the package of fringe benefits attached to employment in a specific firm and individual wage and salary payments. Political proposals to reduce any specific form of social wage benefit is regarded, in effect, as an attack on the labor movement and on the fundamental rights of every worker.

A second, contrasting "working-class" perspective, is that welfare state provisions are essentially instruments of social control used to reinforce the exploitation of the working-class (Rochefort 1981). The early charity organizations, as well as current "means-tested" public assistance programs, are viewed as social control institutions, providing minimal financial benefits with the objective of blunting organized protest from the poor, while undercutting the development of workers organizations and delaying the fundamental reorganization of society (Withorn 1984). Such minimal benefit assistance programs are also viewed as serving to maintain people in a dependent, marginal economic position which in turn assists in maintaining the suplus labor pool.

From this critical perspective the activities of settlement houses and youth serving programs often result in the "creaming" of the more able children of working-class families, encouraging them to pursue upwardly mobile educational and occupational opportunities. In turn, these achievers, some of whom become human service professionals, are likely to become part of the bourgeois "middle-class" and defenders of the capitalist system. Child welfare agencies and juvenile courts are viewed as instruments for imposing middle-class childrearing norms on working-class, immigrant families, or in some instances for removing children from their natural families in order to place them in middle-class institutions and foster homes (Platt 1969). The use of payroll taxes to fund Social Security and other forms of social insurance is criticized as being a form of mandatory savings, imposed on workers (Cates 1983). These savings are intended to assure the availability of a source of minimal personal income after forced retirement from the labor force, rather than treating the costs of forced retirement as a direct cost of economic production to be paid for before the distribution of surplus value profits (Adams 1985).

From this perspective social insurance is a system which is imposed on workers through the control of the political system by capitalist economic interests, rather than a system of benefits achieved through working-class militancy. Workers generally have no direct control over the funds which are withheld from their earnings to fund their retirement, whether through Social Security or through contributory private pension arrangements, nor over the investment purposes for which such funds are used.

Also from this perspective all social wage benefits are considered substitutes for higher real wages so that the total value of real benefits to workers does not really change. Moreover, the costs of benefits for persons who cannot participate in the work force because of physical handicaps, or the presence of young children in the home, are met primarily through payroll and income taxes withheld from workers in the wage and salary sector of the economy. From this point of view it is the members of the working-class who pay the costs of the welfare state and who support the poor while wealthy capitalists avoid their "fair share" of taxes through both legal and illegal forms of tax avoidance.

Regardless of the interpretation of current welfare state provisions, from the socialist perspective the achievement of working-class political control, and the establishment of a socialist society, is viewed as being of ultimate importance. Such working-class control is expected to lead to welfare state policies and programs that will result in: (1) a high degree of equality in the distribution of benefits from economic production, using the tax system and other forms of governmental intervention to re-distribute economic outputs so as to achieve both income and wealth equality; (2) universal income transfer policies that would offset any economic inequalities which might affect those who are not in the labor force, including the disabled and elderly, and (3) direct provision of personal services to everyone without cost through universal governmentally administered educational, medical and social service programs (Gough 1979).

The Welfare Capitalism Paradigm[1]

There is a third perspective on the welfare state, which is often held, among others, by those associated with human service programs in capitalist societies, a point-of-view which differs from both the traditional capitalism paradigm and the traditional socialism paradigm. This welfare capitalism perspective holds that welfare state policies and programs are central elements in the pattern of social provision within a marketplace capitalist economy (Crossman 1952; Gilbert 1983).

Voluntary social welfare services, as well as governmental services, are viewed as significant elements in social provision (Gilbert 1983). A major goal of social reform efforts is the reduction of class conflict and political polarization, this goal being accomplished through a reduction in the extremes of economic and social inequality within the context of a free market economy (Lippman 1937).

The settlement house movement, for example, was viewed by many of its founders as an effort to create a bridge between immigrant working-class families and middle-class business and professional leaders (Davis 1967; Lasch 1965). One objective of the "liberal" social and economic reforms supported by charity organization and settlement house leaders was to limit and contain the class conflict polarization which had developed during the nineteenth century (Fish 1985). This polarization was a result of clashes between aggressive industrial entrepreneurs and the combination of an increasingly militant labor movement and socialist and communist political movements which by the end of the nineteenth century were gaining substantial public support (Lens 1969).

Many of the reform-oriented economists such as Thorstein Veblen, Simon Patten, Franklin Giddings, Richard Ely, John Commons, and Isaac Rubinow had similar interests in modifying the unrestricted competitive operation of a free-market economic system in order to improve the economic postition of industrial workers and to strengthen the political solidarity underlying

American political institutions. Moreover, they identified the "demand side" impact of aspirations for an improved "standard of living" among working-class families as a major force in the growth of a capitalist economy (Schulter 1979).

More recent programs like the Office of Economic Opportunity Community Action Program were similarly viewed by liberal social reformers as instruments for reducing the level of ethnic conflict, which by the 1960s threatened to disrupt the existing social order (Matusow 1984). Social development funds were targeted to low-income black and Hispanic neighborhoods, and residents from such areas were made part of community-wide policymaking bodies, together with public officials and volunteer civic leaders. "Affirmative action" employment programs have been supported to provide individuals from politically and economically disenfranchised groups access to upward mobility opportunities in mainstream political and economic institutions. It is believed that these actions might help to prevent the formation of a permanent "underclass" with the potential of continuous conflict with the rest of society.

From this twentieth century "liberal" welfare capitalism perspective both traditional socialism and traditional capitalism are viewed as simplistic rationalizations that are primarily ideological. They ignore the high degree of interdependence and mutual adjustment among all elements of society which is involved in the functioning of modern societies. Every society is necessarily involved in compromises between freedom and equality, between economic opportunity and economic security. Careful planning and the development of effective "steering capacity" can make it possible to balance these conflicting pressures and adapt to changing economic conditions (Gilbert 1983). From this liberal perspective a broad base of popular consensus and political stability are viewed as more important than ideological consistency in government.

Alternatively both socialist and capitalist ideologists view liberal, welfare capitalism social reformers as "soft-hearted dogooders" who ignore fundamental political and economic realities in favor of various forms of temporary assistance for individuals and "quick-fix" short term remedies for basic contradictions in the society. The result is increasing governmental expenditures and decreasing productivity, viewed from both socialist and traditional capitalist perspectives as the "crisis of the welfare state" (Habermas 1975; Murray 1983; Offe 1984). Central to this debate, however, is the issue of whether the historic analyses of the political economy which underlie the traditional capitalism and socialism paradigms are relevant, or whether recent developments have made both of these paradigms obsolete for the purpose of contemporary analysis of welfare state issues (Bell 1988).

NOTES

1. A related perspective identified as democratic socialism emphasizes a more active leadership role for government in social reform and in the regulation of the economy in the context of a multiparty, pluralistic representative democracy (Harrington 1968; Offe 1984).

Chapter 3

Societal Changes and Their Implications for Political Economy Paradigms

The political economy paradigms described in the preceding chapter had their origins in social and economic conditions of the eighteenth, nineteenth and early twentieth century, during the period of industrial development in Europe and the United States. By the end of the twentieth century many of these conditions have changed dramatically. For example, industrial management and ownership have been separated. The largest absolute share of corporate ownership is now in the hands of institutional interests, particularly large pension funds managed by bank trustees, or is pledged to banks as collateral for the large loans involved in corporate mergers and take-overs.

Managers, including chief executives, are occupationally mobile salaried personnel with limited ownership rights in the companies they manage. Many chief executives, and indeed middle managers as well, have a limited tenure in any single company. The career success of executives may have little relation to the status of corporate owners as a class, or to the economic success of the national economy as a whole. Reich (1983) suggests that as profits from production have decreased in American industry executives have been increasingly involved in "paper entrepreneurialship" to produce short-term bookkeeping profits and to maintain dividends for stockholders, rather than being involved in improving the productive efficiency of the firms that they head.

However, the most significant changes for human service programs are those that have taken place in the organization of the labor force, and in particular in the position of production employees in business and industry. These changes also bring into question many of the basic assumptions of the capitalism and socialism political economy paradigms and the implications

33

of these paradigms for human service programs. These changes are, in turn, a consequence of far-reaching changes in the nature of both national and international economies.

THE POLITICAL ECONOMY OF NATIONAL SOCIETIES

Important changes have taken place in the political economy of postindustrial societies. These changes undercut assumptions built into both capitalism and socialism paradigms. One important change is the emergence of the "mixed economy." Another is the disappearance of the growth surplus in postindustrial national economies.

Traditional class conflict analysis assumes that societies operating under a capitalism paradigm have a pattern of economic activity that is distinctly different from the pattern of the economy which that society would have under a socialism paradigm. The free-market capitalism paradigm assumes that under capitalism the pattern of economic processes is the impersonal result of the economic dynamics of the marketplace which operate according to certain general principles, "the hidden hand" (Smith 1937). This pattern is predictable, based on economic theories, but it is not managed or controlled by any single element in the society.

The capitalism paradigm also assumes that political processes in the society are separated from economic processes, and that while political processes, in general, may support economic activities, they do not control detailed economic decision making. The formal separation of the Federal Reserve Board in the United States from direct political control by Congress is a structural example of this separation of economic processes from political processes.

Both capitalism and socialism paradigms assume that the alternative to a capitalist free-market society is a totally socialist society (Gough 1979). However, all postindustrial societies, both capitalist and socialist, appear to be moving towards a "mixed economy" (Bell 1988; Gilbert 1983). The mix of political decision processes and marketplace decision processes which determine economic patterns in the mixed economy covers a continuum. It includes at one end capitalist societies in which governmental participation in the day-to-day regulation of the economy has, in fact, become very extensive. It includes at the other end socialist societies in which governmental control of the economy is the dominant paradigm but large elements of marketplace economy exist, and are increasingly being given official recognition.

In capitalist mixed economy societies governments are highly involved in the marketplace economy through direct regulation of specific types of business activities, including banking, through control over the monetary system, over interest rates and the availability of credit, and through governmental ownership of a variety of firms that produce goods or services for distribution through the marketplace. To the extent that government is the largest purchaser for particular goods and services, for example, military aircraft, political decisions with negotiated pricing rather than marketplace pricing create the demand which sustains an entire industry. Moreover, to the extent that political processes affect the decisions about money supply, interest rates, the treatment of corporate income for tax purposes, or the conditions of international trade, particular industries receive benefits and others face increased costs quite independent of marketplace supply and demand factors.

In the capitalist mixed economy governmental bodies use contracts with marketplace firms to carry out a number of core governmental functions rather than establishing governmental administrative organizations staffed by governmental employees (Bendick 1985; Ferris and Graddy 1986; Gilbert 1983). These include armament production, management of governmental office buildings, the operation of health care services and the development of new communities. The capabilities and limitations of for-profit production organizations thus often determine the quality of goods and services which result from governmental initiative rather than the quality of production being determined by the administrative competence of elected officials, and appointed public administrators, who can be held accountable through political processes. The production of military equipment is a highly visible example.

In a mixed economy there is often a separation between governmental *provision*, a public policy action by a political unit designed to assure that a particular good or service is available to or provided for citizens, and *production* of the specific good or service (Kolderie 1986; Ostrom and Ostrom 1978). While the decision to provide a particular service, for example by appropriating tax funds for that purpose, may be the responsibility of a governmental body, production may take place under the auspices of a different governmental unit, often at a different level of government, or of a voluntary nonprofit organization or a for-profit firm.

The existence of a mixed economy system in a capitalist society has major consequences for efforts to develop macro economic theories that will predict the actual behavior of the economy, or to develop political theories that will predict the specific consequences of political decisions for the actual implementation of governmental programs. The actual effects of a Medicaid or Medicare policy decision often depend more on the marketplace dynamics of the health care industry than on the intent of Congress. The modest redistribution intent of national social security legislation may be offset by the earnings-based retirement pension plans adopted by employers (Rein 1983a). The stock market value of defense industry stocks, on the other hand, often depends more on budgetary decisions by Congress and the skills of lobbyists than on the managerial efficiency or entrepreneurial ability of corporate executives.

There is also a high degree of interaction between governmental activities and marketplace activities in the provision of social benefits in a mixed economy. Large elements of the population have social benefits provided in the form of wage and salary fringe benefits for employees (Rein and Rainwater 1986). These include retirement pensions, health insurance, employee assistance programs, paid holidays and vacations, stock options, and such perquisites as discount purchasing, company cars and employer provided day care. Such benefits now constitute a sizeable portion of labor costs in both governmental and nongovernmental employment.

Similarily in societies in which socialism is the dominant paradigm competitive marketplace elements are being incorporated into the economic system, in agriculture and retail merchandising in particular. The existence of large-scale "black market" activities, sometimes with the tacit acknowledgement of the government, often extends the range of marketplace activities in such economies.

The emergence of the mixed economy as the dominant societal pattern in postindustrial societies minimizes the likelihood of truly radical changes in either economic policies or in the administration of governmental programs as result of a change in the ideological pattern of political control whether from capitalism to socialism, or vice/versa. Scenarios incorporating the dynamics of revolutionary class conflict are thus of limited value in analyzing the future probabilities for the pattern of societal development in postindustrial societies (Bell 1988).

A second major change in the political economy is the disappearance of the growth dividend in national economies. To a substantial degree both capitalism and socialism assume an indefinitely expanding economy. It was the potential of a very rapidly increasing productive capability under industrialization that made it appear possible to escape the Malthusian dilemma in which an improved economy would lead to an increase in population which would in turn result in increased starvation (Malthus 1958). Moreover, it was the combination of increased production, and the exploitation of expanding markets in developing regions of the world, that created the real possibility of suplus value profits in industrializing economies. This became part of the image, incorporated in both capitalism and socialism paradigms, of the potential for an infinitely improving societal standard of living, although, depending upon the paradigm, with very different assumptions about the preferred pattern of income and wealth distribution.

However, by the mid-twentieth century in all postindustrial societies a substantial portion of any economic growth "dividend" was being absorbed by a combination of military expenditures, which did not result in consumable goods or services, welfare state provisions and the costs involved in protecting the environment against the effects of industrialization and urbanization. Major elements of the welfare state provisons included unemployment compensation, income support for persons retired from the labor force in the form of both social insurance and public assistance payments, military pensions and pensions paid by business and industry out of current earnings, together with expenditures for education for children, for health care, particularly for older adults, and for institutional care of persons with chronic disabilities of all types.

Until the 1970s these welfare state expenditures did not appear to be inconsistent with the possibility of a general increase in the standard of living, and in the United States, an increasing level of expenditure for military purposes and for maintaining the influence of the United States on a world-wide basis through foreign aid. There was a general concept that welfare state provisions could be funded out of increases in the modest social welfare "slice" of a generally expanding "pie." It was recognized that there would always be arguments about the correct allocation of benefits within the total of all welfare state provisions. But with the possibility of a general pattern of increases it was assumed that such arguments could be controlled.

However, by the end of the 1970s there was increasing attention being given to the "crisis of the welfare state" (Gough 1979; Hirschman 1980). The rate of expansion and the rate of increases in productivity in postindustrial economies were slowing down (Reich 1983); the requirements of welfare state provisons were increasing more rapidly than anticipated (Judge 1981). The slowdown in economic growth was a function, in part, of changes in the economic relation between established postindustrial societies and other national economies which reduced the possibilities of a continuing increase in exploitive profits.

There was also the simultaneous growth in the scope and costs of all types of welfare state provisions. This resulted, in major part, from the increase in the life span of retired individuals and pressures to improve the standard of living for such persons, and from reductions in the support provided to such persons through extended families as a consequence of the increase in the employment of women, the increase in divorce, and reductions in the housing space in individual homes. There were also the increased costs of advanced health care technology and increased professional specialization, again largely related to the care of older individuals (Feldstein 1985). The expansion of educational provisions for adolescents and young adults, increased costs of institutional and noninstitutional care for persons with disabilities, and for law-violators, and the costs of structural unemployment all combined to push the costs of human services even higher.

Increasingly economic decisions in postindustrial societies, under either capitalism or socialism, involve absolute choices between current consumption and investment for the future (Thurow 1980). The federal budgetary deficit in the United States involves the use of large amounts of savings for current consumption, (including savings generated in other nations) rather than for future oriented development. This pattern of current consumption, including current production of military equipment, also involves a choice between an improved standard of living for persons in the labor force, and for persons not in the labor force, particularly retired workers. In the United States this involves, specifically, the choice between increased taxes, or, on the other hand, limitations on cost of living increases in retirement benefits under Social Security and other public pension systems. These choices involve real trade-offs as Thurow has pointed out in *The Zero-Sum Society* (1980), not simply political preference choices about the allocation of an economic growth dividend.

Traditional assumptions about a direct connection between the dominant paradigm in the political economy of the nation-state, that is capitalism or socialism, and the scope of welfare state provisions, is no longer valid. Economies in both capitalist and socialist societies have increasingly similar characteristics, involve the same choices and have the same dilemmas.

THE INTERNATIONAL STRUCTURE OF THE POLITICAL ECONOMY

Both capitalism and socialism paradigms assume essentially self-contained national economies. However, the functional structure of both political and economic systems is now predominately international, rather than national. Political decisions in the United States are evaluated in terms of the probable reaction of Russia, or of European members of NATO, as much as in terms of domestic reaction. The national interests of the United States are, in turn, defined as being directly affected by the outcomes of political economy processes in at least half of the other nation-states in the world. Russia has similar direct interests in the political economies of other nations, as far flung as Ethiopia, Cuba and Vietnam.

Nation-state economies are not self-contained. Socialist and capitalist states alike participate in a single international banking and monetary system which handles capital flows across international boundaries, including the Iron Curtain. A single economic monetary exchange system which links the currencies of individual nations together is essential for the flow of international trade. Investment decisions now involve an international network of stock, bond and commodity exchanges. The international banking system reflects a mixed economy pattern of governmental and marketplace institutions. These institutions include the World Bank and the International Monetary Fund which function as semi-governmental components of an international economic governance system, government controlled "national" banks, and multinational private banking systems.

This international banking system is simultaneously involved in credit transactions with national governments, with governmentally owned production corporations and with for-profit marketplace firms. During the 1980s all of the elements in the international banking system have been involved collaboratively in managing the international debt of a large number of national economies, both capitalist and socialist. In many instances this has involved mandating economic, and, in turn, governmental, policies within individual nations, independent of national political processes. However, transnational currency and investment movements often mean that the governments of nation-states, including United States, have limited power to control the pattern of economic events within their nation.

The movement of individuals across national boundaries, a movement which can only partially be controlled by national governments short of constructing a military barrier, also becomes a significant factor in the political economy of individual nations. Social wage benefits designed for native born workers may become a significant factor in improving the economic condition of refugees, or immigrants, from low-income societies. Some of these benefits flow to households outside the national economy with positive benefits for the international economy.

The establishment of a relatively high minimum wage and a wage scale based on that minmum may attract large numbers of new workers from societies with lower wage scales while leaving marginally skilled and handicapped individuals within the society unemployed and dependent on public support. Large wage scale differentials, or tax level differentials, between two nations contribute to the relocation of labor-intensive industrial plants by multi-national corporations. This results in substantial improvements in the economies of some nations but also leads to increased welfare state costs, as a result of unemployment, in others.

Nation-states have become economic competitors within an inclusive international economic system. Economic or political actions within one nation which cause a decline in the level of productivity, or an increase in the costs of production, or in the level of business taxes, regardless of the ideological rationale or social justification for such actions, may result in a competitive disadvantage for that national economy as a whole in comparison to the economies of other nations. The movement of private capital across national boundaries in search of profitable investments, both legally and illegally, also sets limits on the ability of any one nation to make significant redistributions within the pattern of economic benefits within its society. Given the interdependence of national economies the probability of radical and permanent changes in the economic structure of any one nation as a result of a shift in the dominant political economy paradigm is substantially reduced, as illustrated by the experience of France during the early 1980s (Cerny and Schain 1985).

JOB MARKET AND LABOR FORCE

Reflecting the impact of these changes in the international pattern of national economies there has been a marked decrease in the proportion of male "blue-collar" industrial production jobs within the total labor force in the United States (Bluestone and Harrison 1980; Harris 1984). These positions have been at the core of the labor movement and central to the concept of the "working-class." Traditionally these positions required a minimal level of formal education, with job skills largely learned "on-the-job." Job advancement was seldom related to intellectual skills or academic achievement. The level of production, and rewards related to increased production, were largely based on the collective efforts of the work group rather than on the contributions of individual workers.

Since World War II the number of industrial production positions has been affected by a continuous process of automating industrial production processes. The most recent form of this automation has been the introduction of industrial robots. In addition there has been a substantial increase in the proportion of technical and professional positions, particularly in the service industries which have become the largest sector of the American economy (Fuchs 1968; Ginzberg and Vojta 1981). These "white-collar" positions, including many high-skill craft positions in industry, require formal education beyond high school. Career advancement is more likely to be linked to individual technical knowledge, intellectual ability, and individual initiative than to physical strength and endurance and group solidarity. This has also increased the importance of educational services in the society as a whole, reflected in the actions in many states during the 1980s to increase expenditures on education as part of the pattern of competition among the states for economic development opportunities.

The labor market has become increasingly divided into two segments: (1) "primary" labor market positions which have job security, substantial wages and significant fringe benefits, and which are often covered by union contracts, and (2) "secondary" labor market positions that lack job security, have few fringe benefits, have effective pay levels at or near the minimum wage level and are less likely to be covered by a union contract (Bluestone, Murphy and Stevenson 1973). Most of these secondary, low-wage employment positions do not provide sufficient take-home pay for a single adult worker to meet the costs of basic necessities for a two-adult household which includes children. The alternative solution is two employed adults, or a single parent household, and often some form of income transfer (food stamps).

Ethnic minority and immigrant workers are disproportionately concentrated in low-wage labor market positions. Discriminatory practices by both employers and unions often exclude these workers from access to primary labor market opportunities. Many of the increased number of women in the labor force are employed in the low-wage labor market at minimum wage levels in the "light assembly" factories which are characteristic of the electrical/ electronic era (Reskin 1984). In 1983 white women, together with men and women from ethnic minority backgrounds, for the first time, made up more than one half of the total labor force in the United States.

One result of these emerging labor market patterns is that there are in effect two "working-classes" among employed wage earners. One consists primarily of men in those primary labor force positions which do not involve specialized technical or professional competencies and which are covered by union contracts. The other "working-class," which is notable because of the diversity which it includes, consists of most of the women in industry and business, at all job levels, together with men in secondary labor market positions. These two "working-class" groups often have conflicting economic interests; there is little evidence of a common consciousness of working-class solidarity cutting across this division. The proportion of the first "working-class" within the labor force is decreasing; the proportion of the second "working-class" is increasing.

Many young adults with family responsibilities but with limited education and without specialized job skills, who would have been employed as unskilled workers a hundred years ago, are now unemployed and perceived as outside of the regular labor force. They are likely to be receiving major economic support through income transfers from such sources as public assistance programs or government funded job training programs. They are outside the scope of union recruitment and are, in fact, frequently a target of hostility from members of the industrial "working-class."

ORGANIZED LABOR

The role of labor unions has been affected by changes in the meaning of employment and work (Ferman 1984). In the early stages of the Industrial Revolution the shift from independent craftsman or small farmer to factory worker was marked by an increase in the oppressive elements of work—long hours, unskilled mass production technologies, dangerous and depressing working conditions, a pace of work dictated by machinery rather than by the worker. Without mass transportation housing was concentrated near the work locations, often in large tenement buildings, overcrowded and poorly maintained. Work was necessary for survival. But it was also viewed as largely a negative experience, part of the punishment laid on mankind when Adam was driven from the Garden of Eden, according to one form of Christian tradition (Macarov 1970).

Cleaner and safer working conditions, shorter hours, longer paid vacations, and provisions for early retirement with a pension were union bargaining issues, in addition to higher wages. Reform efforts directed at working conditions for women emphasized limitations on hours, provision of rest periods and protection against tasks requiring heavy lifting.

Today the conditions of work in most industrial production settings in the United States have been substantially improved, in both unionized and nonunionized firms, although exposure to toxic substances has emerged as a new workplace hazard. Oppressive working conditions are not a major source of motivation for industrial union organizing today. There has been little pressure from unions to reduce the work week over the past 50 years, though there has been continuing pressure for increases in vacation time.

Moreover, the social importance of being employed, that is being perceived by others as having an occupational role in society, has increased. Today political pressure from ethnic minority groups, and from women, is directed primarily towards gaining access to employment, rather than towards improving income transfer benefits for unemployed persons. Some women's groups have specifically sought to eliminate special protections for women in industry in order to broaden the range of jobs open to women. Organized interest groups among the elderly have successfully lobbied to raise the mandatory age for retirement. In the United States the tyranny of work no longer serves as a major argument for union organizing, nor for the development of working-class consciousness and worker solidarity.

For the large segments of organized labor that are still based on primary labor market industrial production jobs there is a much higher priority of expanding existing benefits, including both wage payments and fringe benefits, and in protecting job security, than there is in expanding the base of the labor movement by organizing workers in the secondary labor market, or in organizing industries in which the workers are predominantly women or from ethnic minority backgrounds. Labor unions, similar to the pattern in other membership associations including professional associations, have become structures for advancing the economic self-interests of their members, rather than providing a social movement base for the development of an inclusive pattern of working-class solidarity.

While production activities in most industries still take place largely in medium-size plants, financial decisions affecting those plants often take place in the headquarters units of conglomerates and multinational firms, and in the offices of the large national banks that are the major source of commercial credit for such firms. Employees of a single plant, however well organized, have limited ability to determine wages and fringe benefits. Decisions to close existing plants, open new plants, or to change production processes are often made by individuals who have no personal involvement in either the factories or the communities most directly affected (Bluestone and Harrison 1980).

One consequence has been that labor organizations have been forced to move towards nationwide bargaining units and nationwide contracts. This requires the development of a large national headquarters unit for the union which is separated from the work locations of union members. Detailed contract negotiations are often carried on by lawyers and accountants who are not union members and who may have little direct contact with the workers being represented. Such negotiations may result in improved job-related benefits but the process of negotiation has little connection with the development of working-class solidarity among union members.

Large numbers of union members who work for governmental organizations, the most rapidly growing segment of the labor movement, do not have legitimated access to the strike as an instrument in contract negotiations, making their position very different from the position of union members in private industry. The illegal use of the strike by such public service workers, while sometimes successful in the short run, has often resulted in a loss of public support for the union regardless of the merits of the individual situation. Such a strike is often viewed as an attack on the general public rather than being a form of confrontation with governmental administrators or elected officials.

Political action leading to the election of sympathetic public officials is often the only way in which such a union can achieve improved working conditions and pay increases. However, successful political action requires the development of a broad base of public support for union objectives. This, in turn, requires the use of language in contract negotiations which is not threatening to the general public, rather than the rhetoric of class conflict and union solidarity. The 1981 air traffic controllers strike is an illustration of the consequences of a faulty analysis of public union bargaining strategies.

Most of the women working in business and industry are not union members, even among those persons whose employment income is the primary source of household support, except in those firms with a long tradition of inclusive union membership. The limited participation of women in unions is a result in part of the lack of direct personal connections with a tradition of working-class solidarity. In part it is a consequence of the domination of the union movement by men, many of whom have been openly hostile to expanding employment opportunities for women and to equal pay provisions. Moreover, the expanding use of part-time employees, particularly women in clerical and technical positions, diminishes the connection between economic benefits and any single employer, and, in turn, with a union that is organized around a single employment location.

Young technical and professional workers are often more interested in career opportunities within an industry than they are in current economic benefits or job security in a single firm. Those opportunities depend more on individual qualifications than on group pressure. Moreover, economic benefits for such workers in nonunion firms are often comparable to those in unionized firms. Participation in organized labor activities to improve current benefits may be viewed as having potentially negative consequences for career opportunities, except in industries which are totally unionized. Universal social wage benefits, such as Social Security retirement benefits, and income-tax deductions, may be more beneficial economically for such persons than job-specific fringe benefits or seniority promotion rights which are part of a union negotiated contract in a single firm.

The organizational maintenance interests of unions, and the perceived self-interest of nonunion workers, coincide in a pattern which separates unions from the most rapidly growing groups among business and industrial workers. This contributes significantly to the lessened significance of the concept of the inclusive "working-class" as a major force in the political economy (Greenslade 1976). In the United States there has also been an increasing separation between the intellectual interpreters of the socialism paradigm, primarily located in academic settings, who continue to emphasize the concepts of the class conscious "working-class," and class conflict, and organized labor which, to a very large degree, operates within the assumptions of the welfare capitalism paradigm (Howe 1985).

THE ECONOMIC POSITION OF INDIVIDUAL HOUSEHOLDS

Although marketplace economies continue to have cyclical periods of recession, many individual households have a substantial degree of buffering against economic catastrophe. The existence of two or more earners in many households contributes to the ability of these households to survive temporary unemployment. Home ownership, which is widespread among wage earners, as well as among higher income groups, provides more economic security than renting. Credit cards and other forms of short-term credit are also important sources of buffering for families with established credit.

Social wage benefits such as unemployment insurance and food stamps have reduced the short-term economic impact of unemployment, and public assistance programs provide marginal economic protection over longer periods of time. Social insurance and income assistance programs for older persons and persons with disabilities relieve employed workers of much of the financial responsibility for older household members, and those with disabilities. Indeed Social Security retirement income coming to an elderly parent may be a significant source of income support in a multigenerational household with an unemployed worker.

One consequence of these several forms of economic buffering is that widespread temporary unemployment does not necesarily lead to political polarization along economic class lines, or to widespread political attacks against the government in power. For example, during the early 1980s in the United States political mobilization among black citizens appeared to be much more a reaction to changes at the federal level in the approach to civil rights issues than a reaction to high levels of unemployment among black workers.

Even among temporarily unemployed workers economic stability and a low rate of inflation may be viewed as more important than steady employment with high rates of inflation, as reflected in the election results of 1984.

THE POSITION OF WOMEN IN THE LABOR FORCE

The increasing level of employment among women has had other far-reaching consequences, including changes in relationships within the household, and in the demand for human services. With an independent source of income, and with access to birth-control technology, adult women have a more evenly balanced choice between marriage (or remarriage), functioning as a single person or functioning as a "single parent." Public attention to the recent increase in female-headed, single parent households with young children overlooks the fact that, in the past, such households were not economically viable on any substantial scale. The high level of employment of women with young children has increased the demand for organizationally produced day-care. The relatively high level of divorce and remarriage has confused patterns of familial responsibility for the care of dependent individuals, both young and old, (usually provided by women) leading to an increased demand for organizationally produced forms of both full-time and part-time dependent care, either in residential settings or through community-based networks of support services. The increased involvement of women in employment, and in career development, has also reduced the ability of the adult household to handle the "resource mobilization" and "coordination" tasks often required in providing care for persons with various forms of disability who are part of the immediate, or extended, family. In turn, this has focused increased attention on a need for organizationally based "case management" services as part of the services for such persons (Weil and Karls 1985).

Women, and in particular women with post-high school education, have also been the traditional source of direct service employees in nursing, elementary and secondary education, library science and social work, as well as in a number of other human service professions. This has been largely a captive labor force for these human service occupations since there was limited access to comparable positions in business mangement, law and medicine, or to primary labor market positions in industry until the 1970s. Pay, working conditions and career opportunities in the employment settings dominated by women have not been comparable to those dominated by men (Boothby 1984), although they have had important advantages for individual women over the unpaid, and largely unacknowledged, role of human service producer within the home (Minton 1984).

Beginning in the 1970s patterns of education, and of employment, among college educated women began to change. Enrollment of women in business and law increased dramatically, and substantially in medicine. By the mid-1980s it was evident that there were beginning to be consequences in those fields that have traditionally depended on this educated labor force of women, particularly in those settings with the most highly structured, bureaucratically controlled environments. This has become most visible in elementary and secondary education. The Report of the Carnegie Foundation Task Force on Teaching as a Profession (1986) with its recommendations for increasing the salary levels and the professional status of teachers, and the education reform measures adopted by a number of states are, in part, a response to an increasing shortage of qualified professional teachers in many school systems.

In social work there has been a steady shift of experienced professional practitioners from traditional organizational settings, particularly in the governmental sector, such as public assistance and public child welfare agencies. On the other hand, there has been a steady increase in private practice arrangements, reflected in the steadily increasing number of professional social workers listed in the nation-wide Clinical Register of the National Association of Social Workers. In nursing there has been increasing discontent with the subordinate role of nurses in most medical care settings, and a development of nursing practice as an independent form of health care service, together with an increasing shortage of nurses to fill traditional hospital nursing positions. Moreover, the developments during the past two decades suggest the possibility of even larger scale changes in employment patterns in nursing, elementary and secondary education, and social work during the rest of this century, particularly if initial efforts to cope with these changes were to result in increased centralization of administrative control in large, male-dominated traditional service organizations, making these settings even more unattractive to college educated women as a setting for a life-time career.

THE BLURRING OF CLASS IDENTITY

An important element in the blurring of class identity and class consciousness is the difficulty in specifying a consistent definition of either "working-class" or "capitalists." Among those who might be categorized as members of the "working-class" in a traditional sense there is, moreover, little evidence of an awareness of common identity (Greenslade 1976).

As indicated earlier there are at least two major subdivisions among wage earners. Men in primary labor market positions have important differences in economic interests from most employed women and from those men who are in secondary, low-wage labor market positions. There are also important differences in interests between wage earners in free-market for-profit firms who have some protected rights in the use of the strike, and indiviuals who work in regulated utilities and governmental organizations who are sharply limited in their ability to resort to the strike.

Many of the married women who are employed in industry may be working for "working-class" wages but view themselves as part of a "middle-class" family, particularly when the combined household income makes it possible for the family to live in a middle-income neighborhood. There are, moreover, large numbers of salaried clerical and commercial workers, technicians and professionals, who may be unionized, or have some form of group negotiating relationship with an employer, but who do not share any sense of class consciousness which includes hourly wage employees in heavy industries.

There are also large numbers of marginally employed, long-term unemployed, chronically disabled individuals, public assistance recipients, individuals employed in the "underground" economy, and illegal immigrants who are viewed as falling outside the conventional definition of the "working-class." In most societies these are the most obvious victims of exploitation and oppression by both private employers and governmental organizations, and the plight of these persons is often cited in socialist critiques of capitalist societies. However, to identify all persons who have low social power and all persons who are victims of exploitation, as members of an institutionalized working-class, or as part of a general category of "oppressed classes," is to assume an awareness of common identity among the members of such groups, and, in turn, between them and industrial workers (Piven and Cloward 1982). A conscious awareness of a common socioeconomic position among all of these groups has never existed.

Given difficulties in defining the boundaries of an operational "working-class," in contrast to a theoretical working-class, the divided loyalties among those who might be considered the core of the working-class, and the decline in industrial union membership, it is not surprising that "working-class solidarity" is not a significant dynamic in the political economy of the United States. And there is every sign that such working-class identity will be even less significant in the future (Janowitz 1978; Offe 1984).

There are equal difficulties in establishing an operational definition of a "capitalist" or "upper-class" institutional structure. There are rich and powerful extended families, the Rockefellers being an example. There are individuals who exercise substantial amounts of economic power at any given time, such as the investment managers of large international banks, the managers of the Federal Reserve system, and the executives of large multinational corporations in electronics, oil and gas, and armaments production.

There are residential communities of very wealthy families, some of whom have been wealthy for several generations and some for only a few years. There are wealthy families in New England and in the South who trace their ancestry to original settlers, as well as wealthy families in these same areas who are very recent arrivals. The existence of these families contributes to the creation of an upper-class, "jet-set" social class ambience which is highly visible in the media.

However, there is little evidence that there is in the United States an institutionalized social structure which cuts across these several groups of well-to-do households. To the extent that there is a stable network of relationships among a particular set of "upper-class" households in the United States it is based primarily on White Anglo-Saxon Protestant cultural identity, as much or more than it is based on shared economic interests (Baltzell 1964). There are sharp conflicts over politics and economic policies among wealthy families, and where there may be broad areas of agreement, for example, in regard to income tax and inheritance tax policies, such positions are also supported by many nonwealthy middle-income households.

In every society there are specific individuals who at any one moment have substantial power over the political and economic decisions that affect the allocation of economic benefits within that society. That is, there is a "ruling elite." There are also formal and informal policy forming coalitions and power blocs which include individuals in positions of economic power, and persons with substantial individual wealth. However, in almost all instances these individuals act as representatives of organizational interests, rather than in behalf of an institutionalized social class structure.

The patterns of exploitation that do exist are controlled by individuals from a variety of family backgrounds who at a particular time occupy organizational role positions through which they exercise control over particular forms of economic and political power. These occupants of powerful role positions include business executives in some settings, labor officials in other settings, governmental officials in some cases and military officers in still other situations. In many ways the concentrations of economic and political resources which exist today are much more powerful than any of the institutional forms of power in the early Industrial Revolution. The power resources of some institutions, which can be used by persons in key organizational roles, for example in the instance of multinational banks, may be sufficient to dictate the economic policies, and in turn the political policies, of individual national governments.

The exploitive and oppressive power that is exercised by individuals in powerful organizational positions is, however, based on their perception of role behavior expectations, rather than on their self-conscious membership in, or identification with, the institutional interests of the "upper-class." The dynamics of exploitation are more directly related to the aggrandisement interests of organizations than to the purely personal ambitions of the individuals occupying key organizational roles, although in specific instances such ambitions may be an important element in dynamics of exploitation. Concepts of the corporate society or "corporatism" provide a more relevant framework for analysis of these organizational power relationships than the traditional concepts of class structure and class conflict (Milward and Francisco 1983).

INTEREST GROUP DIVERSITY

Interest group clashes, such as those over environmental issues, illustrate the diversity of interest group identifications which crosscut postindustrial societies (Janowitz 1978). These include, in addition to economic interests, group affiliations based on ethnic commonality, religion, gender, occupation, hobby, geographic region, age and traditional culture vs. modernism to mention only a few. For a particular individual some of these interest group identifications may be relatively brief and transitory. In other instances there may be a pervasive, life-long consciousness of membership in an interest constituency, and a strong identification with other persons with a similar base of identification and commitment.

While individuals may have a general self-perception of social class status, it is other identifications, not socieconomic class position, around which the individual is prepared to mobilize personal resources to affect public policy around such issues as abortion, affirmative action, or prayer in public schools. Of particular importance at the end of the twentieth century is the emergence of large black and Hispanic constituencies, freed from many of the discriminatory constraints of the first two-thirds of the century. These have become important self-identity constituencies, with significant political power, which cut across socioeconomic levels. The model of individual upward mobility in economic position and social status identity within both groups, and in other similar ethnic constituencies, is more powerful than the pull of "working-class" identity, or "oppressed groups" consciousness.

The diversity of interest alignments contributes to the volatility of political processes in postindustrial democratic capitalist societies. But this volatility is, in general, grounded in a central consensus about the fundamental elements of a mixed economy pluralistic society (Janowitz 1978). The alignment of particular interest groups with particular political parties is often temporary (Lowi 1969). Some interest elements are nearly always aligned with the government in power, regardless of party label; other interests are almost always aligned with the critics of the current government.

Political parties which emerged in the nineteenth century as a framework for aggregating interests at a national level have, by the end of the twentieth century, become a relatively weak form of special interest group. American political parties, in particular, are marked by a lack of consistent goals and objectives, together with an almost total lack of connection between party policy positions at local, state and national levels. To a substantial degree the national parties are reconstituted every four years around the selection of a Presidential candidate. Once selected, the Presidential candidates develop campaign organizations which are largely separate from the party organization, even when the candidate has de facto control of the party machinery.

National political candidates, rather than relying on a traditional political party base, develop individual electoral strategies intended to create, at a given moment, a temporary coalition of interest groups to support a personality oriented campaign directed simultaneously at individual voters in the center of the ideological spectrum and at organizational sources of campaign financing. However, whatever the campaign strategy and the rhetoric, when a particular individual is elected to public office, the governance coalition is usually different from the campaign coalition. The margin of electoral victory in contemporary elections is usually a very small percentage of the voters. Indeed most governments in democratic capitalist societies in the 1980s are elected by a minority of registered voters and may be put into office by a minority of actual voters.

A broader base of supporting interests is necessary to establish and to maintain legitimacy, and to govern, particularly under the electoral system of the United States which does not result in unified control of the executive and legislative branches even when the same party predominates. Electoral winners, in order to govern, must establish coalitions with swing interest groups that may not have been significant in the electoral victory. Thus, regardless of labels and the ideological rhetoric used by successful candidates, there is nearly always a substantial shift to the political center and the development of working relationships with "center" interest group constitutencies. This drawing together for the post-election process of governance diminishes political polarization and blunts radical efforts to change the fundamental characteristics of the society.

THE EXPANDED POSITION OF MIDDLE-INCOME HOUSEHOLDS

Another change in social structure is the increasingly important social and political role of middle-income households. Middle-income households have become the dominant political force in most capitalist postindustrial societies, primarily because of the improved standard of living in the twentieth century. Middle-income households are no longer a limited demographic category existing between a large "working-class" and a small but powerful capitalist "upper-class."

These households are now the population sector that includes primary labor market industrial workers, family farmers and government employees, as well as large segments of business managers, most professional and technical specialists and a large component of retired persons with secure incomes (Janowitz 1978). Although the pattern of income for this group of households has changed during the 1980s with a small segment receiving more income and a larger segment experiencing diminished income, there has not been significant change in the political and social position of these households.

Middle-income households now provide nearly all of the active leaders for the extensive network of voluntary associations, including labor unions, and issue oriented advocacy groups. They also provide most of the "lay" and professional leadership in the voluntary, non-governmental sector of human service programs, as well as the academic leadership of colleges and universities. Given the number of persons in middle-income households they dominate the organizational structure of all of the centerist political parties of democratic capitalist political systems, regardless of party label.

Middle-income citizens have a positive identification with private property, particularly in the form of home ownership and savings accounts of various types. Both forms of ownership contribute to a strong interest in the maintainance of economic and political stability. While generally conservative on tax issues, these individuals may strongly support taxes to fund a particular special interest objective. They are likely to be more concerned with efforts to assure access to opportunity for their children, primarily in the form of education, than they are to be concerned with the amount of accumulated wealth that they might pass on to their children as an inheritance.

Members of middle-income households are simultaneously interested in the production of public goods (education, clean air and water, income security for retired persons) and private goods (automobiles and vacation resorts). Many middle-income citizens are involved in political activities around quality of life issues (air and water pollution) and around the promotion of specialized service programs (handicapped children), as well as around the interests of professional associations and business trade associations. They are, on the other hand, much less likely to be involved with political efforts to promote broad programs of income redistribution in order to achieve greater economic equality within the society as an ethical principle of social justice.

The broad and inclusive nature of the middle-income category provides a wide variety of opportunities for "working-class" individuals to change their social status identity either in a single lifetime, or across generations, without a dramatic change in stratification structure of the society. In many instances a change from "working-class" identity to a middle-income identity, reflected, for example, in a change in residential neighborhood, may not reflect any substantial change in income level or any significant increase in economic security for an individual blue-collar industrial worker. The increasing prevalence of two-income households makes it possible to achieve such life style changes without a change in the type of employment of the primary earner. However, with the change in life-style there may be important changes in self-image and in turn in the response of individuals to economic and political issues (Sennett and Cobb 1972). For example, active participation in a labor union and active commitment to the union movement may be viewed as primarily a "working-class" characteristic, not consistent with a middle-income life style.

SUMMARY

Philosophical and ideological debates about the future of contemporary post-industrial societies have been structured around socialism and capitalism paradigms for more than a century. Each of these paradigms has served as an effective perspective for analyzing weaknesses and deficiences in the economies of societies organized primarily around the opposite paradigm.

Each of these paradigms has also been advocated as a normative framework for the future development of postindustrial societies. However, the changes which have taken place in the social structures of these societies—changes in the structure of the labor force, the development of a mixed public/private economy, the blurring of class identifications, the diversification of interest group loyalties, the emergence of an inclusive and dominant category of middle-income households, and the role of women as active participants in the labor force—contradict fundamental assumptions of both paradigms, including traditional class conflict assumptions (Davis and Scase 1985).

The future of these societies, and in particular the future of welfare state issues, must be considered from the perspective of a paradigm which is consistent with the contemporary characteristics of these societies, rather than from the perspective of paradigms based primarily on the earliest decades of the Industrial Revolution. Of particular importance are the implications of these developments for income transfer issues, and for the issues related to the quality of service produced by human service organizations.

Chapter 4

Redistributional Income Transfers

Among the critical issues in the scope, structure and funding of human service programs are the size and characteristics of redistributional income transfer programs within the society. Indeed, it is argued that this is a central issue in the future economic stability of postindustrial societies (Judge 1981; Spivey 1985). And it is around the issue of redistributional income transfers that the most bitter ideological "welfare state" arguments occur. Proponents of traditional capitalism often identify all transfer programs as "socialistic," while proponents of socialism argue that the failure to provide truly equalizing transfer programs is, from a humanitarian perspective, one of the fatal flaws in capitalist societies. Supporters of welfare capitalism, avoiding both ideological extremes, continually seek to design systems of income transfer which do not constitute a significant disincentive to productive economic activity for households with earned income while providing fair and adequate economic resources for households without earned income.

Redistributive income transfer programs involve two elements, with distinctly different political economy dynamics. One element consists of *labor force transfers* through which cash income, basic necessities, or other economic benefits are provided to persons directly, or potentially, involved in the labor force, or in other marketplace activities, whose wage or salary income, or income from other marketplace activities, is below the median for the society. Such transfers usually also cover provision for the other immediate members of the household. Redistributional labor force transfer programs include unemployment insurance payments for unemployed workers, food stamps and public assistance payments to "employable" adults, family support payments for individuals in job training programs, the earned income tax credit, public housing, and subsidized medical care for "working poor" households.

The second element consists of *categorical transfers* through which basic necessities are provided to specific categories of persons not significantly involved in the labor force or in other marketplace activities. These include

Social Security payments to retired persons, to persons who are permanently disabled and to dependents of deceased workers who have Social Security coverage. They also include Supplemental Security Income (SSI) payments, public assistance payments in behalf of dependent children, and maintenance costs (shelter, food and routine medical care) for persons with disabilities living in public institutions.[1]

There have been major changes during the past century in the characteristics of, and the comparative importance of, labor force transfers and categorical transfers in the economy. These program changes reflect many of the societal changes outlined in the previous chapter, and are part of the context of current public policy controversies over the future development of the "welfare state."

Advocates of the traditional free-market capitalism paradigm claim that governmental redistributional income transfer programs are, in particular, undesirable. It is argued that they have a depressing effect on the economy, that they create disincentives to work and to save, and that the taxes required discourage business entrepreneurship and work effort by employed persons (Gilder 1981; Murray 1983). The traditional rejoinder from advocates of a socialist paradigm is that inadequacy of redistributional income transfers is part of the pattern of exploitation of the "working-class" and of neglect of the poor and the powerless under capitalism, and that such transfer programs should be increased to bring about economic equality in the society (Adams 1985; Gough 1979; Kuttner 1984).

THE DEVELOPMENT OF REDISTRIBUTIONAL LABOR FORCE TRANSFER PROGRAMS

In the intital period of industrialization, in the late 1700s and early 1800s, when capitalism and socialism paradigms were first being set forth, the fundamental political economy issue was the allocation of economic benefits from industrial production, as between the total group of industrial workers and their households and the owners of capital. The distribution of benefits through payment of wages determined by a competitive labor market to workers and the payment of interest and profits to the owners of capital resulted in great wealth for some families and poverty for many industrial workers and their families.

Included in the general population of worker households were families of employed workers with large numbers of young children, as well as temporarily unemployed workers, workers forced out of employment because of age, families of disabled workers, and the widows and orphans of deceased workers. All household members in the families of industrial workers had, at best, a single, subsistence standard of living. The issues that were argued in the 1800s about improving economic conditions for workers and their families involved not only increases in wage levels, but also improved working conditions, unemployment insurance, workmen's compensation for industrial acccidents, medical care protection, sick pay, retirement pensions, and income provision for widows and orphans. The objective of all of these proposals was to raise the basic standard of living of the "working poor" and their families.

In initial efforts to improve the standard of living of industrial workers it was generally assumed by all parties that support for dependent persons would be primarily within inclusive family-related households. It was assumed that there would be the direct sharing of food within individual households, and also that there were slack resources within such households in both living space and time resources of women, which could be used in the care for dependent persons. Any "unemployable" dependent individuals who were not provided for in this way could be provided for through the workhouse, the poorhouse or the asylum, or through jails and prisons.

The effort to raise the standard of living for industrial workers and their families involved choices among three alternatives: (1) the provision of economic benefits through voluntary charity, particularly to very poor families; (2) the provision of benefits as part of the wage package connected to a particular job, that is employment-related "fringe benefits;" or (3) the provision of benefits through governmental action, including the regulation of working conditions and redistributional income transfer programs. Traditional capitalism argued for minimal provison of any economic benefits other than those that resulted from the competitive operation of the unrestricted labor market. Socialist ideology argued for extensive governmental action to improve the standard of living of all workers and to reduce inequality in the whole society.

The strategy that was supported by individual labor unions as they began to be organized, and by many individual employers, was the provision of increased economic benefits through employment-related "fringe benefits." Unions could use the provisions in specific labor agreements for such benefits as an incentive for union membership. For employers such provisions avoided political decisionmaking about economic benefits for workers and maintained a high degree of employer control over the actual benefits provided. Governmental action did take place to regulate some aspects of working conditions, action which was supported by some employers since it reduced the competitive advantage of those firms, particularly nonunion firms, that saved on production costs by operating under sub-standard conditions. Governmental action in the twentieth century to establish a universal minimum wage level, and to establish common procedures for workmen's compensation programs had similar advantages for some employers.

Employment-related benefits became the dominant element in an enhanced standard of living for workers in capitalist societies in general, and in particular, in the United States (Rein 1983a). These included not only negotiated increases in wage levels, but various forms of employer financed insurance including health insurance, retirement plans, and holiday and vacation provisions. As income taxes became widely used in the twentieth century the comparative economic advantage for workers with substantial fringe benefit packages was increased since these benefits were not considered part of the income base of individuals for tax purposes.

While the provision of fringe benefits for *public employees* did involve collective political decisions, in the United States these decisions did not substantially affect employment conditions in the economy as a whole since they involved several thousand different federal, state and local governmental bodies, making the situation of governmental employees much like the situation of those employed in for-profit organizations, with benefits being determined separately in each firm. Increasingly many elements of these employment-related fringe benefit packages have been mandated, conditioned, or stimulated by governmental action, for example, the regulations on overtime pay (Rein 1983a), and have become a major element in the mixed economy characteristics of capitalist societies.

These employment-related fringe-benefits have become a major element in the comparative economic advantages enjoyed by workers in primary labor market positions, including many governmental employees. In many instances within a particular industry the benefits provided by nonunion firms are similar to or better than those provided in unionized firms. The provision of such benefits by management action has become a major strategy for avoiding unionization.

However, the existence of these employment-related economic benefits has not eliminated poverty and income inequality in the society as a whole. Among those who have been left out of the increased standard of living provided through employment-related fringe benefits are workers in low-wage firms and industries that provide few benefits, large families in which the standard wage rate provides inadequate family income, and unemployed workers, including seasonal workers. Also left out are single-parent households with young children in which child-care responsibilities make it impossible to hold a job.

For these groups the basic public policy issue has been the establishment of labor force redistributional income transfer programs administered by governmental agencies, particularly since the 1930s in the United States. These programs have included state-administered unemployment insurance programs, food stamps, public housing, health care benefits provided through a variety of limited state and local programs and available to some labor force related households through Medicaid, public housing programs, the AFDC program, particularly as it applies to single parents with school age children and two-parent families in some states, special economic support programs for migrant workers, and state and local "general assistance" programs.

The modest provisions for improving the standard of living for workers and their families during the early development of the industrial welfare state, whether provided through union-won fringe benefit provisions, private charity, or governmental redistributional policies or programs, primarily involved a redistribution of economic resources within the same generational cohort, involving the owners of businesses and the contemporary group of workers and their families. There was bitter disagreement, however, as to whether the objective of such programs and policies should be, at the most, the provision of a minimal survival level of income for a small group of the poorest families of industrial workers or provision of enough income to bring about a substantial degree of income equality among all households connected to the labor force.

This choice continues to be a central policy issue in governmentally administered labor force redistributional income transfers. Over the past century the combination of union pressure, social reform movements, political agitation, and governmental action have resulted in a substantial increase in both the level and the security of employment-related fringe benefits, *particularly for those in primary labor market positions.*

These employment-related labor force transfer benefits have been largely removed from the current public policy debates about the future of the welfare state, although specific provisions are often the focus of labor-management conflict. In the 1980s, in particular, there has been an increased level of labor-mangement conflict over these provisions within union contracts with pressure from management for unions to "give-back" a variety of fringe benefit provisons which have previously been provided. However, the general concept of the inclusion of such benefits as part of the total wage package has not changed. Indeed, there has been an expansion in many firms of such benefits in the form of Employee Assistance Programs.

On the other hand, although the scope and level of benefits in governmental labor force income transfer programs has been minimal in the United States, these programs have been the focus of continuous political controversy with frequent proposals for reducing or eliminating such benefits altogether (Murray 1983). Perhaps the most important factor in these policy controversies has been the separation of the interests of currently employed persons, particularly those employed in primary labor market positions, whose standard of living depends substantially on employment-related benefits, from the interests of persons in secondary labor market positions and those who are unemployed or only marginally related to the labor force and who are more directly dependent on governmental redistributional programs. One result is that there is no cohesive "working-class" coalition that supports expanded governmental labor force redistributional transfer programs.

Another factor in the limited scope of benefits through governmental programs is the rule-of-thumb guide which is widely used in evaluating the level of support to be provided through governmental action, which calls for transfer benefits for persons who are actual or potential labor force participants to be kept at a level that is below the level of earnings of the lowest paid employed worker. This is viewed as maintaining pressure on those unemployed workers who are part of the "surplus labor pool" to accept any employment available, and as exerting a desirable downward pressure on wage rates in general in the community.

Another important factor is the pattern in which benefit levels and eligibility determination in labor force redistributional programs, with the exception of food stamps, are primarily determined at state and local levels, although there is federal financial participation in several types of programs. This means that policy decisions on eligibility and benefits are fragmented among many different governmental units rather than being highly visible issues at the federal level, as are the decisions on Social Security benefits for retired persons. This also means that such decisions are affected by competition among states, and localities, to attract businesses through the appeal of low tax levels.

In the United States the policy decisions on governmental labor force transfer programs are also affected by the role of agriculture and agricultural wage labor in the economy of the state. Agricultural wages in general are low and include few fringe benefits, and agricultural employment is often seasonal. In turn, the benefits provided through labor force transfer programs in states with large agricultural components in the economy tend to be particularly low, in order to maintain pressure on unemployed persons to take any available low wage job, including seasonal agricultural jobs. In the United States this has included, in particular, states in the South and Southwest in which these economic factors have been reinforced by traditional patterns of ethnic discrimination and exploitation. However, a study by Schuman, Steeh and Bobo at the Institute for Social Research (1986) indicates that while racial equality is supported in principle negative attitudes towards governmental economic initiatives explicitly intended to redress the consequences of past racial discrimination are, in fact, wide-spread throughout the United States. AuClaire (1984) reported resistance to increased taxes for social welfare when linked to on-going military spending, or to benefit individuals from ethnic minority backgrounds.

Proposals for more far-reaching redistributional labor force transfer programs that would sharply increase the level of economic benefits, for secondary labor market workers and unemployed persons in particular, are part of many utopian visions of the society of the future (Gil 1976; Kuttner 1984). However, such proposals, for example, the replacement of AFDC and food stamps with a universal, equalizing "negative income tax," which would require sharply increased *intragenerational* transfers through the tax system from the broad and inclusive group of middle-income households, are not the focus of the current national policy debates about the future of the welfare state. Indeed, Hochschild (1981) reports that there is a general resistance in the United States to proposals for governmental action that would explicitly modify those inequalities in income that are perceived as resulting from marketplace processes among persons in, or potentially part of, the labor force.

However, among all of the factors which have a negative impact on the potential improvement of benefits in governmental labor force redistributional programs the most important is probably the growing size, and cost, of the predominantly *intergenerational* categorical transfer programs (Judge 1981). It is primarily the public policy issues involved in these categorical transfer programs which now dominate discussions about the "future of the welfare state" (Spivey 1985).

THE DEVELOPMENT OF CATEGORICAL TRANSFERS

Current public policy debates about welfare state provisions are primarily centered on *categorial transfers*, not labor-force transfers. The public policy issues involved in categorical transfers are largely a result, first, of the changes which have taken place in the size and characteristics of the economically dependent population outside the labor force, and second, of changes in expectations about the standard of living to be provided for that population (Feldstein 1985).

The relative size of the dependent population outside the labor force which requires economic transfers in some form is substantially a function of societal characteristics which are independent of the characteristics of the dominant political economy ideology. In a low technology, agrarian, labor intensive society, whether capitalist or socialist, there are likely to be a large number of young children living with their natural families, few unemployed adolescents or adults, few retired older persons, and few severely handicapped adults. In this society, moreover, most of the support for economically dependent persons including young children is provided through family households, and the standard of living to be provided for such persons is, therefore, determined by decisions made within each household. Variations in the level of provision for dependent individuals parallel the variations in household income within the society.

In contrast, a high technology, urban, capital intensive, rapidly changing society, whether capitalist or socialist, is likely to have relatively small numbers of young children, with a significant number of these children requiring care outside the natural family, a widespread pattern of delayed employment among adolescents and young adults, retirement before physical disability limits the ability to work, relatively high numbers of adults who are unemployed because of the pattern of constant structural changes in the labor market, and a relatively large number of persons with lifelong disabling conditions whose life expectancy has been lengthened by advances in medical technology. In such societies, the economic support needed by dependent persons is often not available through inclusive family households.

In contrast to the pattern for the distribution of economic benefits among all of the persons who are related in some way to the labor force in which the largest element consists of wage and salary payments and employment-related fringe benefits, the distribution of economic benefits to retired persons and persons with permanent disabilities, as well as to dependent children, are largely determined by governmental policies in income transfer programs, with the exception of the employer share of private employment pensions. Moreover, to the extent that such employer provisions are offset by tax deduction provisions they may also be viewed as primarily a consequence of governmental policy (Rein 1983a). Governmental categorical income transfer policies and programs are, therefore, not only important because of their relative size, but also because of their importance for nearly all persons in the categories affected.[2]

The major effect of these categorical transfers is to transfer economic resources from labor force participants to non-participants. These transfers are also heavily intergenerational transfers since the largest elements are first, payments to meet basic maintenance costs for persons over 65, and second, payments to meet health care costs for such persons. Other intergenerational elements include basic maintenance costs and health care costs for children who require care outside of their family and for very young children in some single parent households, and maintenance costs for some young adults in higher education. Other categorical transfers which are not primarily intergenerational include payments for basic maintenance costs for adults with chronic disabilities who are unable to obtain regular employment, the payment of maintenance costs for adult caretakers in single parent families with very young children who are not available for labor force participation, and the payment of basic support costs for persons in publically administered institutions, including psychiatric hospitals, state schools, jails and prisons.

The increased importance of these nonlabor force, economically dependent population categories in income transfer arrangements reflects a particular set of social and economic developments. There has been a disaggregation of large inclusive households with the establishment of independent households by large numbers of young adults attending colleges and universities, by persons beyond the retirement age, by young unmarried, separated, or divorced mothers and by a number of adults with disabilities. These separate households, in which there is no one directly involved in the labor force, require a consistent source of income for food and housing costs. In addition, the shift from institutional care to community-based care for substantial numbers of individuals with disabilities has required a change from providing food and shelter through institutional budgets to providing transfer payments directly to the individuals involved to meet such costs.

This existence of large numbers of economically dependent individuals in separate households has created pressure for establishing a universal standard of living criterion for income provision for each category of individuals, rather than assuming that the standard of living of particular individuals is tied to that of the family unit to which they may be most directly related. The establishment of a universal standard of provision, as for example in the case of Social Security retirement benefits, may, in turn, result in the formation of additional separate households by retired persons.

A similar development among adults with disabilities has resulted from the establishment of a universal standard under the SSI program (Stone 1984). A universal standard of economic support for single parent households with young children may also result in more adolescent single parents leaving the parental home and establishing their own household unit. All of these developments add to the number of household units that require a regular source of cash income through transfer programs. These developments also increase the size of the political constituencies who may lobby in support of such transfers (Janowitz 1978; Stone 1984).

THE POLITICAL ECONOMY DYNAMICS OF CATEGORICAL TRANSFERS

Pressures created by these changes in the characteristics of the nonlabor force dependent population have resulted in increasingly intense public policy arguments focusing on increasing costs of categorical transfers. This has become a collective choice, or political decision issue, rather than a decision made within individual households (Olson 1982). However, there are no guiding principles under either the capitalism paradigm or the socialism paradigm, either as to the appropriate division between household provision and collective provision of economic support for such categorical dependent persons, or as to the standard of living to be assured. There is no necessary connection between an appropriate level of economic support and the level of earned income of low-wage workers, since these categorically dependent individuals are not viewed as part of the "surplus labor pool."

There is, on the other hand, no clear-cut "social justice" principle, either economic, or political, that defines the appropriate relation between the standard of living for an eighty-year old widow, who has never been "employed" in the labor market, and the standard of living for a twenty-year old single adult, without any household dependents, who is employed full-time (Lane 1986). The long standing theoretical arguments between supporters of the socialist and capitalist political economy paradigms about the distribution of economic benefits are essentially irrelevant in the debates over categorical transfers which are at the heart of the "future of the welfare state" controversy.

Public policy debates about categorical income transfers often ignore certain basic considerations. The fundamental choice issue involved in categorical transfers is the general standard of living to be provided for economically dependent persons outside the labor force. This is often a difficult issue within individual households. It is an increasingly difficult collective public policy choice within the society as a whole. However, given a general consensus on the standard of living to be provided for such persons, the total amount of economic resources used within the society is the same whether the transfers are within households or through governmental programs. The economic impact on employed persons who provide the economic resources is also essentially the same whether the transfers are within a single household, or through a governmental taxation/transfer program. Sharing within a household reduces the level of discretionary spending by those persons who receive employment income directly, just as much as charitable contributions or a tax withholding from a paycheck.

In postindustrial societies, however, specific elements of these arrangements have changed as indicated above so that the proportion of support provided through households has decreased and the proportion of support provided through governmental transfer programs has increased. Because of the increase in the overall size of the economically dependent population and the increased proportion of such persons requiring governmental transfers, the scope of the collective decision issues involved has increased dramatically (Preston 1984).

Moreover, the standard of living expectations, in particular for retired persons and for disabled adults, including provision for both personal and professional care if needed, have increased as the standard of living has increased for "worker" households (Olson 1982; Stone 1984). In many instances these increased standard of living expectations for disabled individuals and older adults are still being met by transfers within the household economy, or through life-time savings or annuities, or life insurance.

The same general standard of living expectations, however, are also applicable to individuals for whom household transfers are not available and who do not personally control any significant economic resources. To meet these expectations requires provisions for regular upward adjustments in transfers consistent with increases in the general cost of living, further adding to the pressures on governmental transfer programs (Feldstein 1985; Judge 1981).[3]

The size of governmental income transfer programs required to meet the costs of whatever standard of living is established as a norm of economically dependent persons living apart from their family has, in fact, very little effect on the economy as a whole. At any given level of taxes and transfers some marginally productive individuals, including persons over 65, may reduce their hours of work or leave the labor force in order to receive a transfer because the transfer income that they may receive is greater than their earnings after taxes.

This is, in effect, a function of an economic trade-off. The value of their contribution to production is at or less than the minimal wage and fringe benefit costs of their being employed, while their minimal costs for living are higher than the amount they can earn through employment. If there is an economic demand for the products which that individual was producing, that demand will be met through increased work effort by a more productive worker, or by increased use of machinery and technology, since neither labor resources nor capital resources are fully utilized in any society. Part of the value of such increased production is then transferred to the individual outside the labor force.

On the other hand, if the lack of systematic provisions for an income transfer program forces marginally productive individuals to work at sub-standard wages, only the form, not the substance, of the income transfer process is changed. The transfer in this instance occurs either by depressing the wage rates for more productive workers or through a decrease in the number of hours worked by more productive workers. In either instance the income of the more productive worker is reduced in proportion to the wages paid the marginal worker. Moreover, economic transfers allocated either through such market-place processes as employment at sub-standard wages, or through governmental income transfer programs, have exactly the same demand effect in the economy; that is, dollars earned, and dollars transferred, have the same purchasing power.

To the extent that substantial numbers of persons dissent from the payment of taxes to maintain a particular level of categorical transfers, however, there may be substantial efforts, either by individuals or through an organized "underground economy," to buffer economic activities from the collection of taxes. The level of taxes may thus have more impact on the relative size of the "underground" economy than on the total work effort or productivity in the society. The relative size of the underground economy reflects, in part, the degree of consensus, or dissensus, within the society about the standard of living to be maintained for persons not in the labor force. A similar process takes place when workers refuse to share their earnings equally with elderly grandparents, or a divorced parent attempts to buffer his/her income against requirements for the provision of a categorical transfer in the form of a child support payment.

Assertions that economic provision for those outside the labor force depresses the economy and reduces the incentive for entrepreneurship are not the central issue in policy decisions about transfer programs and the welfare state. The only significant ways for reducing the relative proportion of economic resources *consumed* by economically dependent households are either an explicit decision to establish a standard of living for such persons substantially below the standard for worker households, or to promote an increase in the death rate among dependent groups through deliberate economic neglect. While in fact this may happen in particular societies, neither the capitalism paradigm nor the socialism paradigm includes nonemployable, economically dependent persons living outside the households of employed workers as a significant element in their political economy theories. The development of a welfare capitalism ideology, on the other hand, has been significantly shaped by a recognition of the need to make systematic provisions for such persons.

The requirement for basic economic provision from some source for economically dependent persons is an unescapable economic fact of life. The comparative level of such transfers, which have changed from being primarily intrahousehold transfers to being a combination of household transfers and collective societal transfers, is increasingly a political choice, which, in turn, is related to other political decisions that affect the general distribution of economic benefits in a mixed economy society. Although there may be marginal variations among societies in the degree of redistribution that results from the tax and transfer provisions for economically dependent persons, the basic support of such persons requires that all persons currently in the labor force share the goods and services which they produce with an increasing number of persons not in the labor force. Any increase in the effective standard of living for such persons comes at the expense of the standard of living for workers and worker households.

Current patterns of categorical income transfers are skewed to middle-income households in spite of modest redistributional provisions in the schedule of benefits in Social Security retirement benefits (Cates 1982). Many individuals employed in secondary labor market positions, agricultural workers, domestic workers, and hotel and restaurant employees, were not covered by Social Security for many years, and workers in the underground economy are not covered at all. The exclusion of unearned income and employment-related pensions in determining eligibility for Social Security retirement benefits favors middle-income retired persons, as do the income tax provisions for exemptions and deductions for older persons which benefit persons with significant personal income the most. The retirement income security provided through the Social Security system, and the security against high medical costs provided by Medicare, and by the Medicaid provisions covering individuals in nursing homes, are as much economic benefits to the middle-income children of retired persons as to the retired persons themselves. Moreover, since middle-income white women as a general group have the longest life expectancies among various gender/ethnic categories they receive the greatest benefits from the Social Security system.

Moreover, it is evident that there is no way, in an open democratic political system, to establish intergenerational categorical transfer policies that do not substantially benefit middle-class households. It is possible to establish a significant level of benefits for lower-income households within such policies; it is not possible to exclude the middle-class from benefits, any more than it is possible to have a labor contract covering an entire firm that provides more economic benefits for unskilled workers than for skilled workers, particularly if the skilled workers pay higher union dues. With the growth of the numbers of middle-income households and the increase of their power in the political system, the system of categorical transfers has become, to a substantial degree, a mechanism through which employed middle-class households forego current income thereby providing a variety of intergenerational income transfers to economically dependent persons from middle-income households as well as to comparatively smaller groups of other economically dependent individuals (Gilbert 1983).

Traditional capitalist and socialist political economy perspectives may provide insights on the discrepancies between the economic criteria that shape *redistributional labor force transfer* programs and those that shape *redistributional categorical transfer* programs. However, neither perspective provides a future scenario that deals with decisions about the actual standard of living to be provided for persons outside the labor force, or about the relative role of household, employment-related, or governmental transfer provisions for such persons. Even welfare capitalism, which recognizes the need for redistributional categorical transfers on a permanent basis, provides no explicit guidance about the appropriate balance between economic incentives for employed workers and a decent standard of living for transfer recipients. These are essentially political choice issues that take the shape that they do as a result of a particular pattern of political forces, including a variety of "special interest" constituencies, rather than being shaped by an explicit ideological paradigm (Janowitz 1978), which is why traditional socialist and capitalist paradigms offer such little guidance in current policy analyses dealing with categorical transfers.

NOTES

1.   There are also policies and programs which result in positive distributional transfers such as income tax deductions for home mortgage interest payments and for Individual Retirement Accounts (IRAs), which add to the effective income of persons whose marketplace income is already above the median.

2.   Income from personal savings, from individual investments in retirement programs or from individually purchased disability or life insurance represents deferred consumption by the individual or household rather than an economic transfer. One approach to reducing the scope of governmental transfer programs is to promote such deferred consumption in the form of savings for retirement, although the encouragement of such savings through preferential tax treatment, as in the instance of the Individual Retirement Account, is, in fact, a form of transfer by governmental policy.

3.   Both the President and the Congress have, in fact, supported the provision of annual cost of living increases in Social Security retirement payments even in those years, such as 1986, in which there is little or no inflation.

Chapter 5

Quality of Service Issues in Human Service Programs

The preceding chapter dealt with one of the critical issues involved in the scope, structure, and funding of human service programs, namely the nature of redistributional income transfers, and factors affecting their future development. The other critical issue is that of the quality of services provided through personal service organizations. There are problems related to levels-of-funding and the inadequacy of current scientific and professional knowledge that affect the quality of services in any particular program area. However, there are also fundamental problems in program design and administrative structure within the human service industries that directly affect the quality of many of the services produced.

In some instances the problems may be attributed to the diversity of organizations, the fragmentation of service delivery systems, and the absence of consistent procedures for enforcing accountability either to service users, or to service funders. However, the most fundamental problems of quality in production are linked to increases in the absolute size of administrative organizations in human service industries and an accompanying centralization of administrative authority. Moreover, the solution often proposed for dealing with the fragmentation of service delivery systems and problems of accountability is increased centralization and more administrative control.

The move towards larger administrative units and intensified administrative control in human service industries is consistent with, and in part a direct result of, the concentration of economic power and administrative authority that has already taken place in postindustrial societies. This centralization of power and authority has taken place in both capitalist and socialist societies, and is consistent with fundamental principles in both traditional capitalism and traditional socialism paradigms.

POLITICAL ECONOMY PARADIGMS AND THE DEVELOPMENT OF CENTRALIZED SOCIETIES

Traditional capitalism and socialist paradigms include very different concepts about the management of the economic system and the preferred distribution of economic benefits within an industrialized society. These differences, and their implications for the total social order, are viewed as so fundamental that they have resulted in a pattern of continuous world-wide conflict during the twentieth century, particularly in the period since World War II. (Both World War I and World War II were fundamentally wars among capitalist societies over issues of economic supremacy, and over access to raw materials and markets in Africa and Asia for purposes of economic exploitation.)

However, both capitalism and socialism paradigms provide rationales for a high degree of centralization of economic power and political authority within the nation-state. The unrestricted functioning of the free-market under the capitalism paradigm results, over time, in a high degree of *economic power concentration*, except when there is action by the political government to prevent it, for example through restrictions on the development of economic monopolies. Political intervention to control economic concentration, however, contradicts the fundamental concepts of capitalism. Such regulatory controls are, therefore, resisted by the advocates of the traditional capitalism paradigm on the grounds that if such concentration results from the "hidden hand" processes of the marketplace that it must be economically efficient, and therefore, should be allowed to proceed.

The concentration of economic power under capitalism can take the form of oligopolies, monopolies, cartels and trusts within a single industry as well as massive concentrations of financial power in the form of multinational conglomerates, cutting across industry lines. It also takes the form of an interlocking concentration of financial resources within the banking system, first within national economies, and then, as is happening in the late twentieth century, on an international basis (Mintz and Schwartz 1986). The current deregulation of banking systems, justified as being consistent with laissez-faire capitalism, appears, in fact, likely to increase the degree of economic power concentration within the United States. While laissez-faire policies free the economy from governmental controls they also legitimate the efforts of powerful economic interests to increase their economic benefits through the use of power rather than through economic efficiency (Adams and Brock 1986).

This concentration of economic power in the nation-state under capitalism is associated with a concentration of political authority at the national level which, in turn, is used to maintain and protect the conditions which are considered essential for economic growth. These include the maintenance of law and order within the national society, the protection of the national system of credit and currency, and, in particular, external protection against economic and military rivals.

In turn, the most important justification for the concentration of political authority, and governmental executive power, in the capitalist nation-state has become the maintenance and control of military forces, and, in turn, the central collection of taxes and the management of material procurement in support of the military. Without a large military establishment much of the rationale for a highly centralized political authority in the captialist nation-state would disappear. The only other rationale for such a concentration of authority becomes the economic redistributive functions discussed in Chapter 4. Indeed, the current policy debate in the United States is not over increasing taxes to pay for increased defense expenditures, but over the balance between defense expenditures, which have been financed by borrowing since 1980, and redistributional expenditures through the Social Security system including medical care, *assuming essentially a fixed level of federal tax revenue.* All other federal expenditures, except interest on the debt, are relatively small compared to these two elements of the federal budget.

One of the major unknowns in the next few decades is the future of the present structure of nation-states, particularly in the instance of those nations in which, given a monopoly by the superpowers on military advanced technology, there is no longer a significant external function for a military establishment, and therefore limited justification for taxes to support such an establishment. Even among the superpowers increasing dependence upon advanced military technology will raise questions about the function of a large standing force of military personnel, and the centrally collected taxes required for its support.

The traditional socialism paradigm assumes *a high degree of concentration of political authority* so that the political state can exercise control over the economy, either directly through ownership of "the means of production," or indirectly through regulatory controls. The justification for central control of the economy is that it is required in order to bring about a new collective social order and to assure an equitable allocation of economic benefits within the society based on equality of status.

However, the resources available for collective allocation depend on the effectiveness of the economy so that control of the economy, in turn, requires active management of the economy. The active management of the economy involves dealing with economic decisions through centralized political decision processes. The socialism paradigm also requires political decisions about the choices between current consumption and capital investment for the future. In the instance of investment it also means making political choices among a variety of investment opportunities. To the extent that the economic effectiveness of such investment decisions requires economic stability over time, socialism requires stability in the political control of the state, and therefore a one party political system. And in a one party political system the organization of dissent into an effective alternative political movement cannot be allowed. The existence of an effective political alternative, in effect, changes the political system to a pluralistic democracy.

The successful management of the economy under socialism requires political attention to the same fundamental necessities as in the centralized state under capitalism, that is the maintenance of internal law and order, a stable currency and credit system, and protection against economic and military rivals. It also requires effective control over the movement of economic resources within the economy in order to finance the administrative costs associated with the mangement of the economy, and to implement the principle of economic equality through redistribution. Moreover, rigorous social and economic controls are required to assure that economic inequalities do not reappear as a result of the development of an uncontrolled "underground" economy.

While a socialist state is based, in principle, on political control by "workers," the industrialized socialist economy, like the capitalist economy, requires stable production conditions within major industries. In a centralized socialist society if the rewards for particular workers are not perceived by them as equitable, and productivity declines, control over the workplace behavior of such workers is achieved through a combination of ideological persuasion and direct control of dissent. Because of the association of political authority and economic power, disagreement with economic policies is by definition political dissent.

To the extent that socialist states come into existence as a result of revolutionary action by a political minority there is a perceived need for the government to protect itself against both internal and external opponents through a combination of military forces and a national police system. Support of the military thus becomes a major source of justification for the concentration of political authority and economic power at the national level even if the socialism paradigm, in principle, excludes "imperialism" as a national policy.

Under traditional capitalism the fundamental paradigm assumes that political power is subordinate to but supportive of the economic processes of the market. Under socialism it is assumed that the political power center should directly control economic power centers. However, in both types of societies the concentration of economic and political power is necessarily associated with the development of a system of social control which has as its objective the support and protection of the particular structure of power concentration in that society. These controls take the form of laws and regulations, and the use of both economic power and political authority, to limit, or eliminate, the impact of dissenters. Even more important is the development of symbols, and intensive processes of socialization about the significance of those symbols, that serve to establish and maintain among the majority of the citizens in both types of societies the legitimacy of the concentration of power.

THE CENTRALIZED SOCIETY IN THE UNITED STATES

The increasing concentration of power in the United States is marked, in particular, by the centralization of economic power in the banking system and the centralization of political authority in the national government. This concentration of economic power and governmental authority has, in turn, been associated with the development of large scale organizational systems in many different sectors of American society, as well as in other postindustrial societies (Adams and Brock 1986; Reich 1983). In the United States these large scale systems include nationwide corporations in steel, automotive production, insurance, television, transportation, and so forth.

These large-scale systems also include multinational corporations, business conglomerates, the Federal Reserve system, bank holding companies, agribusiness combinations, interrelated high technology development networks, interlocking public utility networks, nationwide commercial athletic leagues, and the military procurement and production system. Professional associations and labor unions are not only nationwide in scope, but nationwide contracts have been established by a number of unions. Some of these systems, particularly the commercial banking system, and the United Nations as an intergovernmental organization, are beginning to take the form of comprehensive world-wide organizational systems.

The centralization of both power and legitimated authority in the United States and other postindustrial societies is reflected in the recent surge of corporate mergers, and in the strengthening of a "command and control" pattern of centralized administration. Recent developments in communications technology and computers have supported this pattern of centralization. Much of the formal theory of administration which is now incorporated in the educational preparation of future administrators for business, for public administration, and for the human services, assumes that effective administration takes place primarily within large-scale, hierarchial administrative structures (Neugeboren 1965). These large-scale organizational systems are viewed as essential for the concentration of economic resources required for business and industrial development, and for efficient organizational performance, and are, therefore, assumed to be essential for continued improvement in the standard of living within the society. However, the trend towards concentration of economic power and political authority, and, in turn, in organizational size and complexity, has increased the risk that such centralized power and authority might be used primarily for the personal benefit of particular individuals or groups rather than for the society as a whole.

The increase in organizational size and complexity, which is evident in human service industries as well as in other sectors of the society, has been accompanied by a number of operational problems. These include: (1) low levels of commitment to organizational goals by individuals working within large organizations; (2) high levels of behavioral problems among personnel in large-scale organizations; (3) decreasing levels of productivity (Reich 1983; Spivey 1985); (4) decreased ability to exercise effective administrative control and to insure the quality of organizational outputs as a result of communication lag, communication distortion, and other problems in the communication linkages in the middle of large scale organizations; (5) inability of many large scale organizations to adapt effectively to changes in the environment or to innovate; (6) ineffective use of personnel resources, particularly skilled personnel, in the middle of large-scale organizations; (7) increasing numbers of "employable" individuals for whom there is no meaningful role in the economic production system; (8) loss of public confidence in the ability of both governmental and business administrators to manage these organizations effectively, and loss of confidence in the quality of products produced by these organizations; (9) steady growth in an underground "hidden" economy; (10) low levels of active personal participation in political processes; and (11) substantial, and sometimes violent, dissent within particular societies by groups who are excluded from access to the centers of power and authority.

While these problems are beginning to be recognized as societal level problems in goods producing industries (for example, recent critical analyses of the organizational problems of General Motors), they also have major consequences in human service industries.

CENTRALIZATION IN HUMAN SERVICE INDUSTRIES

Much of the development of the comprehensive "welfare state" in capitalist societies in the twentieth century, and the traditional "liberal" or welfare captialism agenda for the advancement of human service programs, has been linked to the model of a centrally managed society (Hollingsworth and Hanneman 1984). In England the Fabian social reform tradition was based on the concept of comprehensive action by the national government to deal with social problems (Webb and Webb 1920). In the United States, particularly since the 1920s and the enactment of a national income tax system, major social reform efforts have involved initiatives to establish comprehensive nationwide service programs under the sponsorship of the federal government. The initial focus was primarily on establishing comprehensive social insurance programs, but since the 1930s the social reform agenda has been expanded to include national provision of a wide variety of personal service programs. As Kirschner points out (1986) this development which was supported by public service professionals in such fields as public health, city planning and social work, was a contradiction of the emphasis on local control, civic participation, and voluntarism that marked the early developments in these professions.

The results of the social reform efforts in the United States are reflected in federally administered Social Security (OASDI), health care financing

Medicare), and Supplemental Security Income (SSI) systems, the Veterans Administration, and the federal-state public assistance (AFDC and food stamps programs) and means-tested health care financing system (Medicaid). Detailed federal regulatory controls affecting many types of human service programs have been established in such areas as affirmative action, public access for persons with physical disabilities and special education. In other areas, such as community mental health, there were initial steps in the 1960s and 1970s to develop a comprehensive, nationwide federally sponsored system with continuing federal funding, although this development has been curtailed under the administration of President Reagan. In such areas as institutional care of persons who are mentally ill or mentally retarded, and child welfare protective services, the large-scale organizational developments have taken place primarily at the state level.

Professional experts and program reformers have frequently turned to federal agencies, and to Congress, in efforts to enforce uniform regulations on a nationwide basis, or to impose particular program organization structures or innovations in treatment methodologies on program operations at state and local levels. In other instances federal financial incentives have been used in efforts to achieve system-wide changes at state and local levels. The centralization of administrative authority has been reinforced by continuous efforts by the federal government to increase fiscal controls and accountability in programs involving substantial federal funds, even when formal administrative authority is at state or local levels, for example through "quality control" procedures in the AFDC and food stamps programs.

Regardless of the rhetoric about voluntary initiatives at the community level, the development of large-scale private philanthropy, other than the contributions of individuals to local churches, has been increasingly associated with national philanthropic foundations, and a nationwide pattern of systematic fundraising. Examples include nationwide telethons and computerized mail solicitation, and national corporate and labor union sponsorship of combined fundraising efforts like the United Way. National organizations like the Red Cross, Boy Scouts, and Girl Scouts adopt management control structures and procedures comparable to large-scale for-profit corporations. The Independent Sector, organized in 1981, has created a comprehensive national coalition of large corporations, large foundations, and national trade associations representing various categories of nonprofit service organizations. Large nationwide chains of for-profit hospitals, nursing homes, and residential treatment centers use contemporary methods of centralized management.

Several factors have supported the trend towards large administrative units with centralized administration, and intensified administrative control procedures in human service programs. The orginal growth of human service organizations came from efforts to provide such services across the entire society in education, health care and social services. In particular it involved the extension of services to rural areas which had initially been developed in major urban centers. This required state-wide comprehensive administrative systems. More recently, similar motivations have led to the development of large, inclusive, administrative systems covering metropolitan areas through the merger of independent local service organizations. In other service sectors the effort to ensure nationwide consistency in availability and quality of services led to the creation of organizations like the Veterans Administration.

This trend also reflects the current dominance of the instrumental perspective in the development of human service programs (Christian and Hannah 1983), and the application of "economic man" assumptions, with economic rewards and deprivations being viewed as the only significant form of motivation available for guiding the role performance of organizational staff persons. Motivations based primarily on concepts of mutual assistance, commitment to universal social values, or professional competence are viewed as inconsistent with the requirements of effective administration. The "command and control" concepts of standardized assembly line production (Reich 1983) have been transferred to nonstandarized human service production, reinforced by communication technology and computerization which makes it possible to extend the vertical "span of control" of central managers.

The trend towards increased size and centralization of control in human service programs has been, in part, a response to the requirements of dealing with concentrated centers of public funding and authority in state and federal governments and of economic power in business and industry. It is also, in part, a consequence of the dynamics of individual self-interest among organizational administrators and policymakers since size often equals power, and the level of organizational power often determines the economic status of individuals in policy and administrative positions. This highlights the tension between the "economic self-interest" model of individual human behavior and the complex interdependence among individuals and organizations which actually exists in postindustrial societies. Maximizing self-interest by corporate executives in for-profit organizations may, in reality, be a source of serious difficulty for both stockholders and consumers.

However, the maximization of individual economic self-interest as an operating principle for administrators in either governmental or nonprofit human service organizations can have castastrophic consequences for individual service users, and for the public-at-large. Moreover, any effort to make a consistent distinction between economic self-interest motivations in the for-profit sector and public service motivations in the governmental and the voluntary nonprofit sector is essentially irrelevant in a "mixed economy" society. For-profit self-interest decisions have public consequences, as in the instance of the Challenger space shuttle, while, in some instances, individual economic rewards for administrators may be effective in increasing efficiency in the procedures used in governmental and nonprofit organizations in contracting with for-profit providers.

As the size of financial operations involved in human service industries has increased, the concern with financial accountability has also increased. Recent financial constraints on governmental funding have intensified this concern. This has led to a focus on centralized financial accountability controls and standardization of administrative procedures, in particular cost-accounting procedures, with computers now making it possible to produce more and more detailed information more and more frequently. This concern for detailed fiscal accountability is reinforced in governmental agencies by traditional legislative concerns about the possible loss of resources through political corruption or through fraud.

The effect of these concerns is to increase the power of central auditors, with an emphasis on following standardized financial reporting procedures regardless of local administrative conditions. Intensified accountability procedures instituted by categorical funding sources have also been directed at controlling the flexible use by administrators in individual organizations of categorically targeted funds from a variety of funding sources in ways that maximize the total pool of financial resources and stabilize organizational funding levels by ignoring categorical constraints.

Concerns for meeting specialized human service needs for which traditional local services were inadequate resulted, in the 1970s, in the development of separate administrative networks of services for particular categories of service users with federal, federal-regional, state, state-region, and local components (Hollingsworth and Hanneman 1984). These categorical components were linked together by categorical funding and reporting systems, along with distinctive training and technical assistance functions. The specifications for these vertical categorical systems were largely developed at the federal level either in the form of detailed rules included in legislation or detailed administrative regulations.

In a number of these programmatic areas the establishment of complex nationwide vertically integrated systems has been accompanied by the development of accreditation standards for service organizations and accreditation machinery. Increased competition for funds from both governmental and philanthrophic sources has increased the importance of national trade associations in each of these human service networks. Intensified Washington-based lobbying activities and the development of nationwide public relations programs have become high priorities. In turn these activities generate pressures for local units to conform to nationally promoted models of administrative and program performance.

Concerns about particular types of implementation problems, in particular the coordination of the highly specialized services provided by categorical organizational components, have led to recommendations for increased centralization of authority and tighter management of service delivery systems under general purpose governments at state and local levels. In the early 1970s, as a result of initiatives by Health, Education and Welfare Secretary Elliot Richardson, *services integration* became a catchword for the promotion of inclusive management structures and procedures, such as consolidated, or "umbrella" human services agencies at the level of state government (Agranoff and Pattaos 1970; Austin 1978; Austin 1983a). Other recommendations focused on administrative consolidation of service programs at the local level. In England the 1968 Seebohm report resulted in the establishment of consolidated local authority social services departments, replacing separate categorical service programs (Harrison and Hoshino 1984).

Concern about protection of the "rights" of individuals involved in service programs has led to increased use of the courts, in particular the federal courts, by service consumers and consumer advocates to enforce access to services and due process in service delivery. Major class action suits charging deficiences in services have led, in some instances, to the court appointment of masters and monitors. This becomes another form of centralized administrative authority, with the court officers often having the power to override state and local decisionmaking in matters under the court jurisdiction (Moss 1984).

In spite of these pressures towards centralizing administrative authority and control, pressures which have come from both financially concerned "conservatives" and programmatically concerned "liberals," the personal service production system is still a substantially decentralized system in the United States. A major factor in maintaining the pattern of decentralization is the constitutionally defined "federalism" governance structure of the United States that interposes barriers to direct federal administrative control over state and local adminstrative operations.

This traditional pattern of decentralized federalism is reinforced by traditions rooted in the history of many immigrant groups who entered the United States as dissenters from, or refugees from, powerful centralized governments. The diversity of religious traditions also limits the role of institutionalized religion in supporting the authority of the national government. Efforts by Congress and the Executive Branch to exercise indirect control over programs involving federal funds, however, often result in elaborate provisions for proposal review, planning documents, fiscal and program auditing and program evaluation. These methods of control are often more constrictive, and more expensive, than direct administrative control might be.

The key issue, however, is not the degree of administrative centralization that has already developed in human service industries. The critical issue is that of the direction of future development in the organization of human services, and the relation of such development to the solution of the performance problems which characterize human service industries (Reich 1983). There have been a variety of alternative proposals for the direction of future development including: (1) intensification of central administrative controls; (2) the conversion of the entire system of governmental personal service provision to a highly decentralized marketplace system through the use of pre-payment or insurance mechanisms (Hatry 1983); (3) use of purchase-of-service vouchers on an income eligibility basis with services being provided by any licensed, or approved, provider with no centralized planning or control of the service delivery industry (Bendick 1985); (4) the separation of provision from production through the continuation of highly centralized governmental policymaking structures but "contracting out" the production of actual services to a variety of "provider" organizations, both large and small (Bendick 1985; Ferris and Graddy 1986); (5) the elimination of central administrative structures, particularly at the level of the national government, returning to an organizational system of services primarily based on "community initiative," "voluntarism," and "deprofessionalization" (Hadley and Hatch 1981; Harrison and Hoshino 1984; Starr 1985)[1]

However, none of these approaches is based upon a careful analysis of the dynamics of large-scale organizations which underlie many of the organizational performance problems identified with the present system. Nor do they include an analysis of the operational requirements of personal service production which must be taken into account in considering future alternatives either centralized or decentralized.

PERFORMANCE PROBLEMS IN LARGE-SCALE HUMAN SERVICE ORGANIZATIONS

Current concerns about the deficiencies in personal service programs do not focus primarily on questions of economic injustice, although such problems exist. They focus more on problems of implementation. While recognizing that there are many benefits provided by present service programs for particular individuals in specific situations, the criticisms of personal service programs include charges that many organizations provide poor quality services, are insensitive to the personal preferences of service users, are primarily remedial rather than preventive, involve excessive "red-tape," are over-professionalized, are inflexible in procedures, are unable to adapt to new knowledge and new operating conditions, are not cost effective, and are unable to coordinate service activities involving more than one organization (Murray 1984).

Failures in policy implementation have been receiving increased analytic attention in the last few years as it has become increasingly evident that the establishment of service programs to achieve particular public policy objectives often has only a modest relation to program outcomes (Aaron 1978; Derthick 1970; Haveman 1977; Matusow 1984). Many of the implementation problems which have been identified are related to the basic characteristics of large-scale administrative systems, whether that system is defined as a single organization, or as a multitiered, intergovernmental, service providing network. These problems have serious consequences even in the operation of those human service programs which are primarily concerned with the routine administration of standardized income maintenance and social insurance programs, the proto-typical governmental bureau or "bureaucracy." They have even more severe consequences when the model of the administrative, "people processing" (Hasenfeld 1983) bureaucracy is carried over to nonstandardized personal service programs in which the quality of service depends largely on the quality of personal interaction between the service producer and the service user.

The problems of large scale systems are largely a consequence of fundamental human behavioral characteristics of those individuals who must enact the role positions that make up the structure of the organization (Taylor 1983). While many aspects of the performance of a particular organization may be a function of the unique strengths or weaknesses of particular individuals, there are certain widely recurring problems which are related to general human behavioral characteristics. The behavior of human beings in enacting organizational roles is inherently problematic. These problems set limits on the extent to which any intensification of centralized control can effectively remedy the performance problems in human service organizations.

This situation is largely independent of ideological or political economy characteristics of the society although some organizational problems may be more evident in some societies than in others. It is also largely independent of the type of services being produced by the organization. Many of the complexities of large-scale systems are a consequence of numerous efforts to force human behavior to fit the requirements of large-scale organizational management (Brown 1982). The following sections identify briefly some of the more pervasive problems inherent in the interaction between humans and the structure of role positions in large-scale, administratively centralized organizations, and in particular in human service organizations.

Large scale organizations are dependent on complex communication systems (Knight and McDaniel 1979). Without direct person-to-person contact between those individuals initiating action and those individuals carrying out the prescribed action a variety of formal communication structures are required, first for communicating policies and operational instructions, and second, for reporting the results of action. The larger the organizational system the greater the number of intermediate points involved in communication transfers. At these intermediate points information is normally transformed, either through expansion and elaboration as action directives are applied to particular production operations, or through consolidation and interpretation as reports from multiple sources move to a single central source. As a result of these necessary intermediate steps, substantial problems of both *communication distortion* and *communication lag* develop.

The refinement of communication technology means that where electronic transmission of original information is involved there may be very little distortion. However, whenever communication must be dealt with by a person, functioning as a linkage point in a communication network, problems of distortion are likely to occur. Action directives, or regulations dealing with operating procedures often are received by front-line action personnel in a different form or understood in a very different way, from what was originally initiated. Thus when a communication is initiated it is impossible to make a firm prediction as to the percentage of accurate perception there will be on the part of the ultimate recipient of that information who may be either a service worker, or a service consumer. In turn, reports on actions taken, or on service outcomes, may be so modified by reinterpretation, or consolidation, that central administrative units have no ability to predict the percentage of accuracy in the information which they use for planning and decisionmaking purposes.

Not only is communication distorted but there are also significant time delays. A year may pass before a Congressional enactment is translated into final federal regulations enabling the initiation of a particular program. If the original action was responsive to an immediate situation, that situation may have changed extensively by the time the program is initiated. However, once the administrative machinery is aligned implementation is likely to proceed, whether relevant or irrelevant. Similarly requests from direct service levels within the service organization for a decision on a nonstandard situation, if processed through the entire organization, may require months to be cleared through all levels, so that by the time the decision is received at the point of service the issue is moot.

These problems of communication distortion and lag have little relation to the level of organizational commitment among organizational employees, their level of training, or their political ideology, except that if there are individuals within the organization who are actively hostile to the organization or opposed to organizational goals the problems may be compounded. These communication problems are serious in any large-scale organization; in a human service organization in which the effects of miscommunication may have a direct effect on the lives of particular individuals they become highly critical.

There are also general problems in the policy decision process in large organizations. These involve both *excessive specificity* and *inadequate specificity* in decisions. Unusual or disruptive events affecting the organization are likely to result in overly specific policy decisions. Policy or procedural decisions are made on the basis of the factors which are understood to have been involved in the unique situation; the application of those policy or procedural decisions is then made system-wide. Public response to a single situation involving the permitted death of a newborn baby with severely disabling physical conditions led to federal proposals for rulemaking to establish procedures shaped by the circumstances of that single incident which were intended to govern every birth in which there are disabling conditions throughout the United States (Moss 1984). In this instance the proposal for such expansive rulemaking was struck down by the Supreme Court.

On the other hand, requests for policy or procedural decisions coming from several different sources within an organization often result in a decision that is broad enough to encompass all of them, but not specific enough to fit the exact circumstances involved in any one of them. The result is that the general policy is still subject to interpretation at the point of direct application, although the objective in seeking a central decision was to avoid making a unique decision at the service production level.

Another feature of large-scale systems is the necessity of establishing highly standardized personnel systems. Standardized personnel procedures, including many aspects of the "merit system," were established to avoid the personalized and often politicized personnel procedures which are characteristic of many business and governmental organizations. In turn, these standarized procedures have become essential to the operation of large-scale organizations in order to avoid having every personnel decision, including not only employment and discharge but all individual elements of working conditions and fringe benefits, become a unique decision resolvable only at the top of the organization. Given detailed rules, specific personnel decisions can be decentralized within the organization and still be accepted as legitimate in most situations.

However, the effect of such rule-controlled procedures is also to standardize the recognition and reward system so that there is little or no differentiation of rewards either finanical or in status perquisites, in support of organizational commitment, performance competence, or specialized effort. The organization becomes a system of standardized role expectations and standardized role enactments. Given the absence of opportunities to provide recognition and support for above average performance, and thus to strengthen the example of such performance, special achievement can only be recognized substantively by promotion. Promotions may include increased financial benefits and recognition but they also involve changes in the role performance requirements to which the individual is expected to respond. This can result in the widely commented on phenomena of removing the most skillful persons from the tasks at which they are the most skillful and assigning them to responsibilities for which they may be poorly qualified.

The resulting elaboration of intermediate mid-management positions takes many forms in large-scale organizations. Having created intermediate positions an elaboration of control and reporting procedures is required to justify the positions. Moreover, the creation of the single position often leads to the formation of an entire bureau or department with support staff, beginning with a secretary and extending to a variety of other specialized positions. The justification for such a unit in turn, requires a justification of domain boundaries defining the scope of responsibility and authority of the unit. This leads to turf battles with individuals in other organizational positions, since the authority of the newly created position must be drawn from the authority already allocated to existing positions. Thus the occupant of the new position must push for some decentralization of authority from higher level positions and for withdrawing some degree of authority from positions closer to the direct service level.

To the extent that the independent authority of mid-level positions is made commensurate with the qualifications and salary level of the persons involved, the communication network of the organization is made more complicated and the possibilities of communication difficulties increased. On the other hand, if the authority of the mid-level positions is not commensurate with the experience and abilities of the persons in those positions, which is, in fact, a more likely outcome, then a pattern of large-scale wastage of valuable personnel resources develops.

This wastage is likely to become more pronounced as each individual in a mid-management position becomes aware that, given the limited number of higher level positions in the organization, further advancements are unlikely to occur, and that future changes in salary and other financial benefits are likely to be unrelated to quality of performance. The individuals in these positions, cut-off from the recognition and personal satisfactions involved in direct service activities and without significant autonomy or independent authority in their mid-mangement position, may cope in a variety of ways (Williams, Sjoberg and Sjoberg 1983). Some go through the formal rituals of passing instructions downward and reports upward with little investment of effort. For others there may be high levels of frustration and stress, sometimes leading to alcoholism and other behavioral problems. For still others there is opportunity for the investment of energy and initiative in personal interests outside the organization (Cherniss 1980). And still other individuals may become involved in elaborate power manipulation schemes, particularly if there are internal conflicts within the organization as a whole (Williams, Sjoberg and Sjoberg 1983).

Considerable attention has been given to the concept of "street-level" bureaucrats, those persons in large-scale human service organizations who deal directly with the public. A common characteristic of the performance of the persons who are in these positions is a high degree of detachment from the official control structure of the organization as a result of the problems of communication and intermediate management levels noted above (Ouchi 1978). One consequence of this pattern of "loose coupling" may be a high degree of informal, and often illegitimate, power exercised by these service personnel over service users (Lipsky 1980).

Another significant element in the performance problems of large-scale human service organizations is the employment of individuals with specialized professional training who are then subjected to highly standardized role definitions and administrative controls. This can result in a lack of commitment by such personnel to organizational objectives, a lack of initiative in innovation and problem-solving, and frequently to problems of "burn-out" and personnel turn-over (Cherniss 1980). The personal, and societal, resources invested in developing individual competencies required for responsible, autonomous, professional practice are thus often wasted.

The large-scale organization is, by definition, involved with a large number of different external constituencies ranging from policy bodies to service consumers (Martin 1985). Such an organization is likely to be involved with a variety of geographic service areas and to encompass a substantial number of distinct program components, or sub-divisions. Each of these program sub-divisions has its own set of constituencies, including public officials, professional bodies, consumer constituencies, parent groups, and news media. As the program structure becomes more complex, the inclusive goals of the organization become divided into a series of distinctive sub-goals which are the concern of individual sub-divisions. Technical support sub-units which are not directly involved in service production are particularly likely to develop self-contained and self-justifying unit growth goals (Beeson 1983; Pfeffer 1978). Even direct service program components are likely to develop organizational maintenance goals which may be in conflict with the presumed policy goals of the entire organization.

This pattern of sub-unit proliferation, and the dominance of sub-unit goals in day-to-day operation, can result in an organizational condition which has been identified by organizational theorists as "organized anarchy" (Sabrosky, Thompson, and McPherson 1983). Under such conditions there may be a high degree of system stability, as an equilibrium is established reflecting the relative power position of various units (Pfeffer 1978). However, this may be at the expense of the ability of the organization to mobilize its resources for organizational goal achievement (Williams 1980), the ability of the organization as a whole to adapt to new environmental conditions, or the ability of the central administration of the organization to control the quality of production activities at the service level (Aldrich 1978; Hasenfeld 1986).

SUMMARY

In human service programs the exercise of authority through highly centralized administrative mechanisms within large-scale organizational systems may be incompatible with the achievement of the performance objectives of such services. When these structural problems are combined with cultural values which place maximum emphasis on individual *economic* self-interest, the performance problems are compounded. The resultant failures in program implementation have substantially undercut the political credibility of many current programs, and in turn the credibility of political parties and governments identified with a centralized model of the welfare state (Gilder 1981; Hadley and Hatch 1981).

NOTES

1. "Block grant" program reorganizations by the federal government in the early 1980s have primarily resulted in substituting centralized control at the state level for centralized control at the federal level rather than the development of local, community-based approaches.

Chapter 6

The Development of Human Service Programs Under Voluntary Nonprofit and Governmental Auspices

INTRODUCTION

Among the significant political economy factors that shape contemporary human service industries are the existing institutional structures through which human services are produced. These structures were shaped by a historical process of development that has distinctive characteristics within each national society. Developments in the United States have been particularly important because of the international dissemination of the United States experience through the extensive involvement of students from other nations in a variety of professional education programs within the United States since the 1940s.

This chapter examines the initial development in the United States of the voluntary nonprofit human services system and the governmental human services system until the 1930s with specific attention to two factors: (1) the social and economic conditions which drove the development of human service organizations, and (2) the political economy that shaped that development.

Since the earliest period of social development three issues have been part of the social policy context of society. The first is the issue of dependency—that is provision for the care and maintenance of dependent individuals, in particular the person with a handicap, infirm elderly individuals, and the child without a family that can provide care. The second is the issue of basic physical survival under conditions of adversity—when catastrophes, such as flood, famine, pestilence, war, or economic collapse leave otherwise self-maintaining individuals, families, and communities temporarily without the basic necessities for life. The third is the issue of poverty, that is the uneven distribution of the economic resources that result from economic activity so that some households are forced to live at a level that is grossly below the standard for the society.

Until the beginnings of the "modern" era of urban industrialization the care of infirm and dependent persons was essentially met within the framework of the extended family. That family was, in general, located in a single geographic area and part of a single locality community over a number of generations. Survival under conditions of catastrophe, beyond the resources of family or neighbors, depended on temporary access to resources under control of the powerful—the king, the emperor, the nobility, the warlord, the wealthy merchant, the landowner—and in some societies, the organized church. The basic distribution of economic resources, and the pattern of wealth and poverty, was primarily determined through the marketplace, except for those who inherited wealth, under rules defined by the powerful, but justified by tradition and theology. The existence of poverty and the unequal distribution of wealth and power were defined as consistent with the "natural order" over which human beings had no control. Poverty was relieved, if at all, by the charity of the wealthy (Lens 1969).

Changes in society brought disruptions in traditional ways of meeting the needs of the infirm and the dependent, and of those affected by catastrophes, leading to the development of "organized" forms of social provision for such persons. Two alternative social policy approaches developed within Europe. One focused primarily on a pattern of provision of assistance through the local community, involving both local government and private charity, or philanthropy, for example the English Elizabethan Poor Law and later poor law revisions (Mencher 1967). The other approach developed at the initiative of, and under the control of, the national government, for example the development of early forms of social insurance under the German government, in part as a response to the growing socialist political movements in Europe (Dawson 1912).

The development of these organized but quite limited forms of provision for infirm, dependent and temporarily impoverished individuals was viewed as being separate from the capitalist free-market processes that determined the basic distribution of economic resources. These economic processes involved the exchange of individually produced goods for cash payments, the exchange of labor for wages, the exchange of capital or savings for interest, and the exchange of the use of land for rent. By definition the results of these marketplace exchanges, under rules enforced by the police powers of the nation-state, were considered to be a "just" distribution of resources.

Prior to the Civil War the policies governing provision of assistance to persons in need in the United States were shaped by English traditions (Leiby 1978). Basic public responsibility for infirm and dependent persons was organized at the community level. It involved various combinations of "indoor relief," or institutional care—almshouses and workhouses, and limited forms of "outdoor relief" or "poor relief," and to a limited degree specialized state-level institutions, such as the asylum for persons with mental illness (Rothman 1971). There were also many forms of private charity including the charitable activities of churches and church-related organizations, personal charity by wealthy individuals, and the activities of philanthropic corporations established to implement the provisions of bequests provided for in the wills of succcessful businessmen. The level of assistance was minimal and there was a strong preoccupation with the need to ensure that the provision of assistance did not encourage individuals to avoid work (Huggins 1971). These "social welfare" activities were critical for the development of human services because they were among the earliest forms of collective, or community, action beyond the organization of militia, tax collection, and the courts (Garraty 1974). In the period from the Civil War to the end of the century a rapid expansion of these social welfare provisions took place, together with major changes in the organizational pattern of such provisions.

THE DRIVING FORCES

The basic forces that changed the society, and which the United States shared with the countries of Western Europe, were the forces of industrialization and urbanization. The move of population from rural areas to large cities, the replacement of agricultural work by industrial employment in large factories, and the change from an economy based on family self-provision and barter to an economy based on wage income and cash payments for necessities, all contributed to the disruption of traditional communal patterns of care. Extended families and traditional village communities were disrupted by patterns of migration. Factory employment divided the population into the *employables,* who could earn an hourly wage, and the *unemployables,* who represented essentially a cost to the economy.

The population growth of industrial cities resulted in overcrowded housing, disease epidemics that often left children as orphans, and widespread crime and violence. Industrial employment often resulted in illness and disability or early death among children, as well as disability and death from illness and accidents among adults. The massing of workers in the cities also brought the periodic threat of social upheaval as the marketplace capitalist system went through cycles of expansion and contraction—boom and bust (Lens 1969; Piven and Cloward 1971). Financial panics and depressions often left thousands of workers unemployed without resources to support themselves or their families.

These unemployed workers were a sympathetic audience for persons who argued that the existing pattern for distribution of economic resources was unjust. In Western Europe and the United States the protests of urban workers against the injustices of the economic system were interpreted first as being caused by the French Revolution, and then as being caused by the teachings of Karl Marx and Frederich Engels and by the revolutionary events in Europe in 1848 (Lens 1966).

In the United States, during the last half of the nineteenth century, these conditions associated with industrialization and urbanization were augmented by developments specific to this nation, including the Civil War. In the North the War intensified the processes of industrialization and urban growth. In the South the result of the War was to maintain and extend the pattern of rural poverty and isolation and to delay the full impact of urbanization and industrialization, and related patterns of social welfare development, for nearly a century.

A second factor specific to the United States was the impact of immigration that contributed to urban congestion, particularly in major industrial centers, adding the problems of cultural and language differences and ethnic discrimination to the problems of poverty and dependency. Immigration swelled the available manpower resources reducing the relative leverage of industrial workers in the economic system and increasing the potential for economic exploitation. Immigration also brought refugees from political violence, particularly from the revolutionary confrontations of 1848 in Europe. Many of these refugees were socialist critics of the emerging capitalist industrial economic system.

A third factor that drove the development of social welfare in the United States was a concern with the potential for political and social polarization within the national society and the threat of political disruption and violence. The Civil War had demonstrated the fearful costs of political polarization. Events in Europe throughout the nineteenth century including the violence of revolutionary political movements, the effects of religious oppression, conflicts between nationality groups, and attacks against Jews in eastern Europe, highlighted the potential for self-destructive violence within modern societies. Responses within the United States to the problems of urban growth and industrialization reflected, in part, a concern with meeting at least a minimal level of the economic and social needs of immigrant working-class groups in order to minimize polarization and confrontation along cultural and religious lines, or across economic class lines.

THE POLITICAL ECONOMY

The development of social welfare institutions in the United States, and similar developments in education and health, during the last half of the nineteenth century, was shaped by the characteristics of the political economy, particularly in the urban society in the Northeast, the Middle Atlantic regions and in the

Midwest east of the Mississippi. The South was an isolated region dominated by the consequences of the Civil War, in particular by the prolonged effort made by the white society to reestablish boundaries and status relationships between black and white citizens following the withdrawal of Federal troops in the 1870s. This issue dominated the social order in the South at least until the 1930s (Grantham 1983).

One important characteristic of the political economy was the absence of certain traditional sources of provision for persons in need. Most important was the lack of a landed aristocracy with a tradition of feudal responsibility for the inhabitants of inherited estates, a responsibility that often carried over into leadership in private philanthropy in the urbanizing societies of Europe. There was also no dominant and controlling church establishment, unlike most European societies. A community-wide system for meeting the needs of dependent or unemployed persons could not be built around a single religious organization. Not only were there bitter divisions between Catholics and Protestants, but Protestantism was fragmented, and the relations between Protestant denominations were often highly competitive. Organizational structures for dealing with social welfare, health or educational needs could not be taken for granted as givens from a historical past. They had to be deliberately created.

There was also a deliberately fragmented structure of government based on a political philosophy of minimal governmental authority. The result was the establishment of a decentralized federal system in which the national government exercised only those limited powers specifically assigned to it, all other powers being reserved to the states. The states continued to be the fundamental political unit in the governmental system in the United States, particularly for internal or "domestic" issues.

The political philosophy underlying the concept of limited political authority for the federal government was reinforced by the tradition of local self-sufficiency which developed from the frontier experience. From the Mayflower Compact to the establishment of village government in frontier settlements in the Midwest (Smith 1966) local decisionmaking dominated because there was no available alternative. The tradition of minimal governmental structure and minimal governmental involvement in social and economic issues dominated American political philosophy until well into the twentieth century. This philosophy also incorporated a belief in the importance of maintaining a specific division of responsibilities among various levels of government, with local self-sufficiency and a narrowly restricted role for the federal government.

The development of social welfare institutions was also shaped by the distribution of economic resources. The last half of the nineteenth century was a period of rapid accumulation of wealth and of control over economic development by business and industrial entrepreneurs, most of whom did not come from traditional upper-class families with inherited wealth. Social welfare organizations, particularly voluntary nonprofit organizations, depended heavily on these philanthropic individuals for their financial support (Hanaford 1875). After these philanthropists died these organizations continued to be supported by endowment income from bequests from their estates. The beliefs of these successful entrepreneurs about the importance of hard work, thrift and ambition and about the possibilities for individual achievement were reflected in their approach to philanthropy (Huggins 1971). They believed in avoiding governmental controls on business, consistent with the attitudes of their ancestors who had been leaders in the American Revolution. Their objective was to keep government out of domestic issues in general except when government played a role in the protection of private property, for example when there were strikes.

The role of antiestablishment religious beliefs in the early settlement of the colonies was reflected in the freedom of religion provisions in the Constitution. This carried over into a tradition of resistance by lay leaders and clergy to governmental intrusion into any activity sponsored by a religious organization. This antagonism on the part of business leaders, and many civic and professional leaders, towards the concept of government as a potential source of regulatory interference, was reinforced by the dominant role that immigrant voters came to play in the politics of confrontation in local governments particularly in the seaboard cities in the late 1800s. The political cleavages that emerged were primarily cultural: Protestant versus Catholic, English-speaking versus non-English-speaking, northern Europe versus central and southern Europe heritage. There were also differences in economic interests—industrial employers versus workers, property owners versus renters, bankers versus borrowers.

The development of social welfare institutions was also shaped by the intellectual atmosphere of the United States. A belief in both personal and intellectual freedom, protected against intrusive government, was embodied in the Bill of Rights. The importance of the Bible in English Evangelical Protestantism, as well as in all Calvinist denominations, had resulted in support for an educated clergy, and a belief in the importance of fundamental reading skills for all citizens, a skill that was also important in a merchantile economy. Moreover, the diversity of religious beliefs within the United States helped to sustain a tradition of intellectual debate as well as a pragmatic toleration of disagreement, regardless of the bitterness with which particular religious leaders attacked each other as heretics and unbelievers (Hutchison 1976).

The growth in the numbers of successful merchants and wealthy industrialists also resulted in increased contributions for the expansion of private colleges and universities to provide, in part, for the education of their sons and daughters. The increased numbers of graduates from these colleges and universities became a major element in the upper middle-class population living in cities. By the end of the nineteenth century the growing college educated, upper middle-class, urban population began to include significant numbers of women as well as men, although the women were largely excluded from career opportunities in the traditional professions, business and government. However, as part of an educated elite these college educated women were socially and intellectually the equal of their male peers who were in business leadership positions, and who controlled the financial resources needed for philanthropic activities. Many of the women had inherited wealth from entrepreneurial ancestors. They also often married men who had inherited wealth or who controlled corporate wealth.

Key elements in the political economy that shaped the voluntary nonprofit and governmental organizations that emerged to cope with problems of meagerly paid and unemployed city-dwellers, included the lack of traditional structures for charity, the concentrations of wealth, traditions of minimal government, and antagonisms between business leaders and political leaders (Ehrenreich 1985). Also important were the intellectual climate that allowed for debate on public issues, an educated and wealthy upper middle-class population, and the characteristics of the dominant religious traditions.

THE DEVELOPMENT OF THE VOLUNTARY NONPROFIT SOCIAL WELFARE SYSTEM

Between the Civil War and the 1930s an elaborate system of voluntary nonprofit social welfare organizations and similar organizations in such related fields as health care and higher education developed in the United States. There were also important developments in governmental provision of human services, and many of the leaders in the voluntary system were involved in these governmental developments. But the social welfare "system" developed primarily around the network of nongovernmental organizations. In particular it was the leadership from the local networks of voluntary nonprofit organizations that created the elements of a national voluntary system in both health care and social welfare.

The voluntary nonprofit system as it developed in the period following the Civil War had a number of distinctive characteristics. It was primarily urban since persons with the most visible problems, the social reformers with a concern for helping with those problems, and the wealthy philanthropists were all city dwellers. Many of the individual service organizations began as projects of Protestant churches or Protestant denominations (Leiby 1978). Over time, however, the voluntary nonprofit system became predominantly "nonsectarian." That is, it was not identified with any single religious denomination although it included service organizations sponsored by each of the major religious traditions (Marty 1980). It was a system, however, largely created by, and controlled by, men from Anglo Saxon and northern European backgrounds who were primarily Protestant by religious affiliation, although the households served by this system in the largest cities were largely Roman

Catholic and Jewish, coming from central, eastern and southern Europe (Baltzell 1964). This system developed primarily under the leadership of businessmen and professionals, doctors, lawyers, and ministers, who organized and directed initial efforts to meet the needs of city residents (Westby 1966). The service consumers, however, were predominantly from an industrial working-class background.

The involvement of civic volunteer leaders during the Civil War and immediately following did not reflect a pattern of sharp distinction between governmental and nongovernmental sectors. The War stimulated voluntary civic initiatives around the personal needs of the soldiers in the field, and the needs of their families in local communities (Bremmer 1980). Some activities were carried out in cooperation with the national government and some developed completely separately. The activities of civic leaders in both the North and South during the War were similar, except that in the North there was a more highly developed tradition of organized charity and access to greater resources. The work of the Sanitary Commission, and the nursing services organized by Clara Barton, developed from voluntary initiatives rather than governmental action. Other initiatives immediately following the Civil War included the activities of individual philanthropists and the religious organizations that became involved in education and other services for emancipated black citizens in the South (Grantham 1983).

The 1860s brought an increase in the number of state boards of charities, consisting of unpaid civic leaders appointed by the governor to oversee state administered asylums, orphanages and schools for the "feeble-minded" (Leiby 1978). These boards also undertook investigations of social conditions, and, in some states, monitored the local provision of poor relief. Members of these state boards of charities met together in 1874 under the auspices of the American Social Science Association. This meeting, and successive meetings in the following years, led to the organization of the National Conference of Charities and Correction in 1878. This Conference became a core element in the development of the nationwide voluntary social welfare system over the next fifty years (Bruno 1957).

Distinctions between governmental and nongovernmental activities in social welfare became more explicit as activities at the level of state government, and at the local community level, took different forms. State governments even before the Civil War began to assume increasing responsibility for individuals with long-term disability and dependency problems, as well as for criminals and delinquents (Leiby 1978). As a consequence of reform efforts spearheaded by Dorothea Dix, attention was given to the need for more appropriate care particularly for the mentally ill persons traditionally placed in local almshouses, or in jails and prisons. These efforts led, in a number of states, to the establishment of specialized residential asylums that required financial support on a state-wide basis (Rothman 1971).

On the other hand persons concerned with social welfare in the cities were faced primarily with the problems of poverty, and in particular the consequences of poverty for households with children (Leiby 1978). The problems of poverty, as they affected individual households, were presumed to be immediate and short-term, rather than chronic, and were considered to be treatable rather than incurable. It was around these problems of temporary household poverty that the voluntary social welfare system primarily developed, although there were also many specific voluntary activities directed at other problems, such as the problems of orphaned and abandoned children. For persons whose poverty condition was chronic, particularly the physically disabled and the aged, tax-supported almshouses continued to be viewed as the preferred solution (Rothman 1971).

During the period prior to the Civil War a substantial number of voluntary nonprofit associations were established in the major cities of the Northeast and Midwest. As in most aspects of voluntary social welfare in the nineteenth century, many of the best known organizations were those in New York City. The Association for the Improvement of the Condition of the Poor, which traced its beginnings to 1843, was the largest of the New York City charity agencies (Brandt 1942). The largest child welfare agency was the New York Children's Aid Society, beginning in the 1850s, which was headed by Charles Loring Brace for nearly forty years (Brace 1872; Langsam 1964). Other types of voluntary service organizations that were established during this period included Visiting Nurse Associations, the Young Mens Christian Association and the Young Womens Christian Association, the Young Mens Hebrew Association, the St. Vincent de Paul Societies in Catholic parishes, and the Salvation Army (Leiby 1978). Privately supported hospitals, organized at the initiative of physicians and primarily concerned with emergency medical care and the training of surgeons, were established in New York, Boston and Philadelphia.

Charity Organization Societies

The first major system development among voluntary organizations came with the initiation of Charity Organization Societies in a number of large cities (Leiby 1978; Lubove 1965). The creation of Charity Organization Societies in the United States, modeled after similar organizations in England, followed an increase in the number of voluntary charity agencies after the bank panic of 1873 that created widespread unemployment. The COS's were initiated by business and civic leaders as the first of many efforts to apply systematic concepts of business organization and management to charity administration and philanthropy. The objective was to increase efficiency in the use of available financial resources, and to focus primarily on a process of rehabilitation through which the individual or family would again become economically self-maintaining. There was also an intent to limit the demands for charitable contributions and to maintain economic pressure on able-bodied adults to accept any available employment (Lowell 1884; Stewart 1911).

The Charity Organization Societies provided various forms of technical assistance to local charity agencies. At least initially the COS's were not intended to provide "material" assistance directly to individual households. Their technical assistance included systematic case investigation by a staff of agents, referral to other organizations for specific forms of assistance such as medical care, the convening of neighborhood case conferences involving all agencies active with a particular family, and the assignment of a volunteer "friendly visitor" who would provide personal support and guidance to the family and assist in finding resources to help with the specific problems that had led to the financial "downfall" of the family (Rauch 1975; Richmond 1899; Taylor-Owen 1986). The overriding objective was to prevent the family from falling into "pauperism," that is into a condition of chronic dependency.

On the community-wide level the COS developed a case register of households in order to prevent duplication and fraud in the provision of financial assistance, and carried out analyses of case records in order to identify those conditions most frequently associated with poverty. COS board members often provided leadership in social reform efforts directed at basic social conditions reflected in individual family situations (Pittman-Munke 1985). This "scientific philanthropy" approach, including both friendly visiting and social action, in effect created the social services component of charity administration, as distinguished from administrative tasks involved in the direct provision of limited material assistance. However, the actual implementation of the COS model varied widely from city to city, with Boston and Philadelphia COS's being viewed as more consistent with the model than those in many other cities (Taylor-Owen 1986).

While there was a concern with human needs in individual situations, there was a very specific emphasis within the COS movement on maintaining work incentives, and encouraging economic self-support, even in the instance of widows with several children (Stewart 1911). The focus was on temporary assistance not on income redistribution to eliminate poverty. A similar philosophy underlay the work of organizations like the Children's Aid Society, which emphasized "placing out" as an alternative to long term institutional care in an orphanage. Placement of an orphan with a family, in particular farm families, it was thought would teach the child good work habits and encourage self-reliance (Brace 1872). It was around these principles that the voluntary social welfare system developed until the turn of the century (Ehrenreich 1985; Kellogg 1893).

The initial organizational structure of the COS organizations generally involved an all-male Board of Directors that carried much of the responsibility for administration, particularly for fundraising and the oversight of expenditures, as well as oversight of organizational staff members. A typical paid staff consisted of men working as investigators, or "agents," although the men were later replaced by women, and women in clerical posititions. It was also part of the COS plan to recruit women volunteers who would serve as "friendly visitors." Many of the friendly visitors were wives of board members and their acquaintances (Rauch 1975; Smith 1884).

The Settlements

The beginnings of the settlement house movement were in colleges and universities, rather than in the business community (Coit 1891). Toynbee Hall, the first settlement house, located in the West End of London, served as a residence and social observatory for university students. The student motivations involved a combination of religious humanitarianism and an interest in Marxist social philosophies and the labor movement. The objective of settlement "residents" was to become knowledgeable about the social environment of the working-class neighborhood rather than to provide case-by-case assistance.

Settlement houses were established in the United States primarily by two types of individuals who were seeking ways to apply in practice the ideals of Christianity and of democracy: socially minded Protestant ministers such as Robert Woods at South End House in Boston and Graham Taylor at Chicago Commons in Chicago, and educated women such as Jane Addams at Hull House in Chicago, and in New York, Vida Scudder at the College Settlement, Mary Simkovitch at Greenwich House and Lillian Wald at Henry Street Settlement. Settlement boards of directors at first consisted largely of a group of personal supporters of the founder of the settlement with similar social philosophies.

As in the English settlements the volunteer settlement residents in the United States, both men and women, were often college students or recent graduates. These settlement residents were part of the rapidly expanding group of college graduates at the end of the nineteenth century who became active in a wide variety of social reform movements during the Progressive Era. Orientation of new settlement residents involved "walking the neighborhood" rather than participating in formal in-service training. The residents determined for themselves, in consultation with the headworker and more experienced residents, the pattern of their own activities. Some residents were more interested in observation and systematic analysis of social problems than in specific service activities. The pattern of personal relations among the settlement house residents was a mixture of a collegial work organization and an extended family headed by the "headworker." This was in contrast to the more formal administrative structure of the larger charity agencies and the Charity Organization Societies.

Participation of neighborhood families in organized activities in the settlement house, including a wide variety of clubs and classes for all age groups, required some personal initiative. In general the settlement house residents were involved with the more stable families in working-class neighborhoods, families in which there were interests in personal development and social mobility, while the charity agencies, and the COS friendly visitors, were involved with the more disrupted family situations (Chambers and Hinching 1968; Lloyd 1971).

While settlement residents were concerned with the immediate problems of their neighbors in the predominantly immigrant neighborhoods of the central city, they were also concerned with a broad range of social and political issues (Addams 1910; Davis 1967; Wade 1964; Woods 1929). These included political corruption and the political exploitation of immigrant families, prostitution and vice that were often linked with corrupt politics, tenement housing and urban congestion, infant mortality and child nutrition. Particularly at Hull House in Chicago, these concerns also included working conditions in the sweat shops and factories in which the neighborhood women, and often their children, were employed. Jane Addams, and other Hull House residents, became nationally recognized as leaders in social reform efforts concerned, in particular, with social and economic conditions affecting women and children (Fish 1985). Lillian Wald at Henry Street Settlement in New York was identified with the development of public health nursing and school nursing (Wald 1895).

The settlements placed particular emphasis on the importance of organizational independence and diversity rather than on the standardization of procedures and interagency cooperation that the COS movement did. Their lack of dependence on public funds left them particularly free to criticize local governmental officials, and their support from those wealthy individuals who supported their objectives made it possible for them to criticize exploitive businessmen. The loose pattern of affiliation they developed through city federations of settlements, and later through the National Federation of Settlements, left each organization free to act independently on public policy issues. However, it also meant that those settlements that did not have wealthy patrons were in a weak position to compete with larger city-wide service organizations for funding support from individual philanthropists and foundations.

The Turn of The Century

While the scope of voluntary social welfare and health care activities in American cities grew slowly during the 1880s, these activities began to take on a new significance. A brief but severe depression in 1886 led to bitter strikes. The Haymarket Riot in Chicago in 1886, attributed to anarchists, increased public fears of the impact of radical political philosophies from Europe, and of the potential consequences of the increasing polarization between industrial leaders and immigrant workers. Industrial leaders began to give serious attention to measures that would overcome worker hostility and increase worker commitment to higher productivity (Berkowitz and McQuaid 1980). Jane Addams viewed the settlement house movement as, in part, a response to these tensions, providing a way in which concerned men and women from middle-class backgrounds could help to bridge the gap between the middle-class and the working-class by serving as service volunteers, thereby learning first hand about the realities of life in urban slum neighborhoods (Addams 1910; Addams 1965).

The Depression of 1893 resulted in a substantial expansion of voluntary social welfare. This was the most severe and prolonged depression in American history prior to the 1930s (Reznek 1953). Unemployment increased rapidly and led to the establishment of a brief work relief program by New York City in the winter of 1894. The 1893 meeting of the National Conference of Charities and Correction, which had become a major channel of communication among those involved in social welfare, public health, and the administration of state institutions, was marked by a twenty year review of the experience of Charity Organization Societies, and a summary of the efforts of individual cities to deal with the problems resulting from the depression (Kellogg 1893). Emphasis in the Conference was put on the importance of relying on carefully organized private charity to meet these problems rather than expanding publicly administered outdoor relief (Kaplan 1978). With increased demands on the charity agencies because of the large number of unemployed workers, the coordinating methods of the COS's had also gained new support.

During the 1890s increasing numbers of women, some of them college graduates, began to be employed as agents in charity agencies (Taylor-Owen 1986). Similar changes took place in voluntary child welfare agencies in which women replaced the men who had been employed as agents to follow-up the children who were "placed out" to determine that they were not being abused or exploited.

Under Robert deForest as Board President and Edward Devine, an economist with a Ph.D. from the Wharton School in Philadelphia, as Executive Director, the New York City COS became the focal point of the national development of the voluntary nonprofit system in social welfare. In 1897 Mary Richmond, who had initiated an in-service staff training program as the executive of the Baltimore COS, presented a paper at the National Conference on "The Need of a Training School in Applied Philanthropy." In 1898 she became a member of the faculty of the new Summer School of Applied Philanthrophy, which was established by the New York COS. In 1904 this training was expanded to an eight month full-time educational program. In 1910 it was further expanded to a two-year program, becoming the prototype for other schools of social work being established in private colleges and universities in the major urban centers in the East and Midwest (Austin 1986; Meier 1954).

The New York COS Board of Directors also provided leadership in two major reform efforts, one in housing that led to reforms in the New York State tenement laws (deForest and Veiller 1962; Lubove 1962), and one in public health that led to the formation of the National Tuberculosis Society and the Christmas Seal fundraising campaigns.

The pattern of organizational development in other major cities was similar to that in New York City. The core pattern of voluntary services that emerged in these cities included: child welfare foster care and adoption agencies, children's residential insititutions, Florence Crittendon homes for unwed mothers, nutrition and public health programs including free milk stations, visiting nurses, settlement houses, vocational guidance, kindergartens and day care centers, summer camps, visiting teachers, hospital and psychiatric social work, charity agencies and a charity organization society.

Although all of the elements of this diverse system of voluntary nonprofit health care and social welfare services were created in most of the major cities of the Northeast and Midwest, the scope of the actual services provided was often very modest in relation to the total need (Ehrenreich 1985). Although there were similar developments in some cities in the South, including the establishment of charity organization societies, it was on a more limited scale, because of more limited economic resources and because of the pervasive impact of conflicts over the position of black citizens (Grantham 1983).

Many of the service agencies which had been originally established by Protestant churches, or at the initiative of Protestant laymen, began to identify themselves as "nonsectarian" in seeking community-wide financial support. Agencies providing similar types of services were organized by Jewish leaders, with a special emphasis on meeting the needs of Jewish immigrants from Eastern Europe, and by Catholic bishops and wealthy Catholic laymen (Pittman-Munke 1986).

These developments at the city level led directly to the development of a nationwide voluntary social welfare system including a network of national associations, each organized around a specialized area of activity. The American Association for Organizing Charity, with headquarters in New York City, started with 62 organizational members in 1911, increasing to over 200 organizations in 1919. The Child Welfare League, the National Federation of Settlements, and the National Association for the Study and Prevention of Tuberculosis were also among the many national associations which had headquarters in New York City. This proximity contributed to the development of personal linkages among the leaders of the various associations. The New York location of the headquarters of national associations strengthened the role of New York City service organizations in shaping national developments in their respective fields. The National Conference of Charities and Correction, which changed its name to the National Conference of Social Work in 1917, continued to be a major nationwide forum for volunteer lay leaders as well as for the increasing number of professional practitioners in a wide range of human service programs, especially social welfare and health care.

This rapid expansion of voluntary nonprofit activities was supported by the increasing wealth of successful businessmen. One example of the effects of this wealth was the establishment of the Russell Sage Foundation in 1907 by Mrs. Margaret Sage with an initial endowment of $10,000,000 (Glenn, Brandt and Andrews 1947). This Foundation was particularly noted for its support of research on social welfare issues. The Russell Sage Foundation staff provided consultation on charity organization and other social welfare innovations to local communities throughout the nation. Other foundations were established by other wealthy individuals. The Rockefeller Foundation supported developments in the field of public health, the General Education Board, also funded by John D. Rockefeller, performed a similar function in public education and medical education, the Commonwealth Fund in mental health, and the Carnegie Foundation for libraries.

Social Gospel, Welfare Capitalism and Voluntarism

Although new wealth was important for philanthropy the full development of the voluntary nonprofit system during this turn of the century period was particularly shaped by two forces: (1) criticism of social and economic conditions that was stimulated by new social science theories and the "social gospel" movement within urban Protestantism, and (2) the response of business leaders to what they perceived as threats to the existing economic system from labor violence, unionism, and socialism.

The development of rationalism and a historical analysis of the Bible, in contrast to traditionalism and Bible fundamentalism, had been going on within American Protestantism since early in the nineteenth century. At the turn of the century modernism in Protestant denominations became a major factor in national social policy. Students in Protestant seminaries attached to universities, including Harvard and Yale, were exposed to new scientific theories about the natural world and society (Leiby 1984). Some of the ministers graduating from these seminaries began to emphasize the application of the prophetic teachings of the historical Jesus to social conditions in the neighborhoods surrounding the large, downtown churches attended by the families of wealthy businessmen now living in the new suburbs (Rauschenbusch 1907).

These "social gospel" ministers became allies of social workers and civic reformers, providing moral justification for efforts to improve working conditions in factories and living conditions in city slums (Cross 1967; Hutchinson 1968). The social gospel message also drew many young men and young women into the settlements, the YMCA and the YWCA, and other health and social welfare activities and sustained them when they faced the overwhelming human problems in the cities or were being attacked by the defenders of the status quo. For some, including Jane Addams, these religious beliefs led to a commitment to pacifism during the years of World War I.

The progressive reformers and organizers of voluntary nonprofit service organizations were also supported by new social science theories in sociology and economics that questioned the assumptions that were used to justify the existing distribution of wealth in the society. Lester Ward was the best known critic of traditional theories of society, which under the label of "social Darwinism" argued for the social virtues of unrestrained economic competition and for the merits of "survival of the fittest" in strengthening society, regardless of the consequences for particular individuals. Ward's argument, noting the growing importance of the systematic application of natural science in new industrial technologies, was that mankind could use social science and the powers of human reasoning to develop a better society through social innovation and planned reform (Commager 1969).

Francis Peabody, professor of social ethics at Harvard and Albion Small and Charles Henderson, professors of sociology at the University of Chicago, were among nationally known social scientists who combined social theory and the social gospel. Simon Patten, a professor of economics at the Wharton School in Philadelphia (Fox 1967), and a number of other economists, including Richard Ely of the Johns Hopkins University and the University of Wisconsin, and Thorstein Veblen of the University of Chicago and later the University of Missouri, argued that traditional economic theories, based on assumptions of economic scarcity were no longer relevant in an era of massive increases in industrial production (Schulter 1979).

The criticism of existing social and economic systems led to proposals for social reforms. These took several forms: recommendations made directly to businessmen and industrialists urging changes in working conditions; proposals to wealthy philanthropists for creating new human service programs or expanding existing services; reform proposals for cleaning up corruption in local government; and calls for improvements in existing public services, such as public hospitals, schools, police services and the courts.

But the most far-reaching reform agenda dealt with expansion of the regulatory activities of state and local governments to deal with housing conditions, and with the conditions under which women and children were working. There were similar regulatory initiatives in the field of public health (Trattner 1979). At the federal level there were proposals to regulate industrial monopolies, railroads and the banking system.

Many of the social gospel activitists and others involved in social reform efforts were also linked to two broader social reform movements. The first was the women's sufferage movement, a continuation of the struggle for women's rights which had its beginning in the period following the Civil War. The second was the Prohibition movement that was widely supported by social workers, and other social reformers, as well as religious leaders because of the widespread impact of heavy drinking and alcoholism on family life.

On the other hand most of these social reform activities as well as the voluntary nonprofit system of services gave little attention to the condition of black Americans (Allen and Allen 1974; Diner 1970; Philpott 1978). The end of the Populist political movement in the South had been marked by the deliberate encouragement of racial antagonism and by increased violence against black citizens, including numerous lynchings. Systematic efforts in the South to create a legal base through "Jim Crow" laws for a totally segregated society brought little reaction from other parts of the country.

An exception to this lack of reaction was the work of a small group of reformers, primarily in New York City, who established the National Association for the Advancement of Colored People, primarily concerned with political and legal rights issues in the South, and the Urban League, primarily concerned with employment issues in Northern cities (Weiss 1974). Many northern social reformers supported the proposal by Booker T. Washington that black leaders in the South should focus on education and self help rather than on political action (Harlan 1972). Few of the new social welfare agencies, including the settlements, served black families. In the South the limited philanthropic efforts supported by church groups, and by foundations from the North, were primarily directed at increasing educational opportunities for young people from black families.

While the social gospel and new social science theories provided support for social reform activities and the expansion of social welfare programs, the fear of labor violence and political radicalism was also an important dynamic in the expansion of the voluntary social welfare system (Coser 1972; Lens 1966). The political appeal of the Socialist Party, headed by Eugene Debs, grew steadily from 1900 to the presidential election of 1912 when Debs received nearly a million votes. The first events of the Russian Revolution were met with expressions of enthusiastic support by Socialist groups in the United States (Thompson 1967). While many of the Socialist voters were immigrant industrial workers who had been Socialists in Europe, the party was also supported by middle-class professionals and others committed to social reform; they felt that there was little hope for fundamental reform under either the Democrats or Republicans.

Much of the Socialist support was a result of the intense conflict between management and labor over such issues as the eight-hour day and forty-hour week, and over efforts by management during periods of economic recession to cut wages. There were bloody strikes in coal fields and steel mills over these issues. In the early 1900s the International Workers of the World emerged as a militant left-wing group within the labor movement, committed to revolutionary confrontation with capitalism. All of these developments created widespread fears in the business community about the possibilities of class warfare in the United States.

Within business leadership groups one response to the growing militancy of labor organizations was a focus on industrial welfare, which included employer initiated improvement of working conditions, and the provision of health and social services for employees as a form of fringe benefit. However, the industrial welfare movement did not reach most workers, and individual business executives could do little about living conditions in working-class neighborhoods.

In an effort to undercut the appeal of the Socialist Party to social reformers, other political parties began taking over its positions on such pragmatic issues as the forty-hour week, elimination of child labor, workmen's compensation, and working conditions for women. The Progressive Party endorsed many of these issues at its 1912 Convention at which Jane Addams was a delegate, and which nominated Theodore Roosevelt for President.

The social reform movements and the expanding voluntary nonprofit health care and social welfare system were viewed from two different perspectives in the ideological battles between labor and management and between the supporters of traditional democratic capitalism and the advocates of socialism. For many of the supporters of traditional nineteeth century liberalism that argued against governmental intervention of any type in the economic system and against labor unions, social welfare leaders and social workers as well as all of the other supporters of such proposals as minimum wages for women and minimum standards for housing, were heretics and supporters of foreign ideologies.

However, for some business and political leaders like Theodore Roosevelt who viewed the future in terms of an expanding economy, created by a working partnership between big business and big government, limited forms of governmental regulation and control were essential to reduce wasteful competition within major industries and to maintain a positive economic climate for business growth (Schlesinger 1957). Under this "welfare capitalism" philosophy certain forms of voluntary health care and social welfare activity as well as governmentally supported public health and public education activities were viewed as acceptable if they contributed to an increase in productivity, reduced the level of social conflict, and limited the appeal of Marxist philosophies. For example, Roosevelt, and many other national opinion leaders, supported the plan for a White House Conference on Children in 1909, and the establishment of the Children's Bureau in 1912, an initiative that resulted from a concern about the impact of industrialization on both the health and social welfare of children in working-class families.

From the Socialist perspective many of the health and social welfare programs, and the social reform proposals, were viewed as pallatives or social control devices intended to ameliorate the symptoms of social problems without changing underlying economic relationships (Ehrenreich 1985). Organized labor was also skeptical of many of the reform proposals, preferring to gain improvements in working conditions through bargaining and union contracts, rather than through legislation which made such benefits available to all workers regardless of union membership.

The voluntary nonprofit system financially supported by, and therefore ultimately controlled by, the business and professional leaders of the community, became identified as part of the broader concept of "voluntarism," which was viewed as a critical element in the dominant business-oriented social philosophy of American society. Because the voluntary nonprofit system was largely independent of local governments it was protected against political exploitation by political bosses whose base of power was the immigrant voter (Westby 1966). It was also protected against the possibility of control by union supporters, or Socialists, even in predominately industrial communities because of the pattern of self-perpetuating boards controlled by business leaders.

There were strong conservative objections to all social welfare programs and to the social reform activities of social workers, public health workers, and their allies. Many of these objections were from persons who preferred to use the police powers of the state to suppress worker dissent, rather than to compromise economic theories which called for unbridled economic competition, and distribution of economic benefits solely through marketplace processes. In spite of these objections the voluntary nonprofit system, and the concept of "voluntarism," became established as essential elements of American society (Hall 1987). It provided a highly decentralized, loosely-linked system for incremental adaption to changing social conditions in individual communities, a system which was controlled by business leaders and was almost wholly dependent on wealthy families and business executives for financial support (Kolko 1963).

Because of the concerns of members of the boards of directors of nonprofit organizations, as well as staff members, about underlying sources of the problems of individuals and families needing help, the system also provided a framework for nonideological, apolitical social reform efforts. These reform efforts, consistent with the basic philosophy of "welfare capitalism," took the capitalist economic system as a given, and did not raise the spector of revolution and atheism which were associated in the minds of the general public with Marxist political movements (Weinstein 1968). By the time of the First World War the importance of the voluntary nonprofit system was as much a consequence of the role of that system in the larger political economy of the United States as it was of the services that individual service organizations provided.

World War I and the 1920s

By the time of World War I the elements of a complete voluntary nonprofit health and social welfare system were in place. In major urban centers there was a diverse network of direct service organizations. Each specialized type of agency had a national network linking it with similar programs in other cities. Formal academic programs for educating service professionals were being established in many fields. There were associations which brought employed professionals together on a nationwide basis in such fields as medicine, education, nursing, psychology, social work, city planning, and public health (Kirschner 1986). Journals in particular fields of service and national conferences provided channels for sharing information among "lay" leaders and professional practitioners. Philanthropic foundations were providing support for research in medicine, education, and social welfare. These organizations were linked together by networks of personal relationships and through organizations such as the National Conference of Social Work that spanned a diversity of interests.

The war years had important consequences for this system. Home front activities broadened the base of involvement in civic activities beyond those persons who had been primarily interested in social welfare problems. Victory gardens and community-wide fundraising campaigns involved many middle-income citizens, most of whom had had little involvement in charity fund-raising. This experience provided a base for the beginnings of the Community Chest movement immediately following the War through which the financial support of voluntary service organizations became a community-wide fund-raising responsibility rather than primarily the responsibility of a small number of wealthy families and business executives (Cutlip 1965).

The war also brought a split in the leadership of the social welfare and social reform efforts. Lillian Wald, founder of Henry Street Settlement in New York, and Jane Addams, who had served as the first woman president of the National Conference of Charities and Correction in 1909, both took a position as pacifists and refused to support the war effort, as did Eugene Debs, the Socialist candidate for president. They were bitterly criticized by other leaders in social welfare and social reform who actively supported the English cause and helped to organize activities in local communities to support the armed forces. Events in Russia during and immediately following the war years (leading to the control of that country by the Bolsheviks) intensified the fear of Marxism in the United States. Social reform proposals and social welfare programs were attacked as left-wing and communist inspired. The federal government initiated an active campaign in the years immediately following the War to destroy the political structure of both Socialist and Communist movements (Lens 1966). The Klu Klux Klan emerged as a potent political force in the Midwest as well as in the South, attacking Negroes, Catholics, Jews and communists.

Two of the nationwide social movements achieved their immediate goals shortly after the end of the War with the adoption of the constitutional amendments on women's sufferage and prohibition. On the other hand, the movement to adopt a federal constitutional amendment banning child labor ended in defeat. The enthusiasm and momentum around all three movements subsided. Moreover, many of the original generation of women, and men, who had been leaders in social reform and in establishing new service programs at the turn of the century were no longer active.

The loss of enthusiasm and momentum served to cripple many of the social reform initiatives that had been a key part of the developments from 1896 to 1916. One of the consequences was a separation between those professional practitioners primarily involved in the operation of voluntary nonprofit service organizations and those who continued to be active in social reform efforts (Ehrenreich 1985; Lee 1937). Much of the social reform concern that did continue during the 1920s was focused primarily on the drive to establish social insurance programs (Chambers 1963; Lubove 1968).

The 1920s were a period of professionalization in the voluntary nonprofit service sector (Kirschner 1986; Lubove 1965). The turn of the century period had brought a steady growth in the role of employed staff in voluntary nonprofit service organizations, and a decrease in the service role of volunteers. Nationwide associations of employed social workers were organized in the early 1920s with a major emphasis on winning recognition as an organized profession (Austin 1983b). These nationwide professional associations also provided continued support for some of the social reform efforts that the boards of directors of individual voluntary service organizations were no longer willing to support. Similar professionalization was taking place in such fields as public health and city planning in which professional practitioners worked in local governmental settings (Kirschner 1986).

Mental health services based in the community, as distinguished from institutional care in asylums and psychopathic hospitals, became important during the 1920s (Grob 1983). These services included publicly funded outpatient clinics attached to state hospitals and veterans hospitals. Leadership in the development of the field of mental health services came primarily from psychiatrists, like Dr. Adolph Meyer (Lief 1948), who were involved in medical education and in private practice in psychologically oriented psychiatry (as distinguished from neurological psychiatry), together with professional practitioners involved in nonprofit child guidance clinics (Hale 1971). The development of these mental health services created new professional practice opportunities for psychiatrists and applied psychologists, as well as opportunities for professional social workers to practice in settings that were not limited to low-income families.

These mental health settings, together with general hospitals and public schools, became major ancillary settings for social work. In these settings policy control over social work functions was primarily in the hands of other professionals, rather than in the hands of a philanthropic board of directors, and in these settings there was a particularly strong emphasis on the development of a distinctive professional identity for social work (Taylor-Owen 1986).

Social workers, and other professional specialists, gained substantial internal control of the on-going service operations in individual voluntary social welfare organizations and similar nongovernmental organizations in the health field. Experienced individuals with formal professional qualifications were appointed as agency administrators. They often pushed for making explicit the distinction between the role of the board of directors in setting general policy and the role of the administrator in employing staff, and overseeing the implementation of the policy (Lubove 1965). With the professionalization of administration the executive was often the senior professional specialist as well as the administrator, serving as the only link between the board and the on-going service operations of the agency. Thus the pattern began to emerge of the voluntary nonprofit service system also being a highly professionalized service production system.

Although professional staff including the executive gained more authority within voluntary nonprofit service organizations, the fundamental policy control of the voluntary nonprofit system in health care and social welfare became firmly located in the business community during the 1920s. The distinction between policy and administration strengthened the role of the board as the legal entity of the organization and therefore as having ultimate control over financial resources. Businessmen, and particularly corporate managers, came to dominate policy boards as the leadership role of ministers declined, and as the individual wealthy philanthropist became less prominent in agency funding, and corporate gifts became more important. These changes in board membership and the distinctions between the professional functions of staff personnel and policy functions of the board contributed directly to a sharp reduction in the role of voluntary nonprofit service organizations as social reform advocates.

The development of the Community Chest as a single, community-wide fundraising activity led by businessmen evolved from initiatives by Chambers of Commerce in a number of cities to establish a committee to screen and evaluate the numerous charity fundraising efforts which were soliciting local businesses prior to World War I (Cutlip 1965). In part the Community Chest was also an effort to protect sources of financial support for local activities from highly organized nationwide campaigns launched by national social welfare and national health organizations, campaigns which sometimes provided no information about the allocation of their funds or the purposes for which these funds were ultimately used.

The successful establishment of the Community Chest concept was soon followed in most communities by the creation of a systematic process of reviewing the budget of each voluntary agency included in the annual fundraising campaign. Through this process decisions were made as to which community services were to be supported and at what level they would be funded. Many staff professionals and organizational executives were skeptical about the effects of such controls, including the possible curtailment of the freedom of organizational staff members to advocate for social reforms. However, the Community Chest campaign substantially simplified the responsibilities of individual organizational board members by providing a degree of financial security and continuity which was often lacking in the days of individual fundraising by each agency. The organization of Community Funds and Councils of America brought national recognition to the Community Chest movement and brought endorsements from national industrial leaders and such governmental leaders as President Herbert Hoover.

The proliferation of voluntary nonprofit organizations during the first three decades of the twentieth century led, in the 1920s, to the organization of "councils of social agencies" in many of the larger cities. These federated organizations, primarily composed of representatives from voluntary nonprofit service organizations, were intended, in part, to continue on a more inclusive basis the inter-agency coordinating efforts initiated by the Charity Organization Societies. Most of the original COS organizations, by the beginning of World War I, had been merged with one or more of the local agencies that actually provided direct financial assistance to individuals, under the name Associated Charities. By the end of the 1920s most of these organizations had, in turn, changed their name to Family Service Agency, and were emphasizing individualized casework counseling rather than the administration of financial assistance (Waite 1960).

The underlying principles of the voluntary nonprofit social welfare system as summed up in the concept of "voluntarism" took on the status of a national movement in the 1920s (Berkowitz and McQuaid 1980). The meetings of the National Conference of Social Work became a forum for the advocacy of voluntarism. Implicit in the concept of voluntarism was a continuation of policy control of community health and welfare activities by established leaders in the community from business and the professions (Westby 1966), rather than by elected political leaders. The concept of voluntarism was applied, not only to social welfare, but also to public health and health care activities including hospitals, visiting nurses and health education, cultural activities such as museums and symphony orchestras, and private colleges and universities (Hall 1987). The concept of voluntarism was also reflected in the "civic improvement" community council movement of the early 1920s as hundreds of local communities established councils representative of diverse interests within the community to take action on civic projects and to solve local problems (Steiner 1925).

While the domain of voluntary nonprofit organizations had all of the elements of a complete nationwide institutional system, it had major limitations in scope and philosophy. Voluntary nonprofit service organizations were largely limited to urban areas of the North and Mid-west. They did not exist on any significant scale in most rural areas. The system was only partially developed in the South, and there it was much more closely linked to Protestant church organizations (Grantham 1983). The voluntary charity agencies had never been able to raise sufficient funds to respond to the needs of all the families who needed assistance, particularly in times of economic recession. Business leaders defined the fundraising goals of the annual Community Chest campaign to fit the preferences of the business community, rather than to fit human needs as experienced by the service agencies. The distinctions between the functions of professional staff and board members often resulted in cleavages between staff members and the board over personnel and organizational policy issues, and, in turn, in internal organizational conflicts.

There were many "gaps" in the voluntary system, needs for which assistance was needed, but for which no service existed. Many religiously sponsored organizations limited services to members of their faith, or injected elements of religious belief into their services. The problems of black Americans were almost entirely ignored. And these voluntary nonprofit organizations dealt with the problems of industrial workers and their families almost entirely on the basis of the attitudes of business managers towards their employees (Tolander 1973).

Moreover, the existence of voluntary nonprofit service organizations, many of which had originally been created as part of a social reform thrust, had now become a major justification for limiting the role of government, and in particular the role of the federal government, in the provision of health and social welfare services. In the 1920s during the period of Republican control of the federal government "voluntary" welfare capitalism became identified with a political perspective that also included hostility to union organization, a glorification of unrestricted entrepreneurial economic development, a "minimalist" role for government, and in particular the federal government, and protection of the dominant role in the national society of the white, male Protestant "establishment" (Baltzell 1964). These limitations in the voluntary system, and its identification with a conservative political perspective in the 1920s were to become a major factor in the changes that took place in the roles of voluntary and governmental services from the 1930s to the 1970s.

THE PUBLIC SECTOR

Early Beginnings

Although most discussions of the institutional history of social welfare in the United States deal with the public sector as through it were a single sector, there are, in fact, three public sectors: city-county, state, and federal. The history of the organizational development at each level is quite distinct. Many of the most important social policy issues over the past century have involved issues about the division of responsibilities among these three public sectors, that is the definition of "federalism," rather than with the division of responsibilities between public and voluntary nonprofit sectors.

Prior to the Civil War, as indicated earlier in this chapter, most of the provision for persons in need was at the local level under a pattern consistent with English Poor Law, emphasizing the continuing responsibility of each community for the care of its own citizens (Mencher 1967). During the half century before the Civil War the population of local almshouses, or poorhouses, increased steadily. There was continuing concern both about costs and about the conditions under which the insane, the "feeble-minded," dependent widows, orphans, and persons with handicaps were forced to live together in these institutions (Rothman 1971).

In the 1830s, however, some states began to establish public asylums that sought to cure the insane through "moral treatment," rather than simply to house them indefinitely (Caplan 1969; Rothman 1971). A major impetus to the expansion of this system of state "hospitals" was the work of Dorothea Dix, who through her special interest lobbying was responsible for founding or enlarging thirty-two mental hospitals in the United States and in other countries (Leiby 1978). States began to establish other specialized institutions as alternatives to the almshouse. The institutional expansion included penitentiaries and reformatories which were intended to relieve overcrowding in jails and to carry out an active program of correctional rehabilitation (Rothman 1971). By 1863 the state of Massachusetts, for example, administered eleven residential institutions of all types and provided some financial support to six others.

There was little question of the legal authority of the states to act, although there were debates on particular proposals, over the costs involved and over the method of taxation to be used to support such statewide services. As would occur again in the future, local communities were willing to shift administrative and financial responsibility for care of chronically dependent individuals to state government when the costs of care began to have a significant impact on local taxes. Another advantage sought in state administration of institutions was protection against the political spoils system that often dominated the administration of county and city institutions. This was accomplished through the use of an unpaid board of managers for each institution, similar to the boards of directors in private charities, to oversee administration. As the number of state institutions increased the problems involved in their oversight increased. In 1863 Massachusetts established the first *state board of charities* to supervise all of the separate state institutions, and to carry out studies on the problems underlying the growing need for institutional care (Leiby 1978).

During this pre-Civil War period the role of the federal government was limited to the provision of medical care for merchant seamen, who were not the responsibility of either local communities or states, and some assistance to special schools for the deaf. As described previously the Civil War brought a temporary expansion of the federal involvement in public sector services (Bremmer 1980), although the work of the Sanitary Commission and the nursing services organized by Clara Barton were primarily volunteer activities. After the War, however, the Freedman's Bureau was established by the federal government to meet the survival needs, and later some of the educational needs, of freed slaves. The federal involvement in these activities came to an end as "normality" returned in the 1870s, and the federal government withdrew from direct intervention in local affairs in the South (Bentley 1970). A major exception to the limited involvement of the federal government in governmental social welfare programs was the creation of a system of pensions for disabled veterans of the Union Army. By a series of legislative modifications during the last half of the nineteenth century these pensions were extended to all Union veterans, and their widows, providing an early version of old age pensions (Richmond 1930). Confederate veterans were not included.

Shortly after the appointment of the Massachusetts Board of Charities members of that Board issued a call for a meeting of interested individuals which led to the organization of the American Social Science Association. Some ten years later it was Franklin Sanborn, secretary of the Massachusetts Board who invited representatives from the growing number of state boards of charities to meet together under the auspices of the Department of Social Economy of the Association. As described earlier this group established the National Conference on Charities and Correction which became a separate organization in 1879. Part of the rationale for creating the Conference was the hope that the new social sciences could solve the problems that were creating a rapidly expanding need for institutional care (Leiby 1978).

However, the hopes that social science could provide effective answers for the treatment of persons in the state institutions were not realized in the decades following the Civil War (Leiby 1978; Rothman 1971). Moral treatment of the insane was expensive and did not change the condition of most of the persons receiving care in the state asylums. Early hopes that systematic educational treatment could change the condition of "feeble-minded" residents in state schools were not sustained. Theories dealing with the treatment of criminals, whether they involved isolation and meditation, or programs of hard labor, did not produce consistent results. Moreover, regardless of how many institutions the states built they were soon overcrowded (Grob 1973).

In the provision of care for dependent children state governments sometimes found it preferable to pay existing voluntary orphanages or children's homes to take care of homeless children rather than to establish a state institution for this purpose. Thus began a long and continuing tradition of public funding to voluntary nonprofit agencies in the field of child welfare, many of them sponsored by religious organizations. Children's institutions, public and voluntary, faced a situation that was very different from that of the other institutions, since in all cases as the children grew older they left the institution. It soon became clear, however, that state hospitals and state schools for retarded persons, and frequently penitentiaries, were to become involved in life-long care of a continuously increasing number of residents.

While the administration of public institutions was a major focus of attention, particularly in the early years of the National Conference of Charities and Correction, little attention was given to improving the administration of local public poor relief. Those who believed in private charity opposed public "outdoor relief" for reasons of principle, as it was said to encourage dependency and lead to pauperism (Lowell 1884), and for practical reasons, since it could be used as a form of political patronage to support local politicians who were opposed by local business leaders. This opposition resulted in the elimination of outdoor relief in a number of cities. The development of services for poor families, thus became, as described earlier, a major focus of the voluntary nonprofit sector (Kaplan 1978).

All of this was consistent with the general view of social policy. Governmental action, on a minimum cost basis, was considered appropriate for the care of those who were viewed as outside the economic mainstream of society. However, governmental action at any level that might be viewed as intervention into the basic marketplace processes of the economy was opposed, particularly any intervention that might affect the relation of able-bodied persons to the labor market. The existence of poverty and the fear of becoming a pauper were considered to be important forces in motivating people to work, particularly when many forms of employment were both unpleasant and dangerous (Lowell 1884). Although the amount of outdoor relief provided in any instance was meager, there was a constant concern that public provision of poor relief would not be consistent with the basic economic principles that business and civic leaders generally supported (Kaplan 1978).

During the period leading up to World War I the attitudes of most of the leaders in government were consistent with attitudes in the business community. A few political leaders in local government urged the expansion of public services, often as much because of the opportunities for patronage as for the value of the services. However, only an occasional governor like Peter Altgeld of Illinois or Robert LaFollette of Wisconsin actively supported social reform causes calling for governmental initiatives. Moreover, the Populist movement, where it was successful in the Mid-west and West, resulted primarily in strengthening the regulatory powers of government to protect farmers and small businessmen economically, rather than in increased assistance for the poor or handicapped.

The 1920s, Social Insurance and Pensions

The 1920s brought a major shift in the focus of proposals for governmental action with increased emphasis on the issues of social insurance and pensions. The charity organization movement had approached the problem of poverty from the perspective of the individual household and its problems with the objective of reforming individuals. The settlement movement, and many of the "progressive" social reform efforts approached poverty with a concern for oppressive living conditions in the community and the abuse and exploitation of workers in industry with the objective of reforming government, landords and industrial management. The social insurance approach, on the other hand, assumed that many forms of poverty were essentially a consequence of the lack of regular income, income which should be provided through mechanisms other than current employment for persons in particular situations. The solution to poverty was viewed as income transfers rather than as the reform of either specific individuals who were poor, or of specific governmental or business organizations.

The beginnings of social insurance are identified with the government of Prussia under Bismarck. Faced with a growing socialist movement among industrial workers Bismarck enacted repressive antisocialist legislation in 1877 but followed that in the 1880s with a program of national health insurance, accident insurance, and disability and retirement insurance, administered by the German government. These "social insurance" programs were financed by a tax on business and provided coverage to those workers who had a work history (Dawson 1912).

The administration of such comprehensive insurance systems required the large scale, systematically administered governmental "bureaus" that Max Weber described in his writings on bureaucracy (Gerth and Mills 1958). This nationally administered social insurance approach was almost the exact opposite of the local community, "means-tested" approach then in use in England, although England by the early 1900s adopted key elements of the social insurance system. The German approach was based on national action with nationwide uniformity. It was administered by the national government, rather than through a mixture of voluntary and local governmental activities, as in England. It was also part of a centrally managed economy involving a growth-oriented partnership between government and capitalist industrial leaders, in contrast to the English laissez faire capitalist economy with its emphasis on separation between government and business.

Information about the German system of social insurance was brought back to the United States in part by economists who studied in German universities. They, and other reformers who were advocates of social insurance, formed the American Association for Labor Legislation (AALL) in 1906. This became the major instrument for public education and legislative lobbying for social insurance. Many members of AALL were also active in the National Conference of Charities and Correction, and the Conference became a major platform for dissemination of its ideas. One of the Association members, Samuel Lindsay, professor of economics at Columbia University was the first full-time director of the New York School of Philanthropy (1905-1910). Issac Rubinow, economist and social worker and the most widely known advocate for social insurance, lectured on social insurance at the New York School between 1912 and 1915.

Advocates for governmentally administered social insurance viewed it as a fundamental solution to the problem of poverty, and as highly preferable to systematic charity (Rubinow 1913). It provided income as a matter of individual right under a universal program, rather than at the discretion of a charity investigator. It was comprehensive in scope rather than being dependent on the accident of local initiative. It did not involve the stigma of being defined as a dependent person, and in need, in order to obtain financial assistance.

Social insurance as a contributory insurance system with rights based on employment history was distinguished by its advocates from a governmental pension system with funding completely from governmental appropriations in which rights were based solely on an individual's status, for example, being over 65, or being a military veteran. Objections to social insurance were that it imposed costs on industry not directly associated with production, that it transferred income to some individuals who might in fact have other resources, and that it would result in the large scale intrusion of government into business management.

The 1920s were a period of extensive development of proposals within individual states for both social insurance and for pensions even though it was a period in which there was strong resistance to reform proposals at the federal level (Chambers 1963). Much of the leadership in the development of the social insurance proposals came from Professor John Commons, in the department of labor economics at the University of Wisconsin. Under Governor Robert LaFollette the Wisconsin state government initiated a process of collaboration with faculty members from the University in the design of "progressive" legislation. This included the first state social insurance program, a workmen's compensation law passed in 1911.

Workmen's compensation was the first form of social insurance to gain general acceptance, supported by a major lobbying campaign by the American Association for Labor Legislation. Unemployment because of industrial injury was a major factor in poverty among the families of industrial workers. Forty-three states had enacted requirements for workmen's compensation by 1920. Following this success the AALL organized a major national campaign for health insurance, but that was defeated by wide-spread opposition from organized medicine. No other form of social insurance was adopted by the states on a substantial basis until the 1930s, although there were efforts to initiate unemployment insurance in several states.

Proposals for pensions were also pushed at the state level during the 1920s. Some states began to enact old-age pension programs, and most states established some form of pension program for blind persons. This was an important new development because it led to the discussion of poverty and income provision as state issues, rather than as purely local issues. The pension plans that were established usually involved state tax funds in some form, and the establishment of eligibility rules and procedures on a state-wide basis. One major objection to such programs was that the tax costs could affect the interstate competitive economic position of industries within a particular state. There was also a fear that pensioners could become an organized political pressure group lobbying for increased payments, as Civil War veterans had done (Richmond 1930). Organized labor favored pensions over retirement insurance, viewing pensions as a reward paid by society to individuals for a life of hard work (not unlike the rationale for military pensions), this being preferable to the concept of forced savings by individual workers, as required under contributory retirement insurance.

"Widows pensions" or "mothers aid" laws were also enacted in a number of states (Lundberg 1928). This was in part a result of the recommendation made at the First White House Conference on Children in 1909 that children should not be removed from their own homes and placed in institutions or foster homes solely on the basis of the lack of family income. Mothers pensions were often administered through the juvenile court and were defined as a public payment for the services provided by a widowed mother in raising her children.

While debates over social insurance and pensions were going on, local public poor relief programs were steadily expanding, particularly in large industrial cities. A temporary period of high unemployment in 1921 had created additional needs for financial assistance. Then as unemployment began to increase dramatically in the last half of the 1920s, the expenditures of these programs increased again. The work of these "public welfare" agencies received relatively little attention at the National Conference of Social Work or from the new professional associations in social work. However, a text book on public welfare administration was published in 1927, written by Sophonisba Breckinridge, a member of the Hull House group and a faculty member at the School of Social Administration at the University of Chicago.

The 1920s were a period of reorganization in state governments. The objective was to establish centralized administrative and fiscal control over the variety of departments and programs that legislatures had enacted from time to time. Among the results of these reorganizations were the creation of state Departments of Public Welfare, beginning with Illinois in 1917. These reorganizations and reforms were stimulated in part by the theories of public administration that guided the founders of the Bureau of Municipal Research n New York City. They, in turn, helped to create the National Institute of Public Administration in 1922 (Dahlberg 1966).

Key concepts of this new public administration included the centralization of administrative responsibility and accountability, and a clear-cut separation between political processes related to public policymaking and the administrative processes related to policy implementation. Other important concepts included the selection and promotion of public employees on the basis of merit, rather than on the basis of political connections, systematic budgetary procedures through which control of expenditures could be maintained, and the development of rules and regulations to insure impartial and even-handed administration of services affecting the public.

By the end of the 1920s there was a substantial structure of governmental human service programs at the city-county level in poor relief, sanitation and public health, hospitals, education, and parks and recreation, although the most prominent national leaders in many of these fields came from nongovernmental organizations. At the state level there was a developing structure of institutions, regulatory provisions and some pension programs, in addition to the rapid expansion of land-grant state universities. But there was little change in the role of the federal government during the 1920s with the exception of limited federal support for medical services for veterans through the newly organized Veterans Administration. Some federal assistance was provided for vocational education within the states, and for maternal and child health services, primarily in rural areas (Sheppard-Towner Act). The latter program was initiated on recommendations from the Children's Bureau and administered by the Bureau throughout the 1920s. But it was repealed in 1929 in the first year of the administration of President Hoover.

Proposals for unemployment insurance and retirement insurance, and proposals for different types of pension or "aid" programs posed the most critical issues for the future because these programs potentially involved large-scale bureaucratic administrative activities on the part of state and federal governments. In contrast to the police-power activities required by the earlier regulatory reforms the proposals for income transfer programs required major expansion of the administrative functions of both state and federal governments. This became an important part of the public policy debates during the Depression years over "welfare state" issues.

The Depression and the New Deal

When the problems of the Depression first appeared, particularly the growing numbers of unemployed workers in 1929, President Hoover looked to local communities to take action. According to his view the role of the federal government was to support local efforts by lending the moral support of the office of the President and dramatizing the need for action through the media

(Lens 1969). Not only was there positive support from President Hoover for voluntarism (Dexter 1932); voluntary social welfare leaders were also thoroughly convinced of the potential danger of an expanded public poor relief program.

In 1931, however, it became apparent to local business leaders, and to Community Chest officials, that it was impossible to sustain a voluntary charitable effort that was adequate to meet the needs of unemployed workers when such an effort depended on contributions from corporations which were either going bankrupt or were trimming their operating costs by laying off thousands of workers. By this time demands on public poor relief programs had exhausted the financial resources of many cities. State governments had begun to make loans to cities. In turn many states had been forced to borrow money from banks and had reached the limit of the risks those banks were prepared to take. New York was the most active state in developing programs to help local communities under Governor Franklin D. Roosevelt. Following his election as President in 1932 he brought a number of his key state administrators with him to Washington, including Harry Hopkins, the administrator of the New York Temporary Emergency Relief Administration, and Frances Perkins, an economist who had been a student of Simon Patten at the Wharton School.

The first two terms of President Roosevelt involved a series of emergency measures, the Bank Holiday, the Federal Emergency Relief Administration, and the Works Progress Administration. These were followed by legislative initiatives directed at fundamental problems. Some did not survive, like the National Recovery Administration (NRA) and the new communities program. But many of the legislative initiatives resulted in programs that became permanent parts of the governmental structure in the United States, such as the Agricultural Adjustment Act to provide income supports for farmers, the Tennessee Valley Authority, federally supported public housing, the Securities and Exchange Commission, the Federal Deposit Insurance Corporation and the National Labor Relations Board.

The most far-reaching impacts, however, came from the passage of the Social Security Act of 1935. This provided for a system of state administered unemployment insurance programs, for federally administered social insurance for retired workers (and later for the survivors of deceased workers and for totally disabled workers), for federal-state public assistance programs for dependent children, persons over 65 and the blind (and later the temporarily disabled), and federal support for state maternal and child health services and child welfare services. By the end of Roosevelt's second term the basic role of the federal government in American society had changed, as well as the structure of state and local public administration.

With the Social Security insurance programs the federal government became a major funding source for programs that dealt directly with some aspects of poverty. These programs provided financial benefits that directly affected the life of individual American citizens. Particularly important was the fact that the level of the Social Security benefits could be determined by political decisions at the federal level, regardless of the theory that they were a form of "insurance" funded solely through premiums paid by, and in behalf of, particular individuals.

Another major change in the role of the federal government not fully evident until the 1940s and the 1950s was that the federal government had become a regulator of state, and local, governments. Such federal controls had existed previously only during war times. With the establishment of administrative regulations for the emergency relief programs during the 1930s, and then for the federal-state public assistance programs, a major shift in the regulatory focus of the federal government had taken place. In addition to the controls on interstate business administered through independent regulatory agencies, such as the Interstate Commerce Commission, there came into existence an extensive system of controls over specific types of state and local governmental activities, administered through federal cabinet departments. These governmental activities included the administration of the Aid For Dependent Children program, Old Age Assistance and Aid to the Blind, and unemployment insurance programs, as well as local public housing programs.

This regulatory control was exercised through the provision of federal funds with attached regulations intended both to specify the use of those funds, and to establish a set of criteria for federal fiscal audits. These procedures were intended to achieve a significant degree of policy and administrative consistency in the politically decentralized "federal" system of government in the United States. Although no national official could give a direct administrative order to a governor, or indeed to any state or local administrative official, a federal official could, based on Congressional intent, establish rules, and penalties, intended to achieve the same result. The requirements of this system made it necessary to provide a sufficient level of federal assistance, under relatively attractive terms, so that few, if any states would refuse to participate in a particular program. In turn, detailed federal regulations and reporting requirements were established so that it was clear that the state administration was consistent with the Congressional intent.

The events of the 1930s brought public administration concepts into social welfare administration on a large scale, primarily as a result of the policies established by Harry Hopkins (Kurzman 1974). Hopkins had been a caseworker and administrator at the Association for the Improvement of the Condition of the Poor in New York City and at the New York Tuberculosis Association. He had then become a member of the staff of Governor Roosevelt with responsibility for the program of emergency assistance provided by New York State to local communities in the first years of the Depression. During the first two Roosevelt terms Hopkins was the President's closest personal advisor on issues dealing with unemployment and poverty (Hopkins 1936). He was responsible for establishing several key requirements that largely determined the characteristics of the nationwide federal-state public assistance program.

The first requirement was that the federal government would deal only with a "single state agency." The federal government thus avoided direc involvement with the complexities of local politics. It also made the administration of financial assistance a basic function of state government in every state.

A second requirement was that the direct administration of public assistance programs in local communities must be handled by a governmenta organization, rather than being delegated to existing voluntary social welfare agencies, or to local nonprofit corporations set up specifically for this purpose The implementation of this requirement under the Federal Emergency Relie Administration meant the creation and staffing of a completely new governmental agency in local communities almost overnight (Waite 1960). I also meant introducing into many communities a sharp distinction between governmental activities in social welfare and voluntary nonprofit activities where such distinctions had previously often not been made.

Hopkins also insisted on a cash assistance system in comparison to the food orders and other forms of in-kind assistance widely used in local poor relief and private charity programs. He viewed cash assistance as essential to maintaining individual independence and a sense of individual responsibility However, a cash assistance program also increased the need for systematic rules and recordkeeping. As federal regulatory requirements increased, state supervision over local administration of these programs was intensified. The size and comprehensive geographic coverage of the public assistance system and the complexity of the controls resulting from federal regulation made the public welfare agency by far the largest public administration operation in most state governments.

Hopkins also rejected the fundamental voluntary charity organization principle of requiring a combination of individualized social casework and financial assistance. He did not believe that families suffering from severe economic problems should be required to accept counseling services from a social caseworker as a condition of receiving income assistance.

Another federal requirement was that the staff of state and local public welfare agencies be employed under merit system procedures. Hopkins sought to ensure that state and local public assistance programs would not become primarily a political patronage system. This requirement contributed to the hostility of many local elected officials towards the program and towards the federal administrators associated with the program.

By the end of the 1930s a permanent federal-state governmental public welfare administrative system for dealing with income assistance needs had begun to emerge, although initially it had been assumed that this system would only be needed temporarily until there was universal Social Security insurance coverage (Abbott 1941). This system was distinctly different from the voluntary nonprofit system in nearly every aspect. The voluntary system was based on local organizations; national associations headquartered in New York had developed as organizational federations initiated by local organizations in nearly every instance. The public system was based on national legislation, with ultimate administrative authority at the federal level. The system was initiated from Washington, and the pressure for nationwide consistency came from federal personnel.

The voluntary nonprofit system was not geographically comprehensive, concentrating primarily in cities; the public system was legally required to be geographically comprehensive, and, like state governments, it was strongly affected in its policies by the preponderance of rural communities in its geographic service area. By the end of the 1930s the voluntary nonprofit health care and social welfare system was moving towards a pattern of professional, collegial staff relationships in small and medium-sized organizations; the public system was organized around the hierarchial control system of the large-scale administrative bureaucracy.

The voluntary nonprofit system was increasingly relying on professional training and the use of professional judgements in individual case situations; the public system relied heavily on rules and regulations to establish consistent and equitable treatment of individual situations. The voluntary nonprofit system was controlled by, and in practice ultimately accountable to, business and professional leaders in the local community; the public system was controlled by elected public officials at county, state and federal levels, and ultimately accountable to the constituencies that elected them.

Although there were these distinct differences in the character of the voluntary nonprofit and governmental systems, they were not wholly separate. Even though state public welfare administrators formed the American Public Welfare Association in 1930, in part because the National Conference of Social Work controlled by voluntary agency leadership had not given sufficient attention to the urgent problems they were dealing with, many of the supervisors and administrators in the public welfare agencies created during the 1930s came from voluntary social welfare organizations (Waite 1960). These individuals brought with them many of the concepts and traditions of these voluntary organizations and they often maintained their connections with former colleagues in those organizations.

However, the events of the 1930s also resulted in major conflicts among social workers. The first conflict was between those social workers who supported a welfare capitalism paradigm and the New Deal proposals, and those who supported a socialist paradigm and attacked the New Deal reforms as a totally inadequate effort to patch-up a bad economic system (Fisher 1980). The second conflict was between those social workers dealing first hand with the desperate needs of unemployed families and the majority of the academic and organizational leaders in social work associations, who were primarily employed in voluntary nonprofit service organizations and who were concerned with establishing the credentials of social work as a form of psychotherapy (Leighninger 1981).

The third conflict was between social work employees in the new public assistance agencies in large cities in the East who joined labor unions in an effort to improve their salaries and working conditions. They viewed the labor union movement as the most important political force for social reform. Other social workers felt that union membership was inconsistent with public recognition as a professional. Business-oriented voluntary nonprofit board members viewed the union movement as a socialist conspiracy. In the ideological divisions that resulted from these conflicts, social reform advocacy in social work was viewed as being linked to a belief in the political power of the American labor movement, and the expansion of governmental health and social welfare programs. Those who supported professionalism were accused of withdrawing from involvement with families in poverty and of supporting a politically conservative voluntary nonprofit system.

The new public social welfare system, like the voluntary nonprofit system that emerged at the turn of the century, was, in fact, a "conserving" response to the crisis of the Depression (Bernstein 1968), developed within the existing federal intergovernmental framework. Although these reform measures of the 1930s have often been referred to as elements of a "welfare state," they were consistent with the "welfare capitalism" paradigm, intended primarily to protect and reinforce the capitalist, competitive marketplace economic system. They provided greater economic *security* for many individuals and families, but they resulted in little *redistributional change* in the relative economic position of persons within the society (Lens 1969).

However, these "welfare state" measures became primarily identified with the Democratic version of "welfare capitalism." Even more important these measures were key elements in the development of a new national political coalition involving, in particular, industrial workers, the elderly, and voters of ethnic minority background. This political constituency would support Democratic control of the Congress during most of the next fifty years, although the actual leadership of Congress frequently involved a conservative coalition cutting across party lines. The Presidency, in the meantime, alternated between Democrats and Republicans. However, with a few brief exceptions as in the early 1960s and the early 1980s, it was Congress, not the President, who determined the outcome on a broad range of "welfare state" issues, affecting health care, education, and social welfare industries. One consequence was a pattern of continuing conflict over "welfare state" and "taxation" issues between Congress and the leadership of the business community. This conflict strengthened a public perception which identified the voluntary nonprofit system with the business community, and, in general, with a conservative position on governmental social policy initiatives. Social reform advocates, who were an important element in many of the Democratic congressional constituencies, were, in general, critical of the role of business in American society, and of voluntary nonprofit service organizations and favorable towards the expansion of service programs directly operated by general purpose governments. This was in marked contrast to the position of most of the social reformers at the turn of the century.

Chapter 7

The Dual Development of Voluntary and Public Systems 1940s-1980s

THE 1940s AND 1950s

The Voluntary Nonprofit System

The Depression and World War II had little immediate impact on the structure of the existing voluntary nonprofit system. One notable exception was that with the establishment of federal-state public assistance programs voluntary family service agencies ended their involvement in providing material assistance. Temporary war-time programs, including a dramatic, but temporary, expansion of day-care programs for the children of defense workers did not change the local network of voluntary nonprofit service organizations.

With the elimination of temporary financial assistance for low-income families as a major rationale for community-wide Community Chest fundraising, two major causes emerged as the core of such campaigns. One was youth service, "character-building" programs, primarily the YMCA, YWCA, Boy Scouts, Girl Scouts and Campfire Girls. These nationally organized and nationally promoted programs had adopted a basic policy of fundraising through participation in local Community Chest campaigns. The volunteer leadership networks of these organizations, particularly in the rapidly expanding suburban areas of the 1950s, became essential campaign elements as central city Community Chests expanded their fundraising campaigns to include the entire metropolitan area thereby warding off the development of independent campaigns in the new suburbs.

The second major fundraising cause included the American Red Cross and other rapidly growing nationwide organizations which dealt with specialized health concerns, such as the American Cancer Society, the American Heart Association and the March of Dimes. With an increasing number of nationally organized special purpose fundraising efforts, local Community Chests had to compete for both volunteers and donations. During the last half of the 1940s and the 1950s, the Community Chest movement made a determined effort to bring the Red Cross and all of the national health campaigns into a single combined local fundraising effort under the name of *United Fund*.

The American Red Cross made a national policy decision to join the local United Fund campaigns and to give up its separate annual fundraising campaign. The March of Dimes, American Cancer Society, and American Heart Association, all of which had a primary commitment to national support of research rather than to local service programs, refused to give up their separate fundraising campaigns and become part of the local United Fund campaigns. However, by the end of the 1950s the local voluntary health and welfare fundraising system in most metropolitan areas did include the Red Cross and a variety of health causes, including health research.

The effort to broaden the base of support and increase the level of contributions also brought changes in the structure of local fundraising. The Community Chest effort had developed originally around the annual solicitation of businesses, individual households and a limited number of wealthy individuals for one-time contributions. Under the United Fund concept large scale campaign solicitation emphasized year-around payroll deduction pledges from blue collar, white collar, and middle management personnel in large corporations. With this newly developed method of campaign solicitation the proportion of corporate gifts in the total campaign remained relatively stable, while there was a substantial increase in the proportion of the funds raised through individual contributions from corporate employees.

In this process of expansion of fundraising and program development focus of the United Fund (later United Way) had shifted from a concentration on the needs of low-income families in the central city to a focus on a broad range of voluntary nonprofit services for both middle- and lower-income families across the entire metropolitan area. As the corporate employees who contributed to the United Fund moved from the inner city to new suburban communities, it became necessary to demonstrate that their contributions, at least in part, would support services for their families in suburban locations. Campaign appeals shifted from an emphasis on philanthropic fundraising to help the poor to the slogan "It Works for All of Us."

This expansion of fundraising and provision of services to suburban areas occurred at the same time that business leaders in many metropolitan areas began to advocate area wide approaches to land-use planning and economic development. The United Fund was one of the few local organizations which brought business and civic leaders together regularly from across the entire metropolitan area, particularly during the annual fundraising campaign. This increased the institutional importance of the United Fund structure within the metropolitan area, apart from the service organizations which it supported.

This shift of focus in the voluntary nonprofit system was particularly evident in the redefinition of function that took place in family service agencies. By the end of the 1950s these organizations were focusing primarily on their development as a professionalized individual and family counseling service for lower middle and middle-income households on a sliding-scale fee-charging basis (Cloward and Epstein 1965). As part of this development many organizations established branch offices in the suburbs. In a similar way voluntary nonprofit child welfare agencies expanded their adoption programs to respond to the interests of suburban, middle-income childless families who were willing to pay substantial fees for adoption services. Some central city settlements established new "neighborhood center" programs in outlying middle-income areas, while YMCA's and YWCA's built new suburban branches. These moves towards "suburbanization" which usually involved expanding services to middle-income white families and reducing services for low-income central city residents, occurred at a time of rapid growth in the number of low-income black residents in central city areas of the Northeast, Midwest and Far West. This increase was a result of agricultural mechanization and restrictive public assistance policies in Southern states and increased industrial employment opportunities in the North and West.

During the 1940s and 1950s there was also a gradual separation between the institutional structure of traditional voluntary nonprofit organizations and the organized profession of social work. Many of the key agencies in the community-wide fundraising structure, including the youth serving agencies and the health cause organizations, were not significant employers of social workers and were unlikely to have social workers as administrators. Moreover, few professionally educated social workers sought employment as United Fund/United Way staff members. Social workers, on the other hand, were beginning to become involved in the rapidly developing network of community-based mental health services under a variety of auspices, including governmental, voluntary and fee-for-service. Most of these mental health organizations were not part of the United Fund network. Some social workers began to move away from organization-based employment altogether, turning to private practice first on a part-time basis and then on a full-time basis.

Another feature of this period of institutional expansion in the voluntary nonprofit sector was an increased emphasis on the use of more complex technical methodologies in the research and planning projects carried out under community planning councils, or under ad hoc citizen task forces. The new technical planners and researchers employed by voluntary social planning councils were viewed as being primarily accountable to community leadership groups that were rooted in the business community, rather than to their professional peers in the voluntary agencies (Morris and Rein 1968). These planners and researchers also became increasingly involved with issues closely related to local governmental services in social welfare, housing, neighborhood development and public health, rather than those issues connected with intraagency and interagency problems involving voluntary nonprofit agencies. By the end of the 1950s collaborative activities between "social" planners and "city" planners within the context of urban renewal projects had been initiated in several cities (Frieden and Morris 1968).

The voluntary nonprofit system was highly visible and expanding in scope in local communities and at the national level by the end of the 1950s. The annual community-wide United Fund campaign strongly emphasized the support of voluntarism as an alternative to the expansion of governmental services using this theme to appeal to business leaders for support. Voluntary nonprofit organizations were increasingly involved with a range of personal services that would attract financial contributions from industrial wage earners and corporate middle managers who were now the primary source of financial support. With the notable exception of organizations like the Salvation Army and some settlement houses voluntary nonprofit organizations had limited involvement with the problems of persons who were physically handicapped and economically dependent, with children who needed long-term care outside their natural family, or with problems of poverty among the chronically unemployed.

Governmental Services

The 1940s and 1950s were also a period of expansion and development in the public services. The Social Security insurance system became increasingly comprehensive with the addition of disability coverage in the 1950s, and later Medicare in the 1960s. The state-federal public asssistance programs, Aid for Families with Dependent Children, Aid for the Blind, and Old Age Assistance, failed to disappear as social insurance programs came on line, contrary to the arguments advanced at the time of the original Social Security debate (Steiner 1966). This was in part a consequence of the exclusion of particular forms of labor force participation from the original social insurance coverage. These included agricultural and domestic workers.

Moreover, there were increasing numbers of single-parent mothers with young children who were not widows, and therefore not covered by Survivors Insurance, in addition to those widows whose husbands had not had Social Security coverage. During the 1950s a state-federal means-tested Disability Assistance (DA) program was added to the existing public assistance programs. County and state public assistance agencies grew in size and complexity. Half of the states had a state administered public assistance system, the other half utilized a county administration state supervision model.

By the end of the 1950s there was a three tiered system for meeting the income needs of households with inadequate income. First, those persons who were normally employed on a regular basis, particularly in the primary labor market, had access to such systems as workmen's compensation, unemployment compensation, Social Security insurance, and in most instances employer-sponsored group health insurance and company pension plans. Second, those persons who were in clearly defined categories of dependent aged, totally disabled, or dependent children with an adult caretaker, had access to state-federal assistance programs: AFDC, Aid to Disabled, Aid to the Blind, and Old Age Assistance. After 1965 persons receiving benefits under these programs also had access to medical care assistance through the Medicaid program.

Third, individuals who did not fit any of these categories and who had marginal or irregular involvement with the labor market, or households with regular low wage employment, but large numbers of children, had access only to limited forms of private charity, or public "general assistance." "General assistance" was a new term for traditional "poor relief," which was state administered in some states, state-county administered in some, and available only in some urban counties in still other states (Handler and Sosin 1983). Only with the enactment of the food stamp program on a nationwide basis in the 1970s was there federal participation in redistributional income transfers for these individuals and families.

As this complex system of social insurance and public assistance developed, increasing attention began to be given to the question as to whether the purpose of such programs should be the elimination of poverty through income redistribution, that is to offset inequalities resulting from marketplace economic processes by providing adequate income, rather than paralleling and reinforcing such inequalities by providing only a minimal level of substitute income on a "safety net" basis (Plattner 1979). What had often been proposed as a utopian fantasy, a society without poverty, in the 1950s and 1960s began to be discussed as a realistic possibility within the United States (Galbraith 1960; Theobald 1966).

The arguments for major income redistribution were based in part on social theory—the concept of progress means that the society of the future should be a society of equality, and in part on social justice arguments—current inequalities are more often the result of inherited income and accidental advantages than of differences in productive contributions to society and therefore they should be offset by redistribution (Harrington 1968). Later in the 1960s there was also a restitution argument, past economic and legal discrimination against persons from ethnic minority backgrounds, and women, should be redressed by redistributional income transfers to such persons.

While redistribution did not become an explicit objective, a significant degree of redistribution was introduced into the categorical Social Security insurance programs for the survivors of covered workers, and for elderly and disabled persons outside the labor force, the traditional "worthy poor." Benefits under Survivors Insurance were adjusted to reflect family size, and benefits for the lowest income participants in retirement insurance were higher in proportion to their payments in the system than were benefits for higher income participants.

Other income assistance programs dealing with able-bodied adults who were actually, or potentially, in the labor force remained at a minimal subsistance level. Among the households covered by these income assistance programs the proportion of black households increased sharply in the 1960s, particularly in urban areas, after the mechanization of cotton harvesting that revolutionized patterns of agricultural employment in the South. Even with the addition of food stamps in the 1970s there was very little net redistribution of income as a result of the income assistance programs among all households actually, or potentially, involved with the labor market.

The administration of the Social Security insurance program was, from the beginning, defined as a public administration activity rather than as a professionalized activity. Social workers and other professional specialists were not actively involved. The Social Security organization fit the classical characteristics of an administrative bureaucracy, and the introduction of computers only reinforced its general characteristics as a hierarchial, rule-controlled organization with a small group of administrators and a large number of front line workers carrying out highly routinized and rule-defined activities.

State-county public assistance agencies were, on the other hand, an unstable mixture of public administration elements and professionalized elements. The early supervisors and administrators in public assistance agencies who came from voluntary organizations brought with them a belief in the combination of casework counseling and income provision, but there was little support for this service model from the federal level (Steiner 1966).

There was, however, federal support for development of professional public child welfare services under the provisions of Title IVB of the Social Security Act, specifically in rural counties (Rosenthal 1986). Federal grants were used to support the development of a staff of social workers with graduate social work degrees, with responsibility, in particular, for dealing with problems of child abuse and neglect. In some states the federal funds were used to strengthen existing state-wide public child welfare agencies. In other states it helped to establish a new public child welfare agency. These child welfare programs developed initially as a professional, collegial structure rather than as a hierarchial bureaucratic structure.

Within state public welfare agencies that had administrative responsibility for both public assistance programs and child welfare services, the child welfare staff developed a strong sense of distinctive professional identity. This sense of professional identity was often reinforced by disparaging comparisons made between the child welfare workers and the public assistance staff workers who, in general, had no professional training and who were working in a highly rule controlled program with very limited worker autonomy.

During the 1950s a systematic effort was initiated to develop a professionalized service structure within the AFDC program based on the social casework model. The effort was supported by leaders from organized social work and the national network of voluntary family service agencies (Steiner 1966). The arguments for the professionalization of the AFDC program reflected the original premises of the charity organization societies, that is the importance of providing individualized counseling services to households in which the lack of sufficient income was only one of many problems, the resolution of which appeared to be essential if economic self-sufficiency were to be achieved. These arguments were supported by research projects carried out during the 1950s under voluntary auspices which documented that a small number of multiproblem families, most of whom received some form of income assistance, absorbed a high proportion of all community social welfare, health and rehabilitation expenditures (Buell 1958).

Federal support for professionalization of AFDC, it was thought, could also make casework counseling services available to low-income households on a state-wide basis, where they were usually available only from voluntary family service agencies in cities. This legislative campaign resulted in amendments to the Social Security Act, first in 1957 to establish the policy that the provision of "social services" was an integral part of AFDC administration, and, second, in 1962 to provide funding for the costs of such social services on a 75 percent federal to 25 percent state basis (in comparison to the 50-50 percent pattern of federal reimbursement for administrative costs).

However, the professional social work model did not become the standard model in AFDC programs (Steiner 1966). Although some state public welfare departments did increase the number of professionally trained staff, and assigned them intensive responsibility for a small number of selected case situations, the public administration model persisted in most states. Professionally educated social workers, if employed at all, were used primarily as line supervisors in a hierarchial administrative structure. The enforcement of rules and regulations controlling eligibility and the determination of individual grant levels continued to be the primary responsibility of the AFDC staff. Large case loads continued to be the general pattern. State agencies were reluctant to employ and guarantee job security under merit system procedures for a large staff of professional social work specialists, particularly in light of the uncertancy of federal funding policies.

Graduate schools of social work made few changes in their curriculums to give priority to teaching the application of social casework methods to the situation of families receiving public assistance payments (Leighninger 1981). The pattern of social casework training in schools of social work had by the 1950s shifted from the pragmatic, sociologically oriented model of Mary Richmond to a highly psychological model strongly influenced by the theories of Sigmund Freud, and ego-psychology theorists (Hamilton 1940; Robinson 1930). Graduates from these programs preferred positions in mental health treatment-oriented settings, such as child guidance clinics, rather than in public assistance agencies (Ehrenreich 1965).

Moreover, by the end of the 1960s the results of a variety of research projects suggested that psychologically oriented casework counseling was not, by itself, an effective method for dealing with problems of economic dependency particularly in multiproblem households (Mullen and Dumpson 1976). In 1967 Congress shifted the emphasis for AFDC social services, supported in part by federal funds, from "soft" (intangible) casework counseling to "hard" (tangible) services including day care, family planning and employment training and placement.

Another major area of development in governmental human service programs was in community mental health services. World War II like WW I created a sense of urgency about the level of mental health problems found among draftees, and about the need to create alternatives to institutional incarceration in state psychiatric hospitals for dealing with these problems. The National Association for Mental Health, with a broad base of public support and a coalition of mental health professionals, primarily psychiatrists and psychologists, successfully lobbied Congress for the passage of the Mental Health Act of 1946 and for creation of the National Institute for Mental Health in 1949. These developments led to federal funding for professional training for psychiatrists, psychologists, psychiatric nurses and social workers, as well as federal funding for a national study of mental health problems. The report of this study, as well as the report from a similar national study of the needs for services for persons with mental retardation, was submitted to President Kennedy in 1962.

The 1950s were also marked by the development of psychotropic medications that made it possible to control the behavioral symptoms of many forms of mental illness. In turn, this made it possible to treat increasing numbers of persons with mental illness conditions on an outpatient basis, and to release long-term patients from state psychiatric hospitals. This began the process of "deinstitutionalization" of psychiatric hospital patients, although from the beginning there was a lack of community support services necessary to implement deinstitutionalization effectively as well as a lack of coordination among services that did exist.

The 1940s and 1950s also brought the beginnings of federal funding for low-income housing and for hospitals in underserved areas. The Public Housing Act of 1937, and the Hill-Burton Hospital Survey and Construction Act of

1946 also set important precedents for the direct use of federal funds in an intergovernmental and "mixed economy" pattern of human service programs at the local level. The Public Housing Act provided for allocation of federal funds to free-standing quasigovernmental Housing Authorities at the local level, established by, but not under the control of, local general purpose governments. On the other hand, the Hill-Burton Act included provisions that allowed for federal construction grants directly to voluntary nonprofit hospitals in local communities, including hospitals operated under the auspices of religious organizations.

Thus in health care services there began to be a mixed economy blending of governmental and voluntary funds. A similar pattern had long existed at state and local levels in the care of children in residential institutions operated by voluntary nonprofit organizations. On the other hand, a rigid distinction between governmental funding and voluntary funding was maintained for youth serving organizations which depended almost entirely on membership dues and United Fund allocations, and for many other United Fund social service agencies.

THE 1960s—BLACK POVERTY AND NEW FEDERAL INITIATIVES

Community Action

During the 1950s there had been an increasing push for direct federal involvement in the problems of older industrial cities particularly in the Northeast, Midwest and West. These problems included delinquency and gang violence among adolescents, violence associated with racial change and neighborhood transition, student dropouts and violence in schools, high out-of-wedlock pregnancy rates, high infant mortality rates and other health problems, and the physical and economic deterioration of older commercial and residential areas.

In each of these problem areas there were major efforts to pass new federal legislation that would provide funding directly to urban communities, by-passing rural dominated state governments. Urban renewal legislation was passed during the 1950s. Legislation directed at juvenile delinquency prevention was passed in 1961 as one of the first legislative initiatives of President Kennedy. Legislative action on the problems of urban schools was delayed until the mid-1960s because of the controversy over the use of public funds to serve children in parochial schools. Legislation dealing with health services and job training also came in the mid-1960s.

Many of these new federal initiatives were influenced by similar initiatives beginning in the late 1950s by the Ford Foundation in its "Grey Area" and "Great Schools" projects in major urban areas, and also by the Mobilization for Youth project on the Lower East Side of New York for which the National Institute of Mental Health was a major funder (Marris and Rein 1967). These urban initiatives, the planning for which began in the early years of the Kennedy administration, established a new pattern of activity by the federal government (Matusow 1984). This involved the definition of a delimited geographic "target" area as the focus of action, the local development of a systematic, multifaceted and time-limited plan of action, and detailed review by a federal agency of the plans in advance of federal funding.

Total project funding involved various combinations of public and voluntary sources, national and local. The interventions were primarily programmatic, involving a staff of specialists carrying out a variety of technical and professional tasks over a period of several years. Academically based professionals in such fields as city planning, sociology, psychology, social work, health care and education played leading roles at both national and local levels in the original design of many of these projects (Knapp and Polk 1971; Matusow 1984).

The initial planning activities associated with many of these programs all pointed to a common problem—the systemic effects of concentrated urban poverty, reinforced by pervasive racial discrimination in housing, employment, politics, public services and business opportunities (Clark 1965; Silberman 1964). The initial experiences of these governmental and foundation supported projects created the rationale for the Community Action component of the War on Poverty, announced by President Johnson in 1964. Through Community Action the concept of locally controlly targeted intervention supported by federal funds in a limited number of localities on a demonstration basis was expanded almost overnight into a nationwide program, primarily directed at ethnic minority areas in cities. A similar approach was involved in the Comprehensive Community Health Centers program. The Model Cities program, also enacted under President Johnson, was intended to combine the concepts of urban renewal, and social renewal, into a "comprehensive" renewal effort in similar central city areas (Haar 1975).

These federally funded initiatives were, for the most part, not directed at the problems of individuals or of individual households on a case by case basis. Using a variety of approaches they were directed at the interrelated problems of geographically concentrated poverty. Community Action Agencies, Comprehensive Community Health Centers, and later Community Development Corporations represented a new type of nonprofit service organization. They were created as a result of governmental initiative, largely funded by governmental funds, but independently incorporated with an autonomous board of directors.

Because the mandates under which these organizations were established emphasized comprehensive forms of intervention, they required the creation of new administrative structures at the local level organized on a geographic basis, rather than on the basis of traditional functional specializations. This frequently resulted in organizational power contests with the leaders of traditionally structured organizations, such as the office of the city manager, public school systems, public health systems and public employment services. In these contests the newly formed comprehensive organizations were most often the losers on specific planning and policy issues (Warren, Rose and Burgunder 1974).

In addition to the community action initiatives there were also federal efforts to change the patterns of elementary and secondary education which contributed to the complex problems in central city residential areas. The passage of Title I of the Elementary and Secondary Education Act of 1965 required an important political compromise that provided children in parochial schools access to some of the services funded by federal monies without violating the constitutional provisions for separation of church and state. This compromise helped to hold together the liberal Protestant and Roman Catholic industrial worker wings of the Democratic Party political coalition at a time when the civil rights issue was threatening to split them apart. Title I of the Elementary and Secondary Education Act also introduced a redistributional element into "universal" public education programs by providing for "compensatory education" programs in those individual schools with a high concentration of children from low-income families. Provisions for federal funding for school lunch programs, and later, breakfast programs, reinforced this redistributional pattern, a pattern that was widely resisted by local school officials in their implementation of these programs (Matusow 1984). However, the issue of redistributional objectives within public education became an even more complex issue when the federal courts, in their efforts to dismantle decades of ethnic discrimination in education, began to mandate far-reaching changes in the organization of local public school programs, with the explicit objective of improving educational opportunities for black school children. (See Chapter 9).

Much of the foundation for these new federal initiatives had been laid in Congress during the Eisenhower years, or had been established by Supreme Court decisions of the Warren Court that struck down the legal structure of racial segregation. But it was during the administrations of Presidents Kennedy and Johnson that actual implementation took place through the New Frontier and Great Society Programs. This was in part a consequence of the beliefs that both President Kennedy and President Johnson held about the leadership responsibility of the federal government in domestic issues.

The Impact of the Civil Rights Movement

Part of the motive for federal activism was political (Matusow 1984). Racial discrimination in the South and clashes between protestors and local law enforcement officials had been widely exposed through television. The civil rights movement, reflected most dramatically in the 1963 March on Washington, had created a sense of urgency about the need for action by the federal government to forestall urban violence, action that would not be initiated by those cities and states where repressive discrimination was characteristic of all aspects of public life.

The civil rights movement also provided political opportunities because of the increasing mobilization of black voters, who had been an important element in the closely contested election of President Kennedy in 1960. In the South the civil rights movement was primarily directed at knocking out the legal and political barriers that blocked participation of black citizens in the political system, in turn creating a new group of voters within the dominant Democratic one-party political system. In the North the civil rights movement was directed at institutional barriers blocking black citizens from full access to public services, to employment and to business opportunities. These initiatives encouraged the mobilization of urban black voters to support the election of those public officials who would advocate for federally funded programs to change social and economic conditions in local communities.

Commitment to the civil rights movement on the part of new program administrators in the federal government in the 1960s meant that in setting up new programs there were strong pressures to by-pass not only state governments, but also city and county governments, which were often guilty of the most blatant forms of institutional racism. It also meant by-passing most of the local voluntary nonprofit human service organizations that reflected, either explicitly or implicitly, traditional ethnic discrimination patterns in the local community. There was, in addition, a pervasive emphasis on "maximum feasible participation" and "citizen participation" in program planning and in service delivery in the federally initiated and funded programs. This federal emphasis on citizen participation included the funding of advocacy groups that were trying to create alternative power centers at the local level (Clark and Hopkins 1969; Matusow 1984).

However among the federal innovators and their supporters in local communities, there were at least three distinct concepts of the social change process being initiated. Particularly in the early 1960s there was an emphasis on the application of social science theory to social problems through social experimentation, systematic planning, and theoretically oriented program evaluation research with academic theoreticians playing a leading role (Knapp and Polk 1971). The objective was to test alternatives and to develop new knowledge in order to contribute to rational policy development at both federal and local levels (Levitan 1969).

A second concept emphasized special interest political constituency building, for example as reflected in the dramatic Lyndon Johnson/Sargent Shriver approach to the "War on Poverty" community action on a nationwide scale

(Matusow 1984). The third concept was that of a "power to the people" confrontation with "the establishment" across the board in which every federally funded program was viewed primarily in terms of its potential as an arena for a successful attack on existing service programs as well as on local political power arrangements (Clark and Hopkins 1969).

But while there was disagreement about the tactics, there was agreement among everyone involved that the objective of the new federal programs was change. Thus the federal government became the initiator of social reform, taking leadership in, and expanding the mission of, the civil rights movement and other related social and educational reform movements. But unlike earlier periods the major targets for social reform were now primarily other units of government, state and local, rather than "big business."

By the mid-1960s the initial intention to deal separately with such problems as delinquency, neighborhood deterioration, and urban schools became largely subsumed under efforts to deal with the pervasive problems of poverty in black urban neighborhoods and the barriers to social and economic advancement resulting from longstanding patterns of discrimination and powerlessness (Clark 1965). However, it was evident from the beginning in the early 1960s that a few individual federally supported demonstration service projects would not change fundamental patterns of discrimination, exploitation and poverty in local communities. It was also clear that the decisions of the Supreme Court knocking out the legal supports for racial segregation would not be self-enforcing. Urban riots and the "black power" movements in the mid-1960s added a sense of urgency to the growing recognition that something more was needed to bring about a general pattern of change within the society.

Four strategies emerged in efforts to support and institutionalize a continuous process of change in the existing patterns of ethnic discrimination. One strategy was to support political mobilization among black citizens in order to force local and state governments to pay attention to black demands. The Voting Rights Act of 1965 was one part of this strategy; the unofficial political coalition building activities of Community Action Agencies in some cities also contributed to this process (Austin 1972). A second strategy was the use of the federal courts, in part through class action suits initiated with the assistance of Community Action Legal Services lawyers to enforce constitutional provisions, particularly on reluctant public officials. A third strategy was the use of federal regulations to force federally funded programs, and contractors with the federal government, to demonstrate that they were in compliance with civil rights requirements. This in turn required extensive reports and additional federal staff persons to investigate compliance with the regulations. The fourth strategy was the inclusion of "citizen participation" requirements in a wide variety of federally supported programs.

In part these citizen participation requirements reflected a philosophical belief in broad involvement of all citizens in public decisionmaking, in contrast to the delegation of decisionmaking authority involved in a representative governmental system. But more generally these provisions reflected an attitude of distrust among both federal and local reform leaders towards administrative and policymaking officials, resulting in an insistence on "lay" oversight to review the recommendations of professional and administrative specialists. This distrust was based in part on the evidence of exploitation of the poor by public officials through public policies favoring business and financial interests, for example, in many of the approved urban renewal projects. However, the strongest motivation behind the citizen participation provisions in the 1960s was the distrust by liberals and black citizens of the existing white establishment, including both governmental officials and volunteer civic leaders (Altschuler 1970).

The Aftermath

Retrospective analysis suggests that the citizen participation provisions in the 1960s, and direct support for low-income citizen advocacy groups had only limited impact on service agencies and the characteristics of human service programs in most communities (Kramer 1969; Rose 1972). Some analysts blamed President Johnson's Great Society programs for creating urban violence by raising the level of expectations too rapidly (Banfield 1970; Moynihan 1969). However, these programs did have an important, though indirect, impact on the process of black political development and mobilization, particularly in cities. Increased political participation by black citizens, in turn, had a real impact on the characteristics of human service programs in many cities over the next decade, particularly when reinforced by supportive decisions in the federal courts (Matusow 1984; Warner 1977).

Federal legislative requirements for citizen participation, like many other innovative elements in the federal initiatives in the 1960s, became in the 1970s the basis for detailed federal regulations, universally applicable, followed by reporting requirements to demonstrate compliance. They also became the basis of procedures for reviewing the reports, procedures for taking corrective action if there was evidence of noncompliance, including due process procedures, procedures for appealing decisions made by federal administrators, and procedures for withholding federal funds if lack of compliance was established. The role of federal officials in the 1970s became primarily that of rule enforcers rather than innovators. Moreover, the establishment of Legal Services resulted in a wave of class-action advocacy law suits in the federal courts. These law suits contributed to an increasingly complex definition of civil rights as including the right of an individual to have "due process" in access to governmentally funded services, and in administrative procedures, and a "right to treatment" in a "least restrictive setting." These law suits not only attacked patterns of ethnic discrimination but also traditional patterns of program administration and professional decisionmaking within service programs (Moss 1984).

Faced with these pressures administrators in state and local governmental service organizations focused increasingly on technical compliance with regulations and legal decisions while seeking ways to buffer themselves against external pressures for substantive changes from both federal sources and local "citizen" constituencies. Organizational buffering processes were common across all programs areas, and were as likely to occur where there was similarity of ideological and political attitudes between federal and local officials as where there was strong disagreement.

The result, however, of all of the federal prescriptive regulations and federal court decisions dealing not only with citizen participation but also with affirmative action, the review of planning proposals, the provision of barrier-free access to federally funded services for individuals with physical disabilities, and other program procedures, was an increasingly complex system of constraints on state and local governmental organizations intended to offset the effects of institutional racism and underfunding of programs that had often developed under traditional, majority control legislative processes. On one hand, governmental service organizations, such as local school districts and state public welfare departments, were viewed as being administrative elements in nationally defined service delivery systems, and therefore nationally accountable for the quality of services produced. On the other hand, they were defined as autonomous governmental organizations democratically accountable directly to local "citizen" constituencies demanding changes, as well as to their own legislative bodies, which in many instances reflected traditional attitudes both about the appropriate position of ethnic minority groups and the politically acceptable level of taxation.

The effect of these conflicting expectations was an increase in the environmental contingencies impacting administration in government funded service organizations, and a decrease in the relevance of many of the most traditional public adminstration concepts. In particular they increased the impact of the political economy on the organization, and the importance of political negotiation skills on the part of executives in public agencies, even at the expense of administrative skills. It often became essential for executives to take the initiative in efforts to obtain matching funds from local governmental bodies or in other efforts to modify characteristics of the local task environment of the organization in order to ensure organizational survival. This often meant crossing the traditional public administration boundary between the political processes of policymaking and the processes of administrative implementation.

Mental Health and Mental Retardation Services

The 1960s brought new developments in mental health services and services for persons with mental retardation. Following the endorsement by President Kennedy of the national studies dealing with mental health, and with mental retardation, and the passage of the Mental Retardation and Mental Health Facilities Act in 1963, studies were carried out in each state to establish comprehensive plans for services in each of these two service areas. The mental health plans emphasized prevention and community-based psychiatric treatment services for persons with mental health problems through a system of community mental health centers. Federal legislation was passed which provided initial funding for staffing such services.

These federal initiatives led to the development of a major new network of community-based, government funded services that provided alternatives to the institutions that had been the major source of care for over a hundred years for persons with severe mental illness. In mental retardation the initial emphasis was on the development of "university-affiliated facilities," research and diagnostic centers based at universities throughout the country, and on the use of federal funds to support demonstration programs involving services in the community. In many states the scope of responsibility of the newly established community mental health centers was defined as also including the development of community services for persons with mental retardation.

Like other initiatives in the 1960s the emphasis in federal initiatives in mental health and in mental retardation was on the development of services by local communities, largely by-passing existing state service organizations, although state funding support was expected. Moreover, the adminstrative structure of the community mental health center was more like the professionalized voluntary nonprofit service organization than a public administration bureaucracy. Some community mental health centers were administered under the auspices of a medical school and its affiliated teaching hospital. The staffing of the community mental health centers often reflected the multidisciplinary pattern involving psychiatry, psychology and social work which had been established in the child guidance clinics in the 1920s. Rather than being clearly under the domain control of a single profession community mental health became an arena for competition among these three professions, two consisting largely of men and the third consisting largely of women.

Federal, and state, funding for community mental health services, together with the growth of mental health coverage under health insurance programs, including CHAMPUS (Comprehensive Health Services for Dependents of Military Personnel of the United States) and the development of a wide variety of private fee-for-service mental health services, made this the largest growth area in the human services in the late 1960s and 1970s. Unlike the problems of poverty, the problems of mental health, and related problems of alcoholism and drug abuse, as well as problems of mental retardation and other forms of developmental disability were viewed as cutting across the total society. Thus the new community based services funded largely by the federal and state taxes paid by middle-income taxpayers were available to middle-income families at no cost or with a low sliding scale of fees, as well as to low-income families.

The developments in mental health contributed to a conflict within the profession of social work that had its roots in the 1930s but had become visible again in the 1960s (Ehrenreich 1985). The conflict was between those who viewed social work as primarily a social reform movement concerned with families in poverty and with public policies that dealt with problems of poverty and income assistance, and those who viewed social work as primarily a form of psychotherapy dealing with individuals at all income levels who had psychological and behavioral problems.

The expansion of funding for mental health services enlarged the employment opportunities for professional social workers as psychological counselors and contributed to the elaboration of the organized profession. In the late 1960s and early 1970s the organized profession launched a nationwide campaign to establish state professional licensing for social workers. These developments were attacked by those who viewed professionalism as "elitist," and the move towards mental health psychotherapy as an abandonment of the historic "mission" of social work (Ehrenreich 1985).

Changes in the Voluntary Nonprofit System

The dominant leadership role of voluntary nonprofit organizations in health and social welfare services in local communities came to an end in the 1960s. When new federal initiatives appeared in the early 1960s calling for comprehensive community planning for health services, for mental health and mental retardation services, and for antipoverty and delinquency prevention efforts, many United Fund supported community planning councils made bids to be recognized as the key local organization for community-wide social planning.

However, many of the academic theorists and policy analysts who were involved in shaping these new initiatives under the administration of President Kennedy were openly critical of the traditional philosophy of voluntarism and of the role of voluntary nonprofit organizations and the existing community planning councils. These organizations were viewed as primarily representing the attitudes and interests of voluntary nonprofit board members, and, in turn, the business community, with a distinct preference for modest incremental changes rather than nontraditional innovations and fundamental institutional change. The consensus planning procedures used by these community planning councils in the 1940s and 1950s were viewed as having produced few significant solutions to the growing problems of delinquency, urban poverty and institutional racism (Morris and Rein 1968). Most of the community planning councils also had limited credibility with local public officials and local political leaders. The business and professional leaders of the community planning councils often seemed to endorse the "government is an unfair burden on the taxpayer" rhetoric that was a common theme in the annual United Fund appeals to business leaders.

By the end of the 1960s community planning councils in larger cities had been largely passed over in the federally funded planning and development projects. On the other hand, many of the experienced lay leaders from the voluntary nonprofit sector were appointed as individuals to the planning bodies and policy boards established under new federal initiatives, and professional staff members of voluntary nonprofit organizations often headed up the planning staffs.

Community planning councils were also attacked in the 1960s by black leaders as being an integral part of the pattern of institutional racism that was pervasive in most communities prior to the 1960s, regardless of the personal values of individual board members or professional staff members. The councils, and the United Funds, had a persistent pattern of including only token representation from the black community on policy groups, long after black citizens had become a major constituency among the users of community services, and a significant source of pay-roll deduction contributions in most industrial cities. United Fund organizations had also been slow to push for desegregation in service programs, to increase the accessibility of services in black neighborhoods, or to provide funding support for new service organizations established through the initiative of black citizens. This led to the establishment of Black United Way organizations in a number of large cities in the 1970s with fundraising campaigns that competed directly with the existing United Ways for access to corporate gifts and for the contributions of industrial wage earners (Davis 1975).

The 1960s were a period of innovation in the governmental sector, as the Progressive Era had been a period of innovation in the voluntary nonprofit sector. Some of the innovations at a programmatic level survived (Legal Services, Head Start, Community Mental Health Centers). Others have largely disappeared (Community Action Agencies, Community Health Centers, Model Cities). However, the legislative acts dealing with civil rights, discrimination, and affirmative action, as well as the Medicare/Medicaid provisions for financing health care were policy-level innovations which led to fundamental changes in the society.

A multilayered system of governmental human service programs began to emerge in the 1960s, involving Washington federal agency headquarters, federal regional offices, state agency headquarters, state regional and area offices, county governments and city governments. Although this system was often viewed as separate and distinct from the voluntary nonprofit system, it was in fact very much influenced by it. Many of the initial program planners and program administrators in federally initiated activities had gained their "know-how" in voluntary nonprofit organizations. Voluntary agencies received contracts for service production under new federal programs. Moreover, the self-contained nonprofit corporation, funded by federal grants, became a favorite form of administrative organization in the public sector, in preference to the traditional governmental bureau that was directly accountable to an elected, or appointed, public official. This was an early stage in the "privatization" of governmental service programs that became a major public policy issue in the 1980s (Starr 1985).

In some of the new programs, like Model Cities, these nonprofit corporations provided a framework for participation from several governmental units, or from a combination of governmental units and special interest constituencies, in a single policy body. In other programs the nonprofit corporation structure was used to buffer the organization against political control by local governmental officials, and against the administrative complexity of existing governmental agencies.

In effect, however, the use of the nonprofit corporate structure for such programs as community action and community health centers, and in some states for community mental health centers, created autonomous, and essentially "private," organizations supported by tax funds that were not directly accountable to any legislative body, except indirectly through the United States Congress. The development of these nonprofit corporations, and their efforts to maintain themselves financially after start-up federal funding disappeared, contributed substantially to the increased complexity of intergovernmental relationships in human services industries and to the mixed economy pattern of human service program auspices that is analyzed in Chapter 8.

THE 1970s AND 1980s

The Growth of the Public Sector

Retrospective analysis suggests that the citizen participation provisions in the 1960s, and direct support for low-income citizen advocacy groups had only limited impact directly on the programs of existing service organizations and the characteristics of human service programs in most communities (Kramer 1969; Rose 1972). However, these programs did have an important, though indirect, impact on the process of black political development and mobilization, particularly in cities. Increased political participation by black citizens, in turn, had a real impact on the characteristics of human service programs in many cities over the next decade, particularly when reinforced by supportive decisions in the federal courts. However, the "proactive" initiatives of the 1960s, which were accompanied by outbreaks of violence in a number of cities, also disrupted traditional social and political patterns in many urban communities. A steady succession of writers from Moynihan (1969) and Banfield (1970) to Charles Murray (1984) have written disparagingly of the innovations of the 1960s and, noting the continued existence of large numbers of low-income families, have declared that the "war on poverty" and the "welfare state" were catastrophic failures. Others, including Warner (1977), Matusow (1984) and Schwartz (1984) making a more detailed analysis, have noted both successes and failures, or highlighted unrecognized accomplishments and results.

However, whatever the judgement which is made about individual programs, the events of the 1960s, and the reactions to them, set in motion a sequence of developments that dramatically changed the characteristics of both the voluntary nonprofit human services system and the governmental human services system. Indeed, by the mid-1980s most of the traditional distinctions between the voluntary nonprofit system and the governmental system had been modified, leaving a more complex "mixed economy" human services system, including significant for-profit elements (Austin and Hasenfeld 1985; Gilbert 1985; Kramer 1985).

During the early 1970s there was a continuous process of converting experimental and demonstration programs initiated in the 1960s by the federal government into ongoing authorizations using a variety of administrative and funding mechanisms. Some programs were transformed into formula grants, such as the Community Development Block Grant that replaced a number of categorical urban development programs including urban renewal and Model Cities. Some programs continued as a system of direct federal grants to individual communities or individual operating organizations, such as community mental health centers, migrant health centers, Head Start and Legal Services programs. Some programs were replaced by another version, as for example in the replacement of the Manpower Development and Training Act (MDTA) by the Comprehensive Employment and Training Act (CETA). Community Action Agencies in the larger cities were generally absorbed into city government with funding coming from a variety of federal sources. Federal support for compensatory education was extended to include federal grants for a long list of special services within public schools. Federal funds under the 1965 Older Americans Act were allocated through State Aging Agencies to both governmental and voluntary nonprofit organizations serving older adults.

One of the most far-reaching program changes during the early 1970s was the shift from federal-state categorical public assistance programs for individuals outside of the labor force who were disabled (Disability Assistance), or over 65 years of age (Old Age Assistance), or blind (Aid to the Blind) to an inclusive federally funded and federally administered means-tested program, Supplemental Security Income (SSI). Unlike the programs it replaced SSI had a single set of eligibility criteria and a single system of benefits on a nationwide basis. A dramatic expansion of the for-profit nursing home industry took place as a result of the automatic qualification of SSI recipients for Medicaid which included payment for long term health care for individuals with limited income.

In turn, the combination of SSI assistance payments to individuals with chronic disabilities, the Medicaid provisions for long term care, and the development of a variety of new forms of residential care, made it possible to reduce dramatically the numbers of the individuals in large state-administered residential institutions. A significant share of the continuing food and shelter costs for such persons living in nursing homes, in Intermediate Care Facilities-Mentally Retarded (ICF-MR), or in community residences, was in turn shifted from state budgets to the federal budget.

Where state facilities were approved as an Intermediate Care Facility-Mentally Retarded, Medicaid reimbursement went directly to the state. There was an assumption that the state funds freed up through the availability of these federal funds paid to the states through SSI and Medicaid would be used to expand service program resources in local communities, replacing the start-up funds for such programs provided under federal mental health and developmental disability programs. To a large degree this did not happen as the costs of existing state-administered institutional programs increased steadily even with smaller numbers of residents.

The adoption of Title XX of the Social Security Act in 1972, replacing the provisions for social service funding under Title IVA (AFDC), provided greater flexibility to the states in defining the type of social service programs to be supported by state-federal funding. The level of federal matching funds for social services, which had been open-ended, similar to the federal funding for AFDC case payments to families, was capped, but at a level that was much higher than the level of expenditures in 1969, just before a runaway expansion began in the state administered social service programs which drew 3-for-1 federal matching dollars (Derthick 1975).

As a result of this elaboration of health, education, social service, and manpower training programs, along with the implementation of other legislative initiatives of the 1960s, the federal government became a major rule-maker for, and regulator of, state and local governments (Lovell and Tobin 1981). The Voting Rights Act of 1965 led to a continuous monitoring of local governmental voting procedures in a large portion of the country. The federal court decisions on civil rights, and on the rights of institutional residents to receive appropriate care and services in "least restrictive" settings often required continuing court supervision of state and local governmental activities, including the administration of residential institutions, as well as school assignments and bus transportation arrangements for children in elementary and secondary schools.

Initial nondiscrimination and affirmative action regulations directed primarily at discrimination against black citizens were extended to cover other ethnic minority groups, elderly persons, women and individuals with handicaps. Citizen participation requirements, requirements for comprehensive planning, and requirements for interprogram coordination were also made part of each categorical program. Some legislative acts, like Public Law 94-142, the Education of All Handicapped Children Act of 1975, established a broad mandate on local school boards to provide equal education for every handicapped child, without providing substantial federal financial support. Sec. 504 of the Rehabilitation Act of 1973 mandated programmatic and physical access for individuals with handicaps to every activity and facility involving federal funds. Environmental protection was added in the 1970s to the areas of federal intervention and control.

Many of the federal program development initiatives in the early 1970s came primarily from Congress, often over the objections of the Nixon administration. Each initiative represented a specialized political coalition including a network of special interest organizations, a Congressional sub-committee and its staff, and federal administrative staff, usually below the level of presidential appointments. A persuasive case was made in each instance through the Congressional sub-committee for the urgency of, and the logic of, federal intervention in each categorical area. Little attention, however, was given to the system effects of the total of all of these federal initiatives (Gilbert 1985; Lovell and Tobin 1981). Separate categorical initiatives at the federal level impacted a single set of state and local governmental bodies. Efforts to develop interagency coordination at the federal level even when mandated by Congress were largely unsuccessful (Friedan and Kaplan 1975).

Funding from multiple sources also encouraged program administrators to develop sophisticated methods for cost shifting and cost sharing among programs in order to maintain program continuity under a system of overlapping and irregular funding cycles. Federal categorical administrators responded with detailed regulations intended to prevent such juggling of funding from multiple sources. Service activity reports were repackaged by operating agencies in various forms, with minor changes in the definitions of user catgories, to meet the requirements of different categorical programs. Grant proposal writing became a specialized activity, relatively independent of program development and program administration, with substantial portions of such proposals taking the form of automatic and pro forma promises to comply with a lengthy list of federal mandates (boilerplate).

In addition to the impacts of the numerous procedural requirements on state and local agencies, there was also a steadily expanding fiscal impact on the federal budget, as both the scope of the categorical programs was enlarged and the level of program utilization increased (Gilbert 1986). However, in the early 1970s it appeared that an expanding economy and a steady increase in federal income (both in part a consequence of inflation) could make it possible to fund these programs from a modestly expanding "slice" of an ever larger "pie."

Governors and state legislators in many states responded to the proliferation of federally initiated programs with administrative reorganizations intended to reestablish state government policy control. One result was the establishment of state "umbrella" human services agencies in which a number of existing state agencies were placed under the authority of a single "human services" cabinet officer directly accountable to the governor (Austin 1978; Hagen and Hansen 1978). The degree of administrative consolidation in these state human services agencies varied from the creation of a small budget and planning unit for coordinating fiscal planning and for dealing with the governor and the legislature, but with no substantive changes in the structure of existing operating agencies, to the actual merger of existing service agencies at the operating level (Florida) (Immerschein, Polivka, Gordon-Girvin, Chackerian and Martin 1986). In addition to initiatives within individual states there were efforts by the federal government, particularly under Elliot Richardson as Secretary of Health, Education and Welfare, to create more inclusive and effective governmental service delivery systems at state and local levels through the support of "services integration" innovations.

State and local general purpose governments developed strategies to cope with unwanted federal mandates, uncertainties in federal funding, and inconsistencies in federal administrative processes. These strategies involved various buffering procedures intended to limit or delay the impact of federal controls. State and local agencies developed their own direct linkages with administrators in Washington, bypassing federal regional offices on policy issues. These agencies also turned to members of Congress for assistance in resolving procedural conflicts with federal agencies, or in delaying negative decisions. On some issues administrators of state agencies worked together on a nationwide basis to promote Congressional action intended to counteract proposed federal regulations.

By the end of the 1970s a major area of controversy in the structure of human service programs was around intergovernmental relationships within the public sector, specifically the relation of the federal government to states, counties and cities. Rather than being a collaborative relationship to achieve common objectives, the relationship in many program areas was one of constant conflict over the enforcement of existing regulations and the wording of proposed new regulations, with frequent federal threats to withhold funds to punish state and local public agencies considered not to be in compliance.

Program administration at state and local levels had become increasingly regulation focused rather than program focused. Discontent on the part of individuals involved in state and local program administration, and persons concerned with human needs and quality of services, became part of the backlash that came at the end of the 1970s against the expanded federal role in human service programs. Elected officials at state, county and city levels found themselves increasingly constrained by federal mandates, both substantive and procedural (Lovell and Tobin 1981). Funding and programatic decision cycles in local governments were often determined by federal deadlines.

It had become evident that no federal public policy enactment was self-implementing, and that, in fact, the complexities of administering direct service programs at a local level through the model of a massive, centrally controlled, rule regulated yet loosely linked federal-state-local administrative system made effective and consistent implementation almost impossible.

In the early 1970s some elements of a comprehensive governmental human services system had begun to appear, and the term "welfare state" was increasingly used, in particular by political critics of these developments. These organizational and administrative innovations, however, were not reinforced by the development of institutional elements required for a fully elaborated system. Many of infrastructure elements that were part of the voluntary nonprofit social welfare system at its height in the 1950s had not developed in the public sector by the end of the 1970s. The interstate networks among governmental categorical program agencies, as exemplified by the American Public Welfare Association (APWA), were preoccupied with efforts to negotiate regulations and cost-sharing arrangements with federal officials. In general, there was only limited attention to information sharing among the states about the operational issues involved in the development and management of effective service systems.

Congressional committees gave little consistent attention to the qualitative improvement of state and local programs and the development of information sharing networks. Within individual governmental human service organizations the concerns of administrators and of direct service practitioners were very different, and often antagonistic. There was no membership association, national forum, conference, or publication, that linked human service practitioners in the governmental system across categorical lines, or across federal, state, county and city lines.

Most important, however, the role of the executive branch of the federal government had shifted by the end of the 1970s from a leadership and developmental role to a constraining, and often antagonistic, role in the governmental human services system. Increasingly both politically appointed policymakers, and the federal personnel responsible for administration of program guidelines and funding regulations, dealt with state and local public administrators as either an interest group lobby only interested in obtaining federal funding to avoid the need for increased state and local appropriations, or as unmoveable bureaucrats unwilling to make modernizing changes in local service programs. The class action suits brought in federal courts to force changes in state and local human service programs further intensified the role of the federal government as regulator of state and local governments (Moss 1984). In some cases federal court "masters," or monitors, became direct participants in state legislative and administrative policymaking.

The involvement of governmental service organizations in efforts to shape the content of professional education to fit the needs of governmental programs was very uneven. Voluntary nonprofit organizational settings were still the preferred settings for practicuum or internship experiences in most professional education programs, including the extensive professional education activities funded by the National Institute of Mental Health in medicine, nursing, psychology and social work. Efforts by the federal government to involve academic institutions in infrastructure development, for example in the operation of a nationwide system of regional technical assistance resource centers dealing with child protective services, were inconsistent, with annual changes in program objectives and unpredictable funding.

By the end of the 1970s the expansion of public human service programs, particularly at the federal level, was coming to an end. In part this was a consequence of the sharply increasing budgetary costs of such entitlement programs as Medicare, Medicaid, and food stamps. In other program areas the extension of limited pilot or demonstration programs to cover the entire country sharply increased program costs. Substantial increases in the numbers of persons entering the labor market, including large numbers of women, created significant levels of unemployment and associated income assistance costs in spite of the fact that the economy was also creating large numbers of new jobs (Schwartz 1984).

Individual taxpayers were experiencing the impact of a steady rise throughout the 1970s in the rate of wage deductions for Social Security participation. Taxpayer "revolts" in some states against increases in local property tax rates suggested that there were political limits on the ability of state and local governmental bodies to increase tax levels to meet the steadily increasing costs of human service programs, which were, in part, created by matching fund requirements in federally initiated programs.

Antagonisms between state and local officials and federal officials resulted in prolonged contests, including law suits, over the wording of legislation and regulations, rather than unified support of basic federal provisions. Widespread media attention was given to policy analysis studies that cast doubt on the results being achieved in many of the categorical programs. There was ambivalence in "liberal" political groups, which were an important element in Congressional constituencies in many states, between "social reform" support of human service programs, and "populist" opposition to a large, self-maintaining, inefficient federal bureaucracy, a theme which had begun to be developed by "public choice" economists, such as Buchanan and Tullock in the 1960s (Tullock 1965). This ambivalence was reflected in the successful 1976 campaign of President Carter in which a central theme was an attack on the "Washington establishment."

This ambivalence over continued expansion of governmental human service programs was particularly evident in the women's movement, in groups primarily concerned with peace issues and with protection of the environment, and in ethnic minority groups, given the overwhelming character of the leadership of the federal executive branch as white and male, and largely committed to the support of the business sector and a large defense establishment. It was also evident that the expansion of governmental human service programs during the 1970s had not solved the fundamental problems of poverty among black and Hispanic families in metropolitan areas (Orfield 1985).

Changes in the Voluntary Nonprofit System

While governmental programs were expanding in scope and complexity during the 1970s, critical changes were taking place among voluntary nonprofit organizations (Kramer 1985). One change was the increasing size and scope of the voluntary nonprofit sector that was estimated in 1982 to include some 125,000 organizations with combined budgets of $131 billion, 5 percent of the gross national product and roughly equivalent to the total of all expenditures for local government in the United States (Abrahamson and Salamon 1986). Another change was in role of governmental funds in the program operations of traditional voluntary nonprofit organizations. An analysis of the income of member organizations of the Child Welfare League for 1979-1980 indicated that 55 percent of their income came from governmental sources (Haddow and Jones 1981). A 1982 study by the Urban Institute reported that among all nonprofit organizations 41 percent of their income came from governmental funding with 28 percent from service fees and only 22 percent from voluntary contributions (Abrahamson and Salamon 1986).

The largest amounts of governmental funding for voluntary and nonprofit organizations involved the purchase of health care services under Medicare, Medicaid, and CHAMPUS. Here the role of government was similar to that of Blue Cross/Blue Shield and commercial health insurance programs. The expanding role of governmental programs as the largest purchasers of health care, however, made governmental regulations particularly significant for all elements of the health care industry.

A more complex pattern of relationships developed around the contract purchase of social services by state and county social service organizations from voluntary nonprofit organizations under Title XX of the Social Security Act (Bendick 1985). In some jurisdictions the move to contract for social services also reflected a policy decision to reduce the scope of governmentally administered programs, as for example, in the replacement of state juvenile correctional institutions in Massachusetts by contracts with voluntary nonprofit organizations to provide non-institutional services (Massachusetts Taxpayers Association 1980).

By the end of the 1970s political and fiscal pressures on state governments were sometimes resulting in mandates to state human service organizations to make across the board reductions in the number of state employees, thus adding an additional incentive for replacing direct administration of services by contracted services. The management of service provision through contract managers introduced into state and county administration some of the same complexities that had developed in the federal-state, and federal-local relationships, that is the management of service programs through regulation, monitoring, and audit/evaluation rather than through direct administrative control (Ferris and Graddy 1986).

This pattern of governmental contract funding with voluntary nonprofit agencies became another major factor in the blurring of the distinctions between the voluntary sector and the governmental sector (Benedick 1985; Starr 1965). Within individual voluntary nonprofit organizations this development also blurred the roles of policy boards and executives, with the executive often carrying major responsibility for negotiating both financial and policy issues with the contracting agency, subject only to nominal approval by the policy board.

The 1970s were also marked by an elaboration of the scope and diversity of the voluntary nonprofit sector within human service industries. Each nation-wide categorical service program enacted by Congress was linked to an elaborate network of local, state and national advocacy groups, including both parent associations, as in the instance of children with developmental disabilities, and self-advocacy associations, as in the instance of physically handicapped adults and older adults. Traditional national advocacy organizations like the NAACP were joined during the 1970s by women's advocacy organizations such as the National Organization of Women, the Grey Panthers and the American Association for Retired Persons as well as groups speaking for Mexican-Americans, Puerto Ricans, Asian-Americans and Native Americans. There were also advocacy organizations organized around single issues like wilderness preservation, gun control, drunken driving and abortion. Many of these advocacy organizations also administered service programs, frequently with a combination of federal and/or state funding and voluntary contributions.

A network of "alternative" service organizations also emerged, based in part on the counter-culture movement of the late 1960s and early 1970s (Powell 1986). These alternative, or "community-based" services included "wholistic" health services, drug abuse services, shelters for runaways, community mental health crisis centers, and storefront service centers for Vietnam veterans, among others. Closely related to the alternative life-style services were new services for women including rape crisis centers and family violence centers created primarily through women's movement networks. In some communities these community-based nontraditional service organizations, as well as more traditional agencies, while continuing to solicit voluntary contributions, also lobbied successfully for grants from city and county governments, which often used federal revenue-sharing funds for this purpose.

One result of all of these developments was a new definition of the voluntary nonprofit sector at the local level in which traditional voluntary nonprofit service organizations receiving funds from the United Way became only one sub-set of nonprofit service organizations within a larger network (Rabinowitz, Simmeth and Spero 1979). Consistent with this development United Way funding organizations reduced their financial support for community planning councils. Independently incorporated planning councils were merged with the United Way organization with their functions primarily limited to carrying out quality-control, problem-solving studies related to United Way funded organizations.

The growth of voluntary nonprofit service organizations and advocacy organizations was both a cause of, and in many instances a result of, the politicization of policymaking in the human services as governmental program auspices and funding became more extensive. This in turn was linked to a general growth of special interest groups, Political Action Committees (PACS) and special interest coalitions in the political system, and a decline in the role of political parties (Lowi 1969). One clear reason for the decline in the role of traditional political parties in shaping public policy was their failure to develop any consistent procedure for linking local, state and national concerns into a coherent intergovernmental policy perspective, consistent with the intergovernmental nature of public programs.

Special interest advocacy groups, on the other hand, were able to develop inclusive policy approaches within their area of interest, as for example in the case of the Association for Retarded Citizens that developed policy positions linking legislative and administrative issues at the federal level affecting services to persons with developmental disabilities to legislative and administrative issues at the state level, and to implementation issues in service programs at the local level.

The growing importance of these voluntary, special interest networks in the national society was reflected in the process of reorganization within the voluntary sector at the national level which went on during the 1970s. The result was the formation of a new coalition organization, Independent Sector, with a membership in 1985 of over 600 national associations, foundations, and corporations. These organizations, including both philanthropic funders, such as foundations and corporations, and national associations of nonprofit organizations, ranged from Aetna Life and Casualty and the Exxon Corporation to Zero Population Growth and the World Crafts Council, from the Family Service Association of America to the National Council of La Raza. Included in this coalition of nonprofit organizations were not only traditional human service organizations but also organizations of museums, symphony orchestras and universities. One of the most important areas of shared interest in this diverse coalition was tax policies dealing with charitable contributions (Simon 1987).

Much of the leadership in developing this new coalition in the voluntary sector came from philanthropic foundations. Just as foundations created by wealthy individuals were an important source of philanthropic initiative at the turn of the century, corporate foundations and community foundations became increasingly significant as a source of support for voluntary activities in the 1970s, reflecting the results of corporate prosperity in the 1950s and 1960s. These foundations became an important source of flexible financial support for philanthropic activities, particularly new program initiatives, at a time when other sources, including the United Way, were largely committed to the continuing support of existing voluntary nonprofit organizations.

While there was a general pattern of growth in the number of voluntary nonprofit service organizations by the end of the 1970s there was little left of a distinctive and comprehensive voluntary nonprofit *system* (Kramer 1985). The National Conference on Social Welfare, a little over one hundred years after its formation as the National Conference on Charities and Correction, ceased to exist as an annual conference after 1983, while the number of separate conferences dealing with specialized human service issues increased steadily. National trade associations of voluntary nonprofit organizations, faced with increasing costs during the inflationary years of the 1970s and stable or reduced income from membership payments, made cut-backs in their operations with resulting reductions in their influence on national developments. Reflecting the increased impact of the federal government on the voluntary sector, many national associations, previously headquartered in New York City, moved to Washington, D.C. or opened Washington offices.

Local voluntary nonprofit organizations had stronger linkages with governmental organizations in the same field of service than they had with voluntary nonprofit organizations in other service areas (Gronberg 1982). Professional social workers who had provided many of the operational linkages within the voluntary nonprofit system up through the 1950s were now involved in both governmental and voluntary sectors, particularly in the mental health field, with individual professional practitioners frequently moving from one type of setting to the other, but within a specialized field of practice. Schools of social work, while using many voluntary nonprofit organizations for field training experiences for students, were not closely tied to the institutional elements of the voluntary nonprofit system. Moreover, many of the key United Way agencies, such as the youth-serving agencies, did not employ any significant number of social workers and were not used as training centers by the professional schools. While the number of voluntary nonprofit organizations expanded steadily during the 1970s, the system linkages among these organizations as a group steadily weakened, even with the creation of The Independent Sector.

System Changes in the 1980s.

The first half of the 1980s brought an acceleration of trends already evident by the end of the 1970s. President Reagan was elected on a campaign platform that called for drastic reductions in the scope of federal financial participation in human service programs of all types. Many of his advisors favored major reductions in all forms of governmental involvement in the "welfare state" (Anderson 1978; Gilder 1981). The Omnibus Budget Reconciliation Act of 1981 (OBRA) led to a dramatic shift in the role of the federal government in the public human services sector (Palmer and Sawhill 1982). For those categorical programs that were consolidated into a series of "block grants" there was, on the average, a 20 percent reduction in the level of federal funding in comparison to the preceding year, a larger proportional reduction if the impact of inflation was taken into account. And for all federally funded service programs there was a 38 percent cut in federal funds over a three year period (Bendick and Levinson 1984).

There was also outright repeal of the original authorizing legislation for a number of categorical programs as well as elimination of many of the detailed rules and regulations associated with particular programs. The Mental Health Systems Act of 1980 that had been intended to provide a permanent framework for federal funding for community mental health services was repealed. There was a shift from efforts to control medical care costs through planning and regulatory controls administered by local Health Systems Agencies to control through the use of the competitive marketplace.

One consequence of these federal funding and policy changes was that most federal program funds were directed to state governments which, in turn, became responsible for the pattern of allocations to local communities. This largely eliminated the direct federal-city connections which had been established in the 1960s and 1970s in human service programs. In general, programs for older adults, including Social Security benefits, SSI and the Older Americans Act were less impacted by these changes at the federal level than programs serving children and young families. On the other hand, cost-containment and program coverage in Medicaid, and Medicare, which did affect older citizens, became continuing issues throughout the Reagan administration.

Other steps were initiated by President Reagan to reduce the federal role in enforcing mandates in such areas as affirmative action, protection of individuals with disabilities against discrimination, and "citizen participation."

These changes in the policy posture of the federal government were accompanied by cut-backs in the level of federal staffing, particularly in federal regional offices, staff re-organizations and freezes on travel funds for federal personnel. In several instances the Justice Department supported legal initiatives by local groups to overturn existing judicial rulings upholding particular federal regulations, for example, those dealing with affirmative action.

Consistent with the philosophy that public assistance programs should provide only "safety-net" support, changes in eligibility in entitlement programs were made to restrict participation by "working poor" families, who had been able to supplement low or irregular earnings from employment with financial assistance through AFDC or food stamps. President Reagan argued that private market provision of all types of services should be used as extensively as possible for middle-income families and that the programs of voluntary nonprofit organizations could be expanded to meet the needs of those low-income families who were no longer covered by governmental programs after more restrictive eligibility requirements were imposed (Burt and Pittman 1985). The impact of these changes in federal income assistance programs was intensified by the economic recession of 1981-1982.

The years following 1981 were marked by a continuation of these new federal policies, but without the dramatic changes instituted in 1981. Proposals by the administration for additional "block grant" program consolidations and elimination of federal funding for particular human service programs were largely rejected by the Congress. Administration attempts to weaken or eliminate the federal role in guaranteeing free and appropriate education for all handicapped children, as set forth in P.L. 94-142, were halted by an all-out show of opposition from parents of such children. The effects of inflation, however, continued to erode the effective level of federal financial participation in state and locally administered human service programs (Burt and Pittman 1985). Although proposals to restrict, or eliminate, federal mandates in such areas as affirmative action, were, in many instances, blocked by Congress, staff support for enforcement of such mandates continued to be reduced. By the mid-1980s the deficit reduction requirements of the Gramm-Rudman bill threatened to create another round of across-the-board cuts in federal funding for state and local service programs in all human service areas, while providing some protection for "safety-net" programs.

The most significant development in the 1980s, however, was the deliberate choice by President Reagan to turn away from a leadership role for the Presidency, and for the executive branch, in dealing with internal or domestic issues within the United States, with the exception of drug abuse. Leadership and initiative in dealing with domestic issues whether through regulatory action or operational service programs was essentially abandoned to the governors and legislatures of the fifty states, although President Reagan, like President

Hoover, emphasized the virtues of "voluntarism" as a solution to problems of unemployment and poverty. His recommendations, however, ignored the extent to which the scope of services actually being provided by voluntary nonprofit organizations depended on funding grants from the federal government, and other governmental sources.

On a nationwide basis contributions for voluntary organizations increased at a rate equal to inflation, but not at a level sufficient to replace federal funding cuts (Abrahamson and Salamon 1986). The major results of the federal cuts included some increases in local and state governmental expenditures for human services, together with reductions in the level of services (Burt and Pittman 1985). Social problems closely associated with poverty increased for many groups of people: homeless individuals and families, female-headed single parent households, teen-age pregnancy, malnourished children, teen-age unemployment and families and individuals dependent on emergency feeding programs. Central cities in large metropolitan areas which included large numbers of black and Hispanic households, and economically depressed rural areas were particularly hard hit.

Nonprofit organizations continued to seek funding support through grants and contracts with state and local governmental agencies, sometimes resulting in further reductions in direct operations under governmental aupsices (Poole 1985). State-level advocacy organizations and trade associations of nonprofit organizations became more important as the role of national associations in promoting federal funding became less important. Increased attention began to be directed towards a redefinition of the place of voluntary nonprofit organizations, given the scope of governmental programs (Ostrander 1985; Tobin 1985).

Increased contributions to voluntary organizations replaced some 25 percent of the decrease in governmental funds in nonhealth care areas. The balance of the decrease in governmental funding was largely offset by increased "commercialization," that is through increases in fees and other charges, or through the creation of for-profit subsidiary activities (Gilbert 1985). This represented a further modification of the traditional structure of nonprofit organizations from one largely supported by sources other than user fees to one in which user fees, and related "sales" income, become sizeable sources of income.

Another important development was the growth of for-profit human service firms, particularly in the health care and mental health areas, but also in day-care and in residential institution services of all types. Within a number of human service industries these for-profit firms were actively promoting the "privatization" of governmental services and aggressively competing with voluntary nonprofit organizations for governmental contracts, as well as for contracts with for-profit business firms to provide services under Employee Assistance Programs (Gilbert 1985). (See Chapter 8). Indeed, development of personal service programs for employees within business firms, either in-house or on a contractual basis, was viewed by some as the next major area of growth in human service programs (Stoesz 1986). In the health care industry, in particular, for-profit firms were beginning to have an impact on the characteristics of the industry as a whole. On the other hand, for-profit organizations made little impact on the organizational pattern of the elementary and secondary education industry.

By the mid-1980s health care for low-income families and for older adults, involving a complex set of "mixed economy" relationships among the several levels of government, and among governmental, voluntary and for-profit organizations, had become the most critical domestic policy issue. The number of for-profit organizations in health care increased dramatically, responding to increases in the scope of both commercial and governmental insurance and other third-party health care programs, such as health maintenance organizations (Gilbert 1985). Federally initiated cost-control measures, such as Diagnosis Related Groups (DRGs), created large-scale, and often disruptive, changes in the health care field, shifting health care expenditures in many cases from acute care hospitals to home health care and nursing homes.

The development of third-party payment systems led to shifts from direct public provision of hospital and ambulatory health care to low-income families to the purchase of such health care from nonprofit and for-profit organizations, particularly in cities. Hospitals began to compete aggressively for insurance covered patients, while actively avoiding patients without such coverage. There was a reduction in health care resources in some rural areas as small hospitals closed down when patients with insurance coverage chose to use urban hospitals. Federally supported training programs for health care personnel, together with the changes in health care procedures, resulted in a "surplus" of physicians, and in reductions in hospital employment for nurses, leading to intensified conflicts within the health care sector over the definitions of professional domain boundaries, with these definitions increasingly controlled by governmental policies.

By the mid-1980s, as a result of the combination of the withdrawal of federal leadership involvement, pressures from advocacy organizations and other special interest groups, and class-action court cases, state governments were becoming actively involved in new program and policy initiatives in such human service areas as adult and juvenile corrections, mental health services, mental retardation services, elementary and secondary education, health care for low-income families, services for older adults living in their own homes, job-training for mothers receiving AFDC payments and child welfare. These initiatives were very uneven, with only limited sharing of information across state lines. Cities were attempting to cope, largely on their own, with the many related problems of the rapidly increasing numbers of homeless people. But both states and local communities were faced with the fact that the macroeconomic policies of the federal government and cutbacks in the scope of such programs as food stamps, public housing and AFDC were significant factors in creating and maintaining the problems they were forced to deal with. In turn, it was initiatives from state governments, rather than from the federal government, that began to shape proposals for major changes in the AFDC program in 1987.

SUMMARY

The 1950s represented the high point in system development among voluntary nonprofit human service organizations in the United States. This was accompanied by a strong emphasis on the distinctions between voluntary and governmental programs with arguments primarily emphasizing the advantages of nonprofit organizations. The 1960s and early 1970s brought a dramatic expansion of governmental services, primarily as a result of governmental initiatives. These developments were initiated by Presidents Kennedy and Johnson, often with reinforcement by the federal courts. They were expanded and institutionalized by Congress. This period of expanding governmental programs also was accompanied by a strong emphasis on distinctions between governmental and voluntary nonprofit service organizations, but with arguments emphasizing the advantages of governmental services.

By the end of the 1970s many human service industries, in reality, had substantial mixed economy characteristics. Intergovernmental funding and administration mixes were combined with public-private contracting relationships. The voluntary nonprofit system had lost many of its distinctive system characteristics while expanding and diversifying. The governmental system had never developed a complete set of system infrastructure elements. A mounting wave of attacks on the ideological concept of the "welfare state," and on the economic assumptions underlying the expansion of governmental programs, came to a head in the 1980 election of President Reagan.

Over all the 1980s have been a period of continuing increases in total expenditures within human service industries but with important shifts. The largest growth areas have been health and mental health services, with proportionally reduced expenditures for direct assistance to low-income families with young children. Limits on federal expenditures have resulted in an uneven pattern of increased state and local funding, and a hold-the-line level of voluntary contributions, given the effects of inflation. The 1980s have also been a period of continued elaboration of the mixed economy characteristics of human service industries with an expanding for-profit sector. Governmental "provision" of the policy legitimation and funding for basic services, and "production" of those services by a diverse network of governmental, voluntary nonprofit and for-profit organizations had become the dominant pattern. This, in turn, created complex issues of policy control and accountability. However, it had become evident by the mid-1980s that human service industries were a major element in the political economy of the United States, as well as in other postindustrial societies.

Chapter 8

Comparative Analysis of Human Service Programs by Accountability Structure

Each of the thousands of service producing organizations in the human service industries in the United States has unique characteristics. But among this total group of service producing organizations there are also consistent patterns of similarities and differences. An understanding of these similarities and differences is important both for an analysis of the characteristics of a particular human services industry and for understanding the specific political economy context of any single organization.

The analysis of similarities and differences requires a system which can be used to locate any one organization in relation to all other human service organizations. There have been a number of efforts to establish a typology, or taxonomy, for the classification of service organizations, that is all inclusive and exhaustive and based on a single set of variables (Haynes and Sallee 1975; Human Services Coordination Alliance 1976; United Way of America 1976). Such a complete taxonomy would be similar to those in the natural sciences, for example the periodic table of elements or the botanical taxonomy of plants. However, no system of analysis dealing with social structures can ever be as clear cut and exact as those in the natural sciences.

Social structures, created through the dynamic social interaction of human beings, do not present the degree of consistency that is exhibited in natural science. Definitions of social structures are entirely a function of language; they change in meaning over a period of time and take on different meanings in different societies. For example, persons involved in voluntary nonprofit service organizations often refer to such organizations as "private" in contrast to governmental or "public" organizations. Public administration theorists, on the other hand, refer to for-profit business firms as the "private sector" (Rainey, Backoff and Levine 1976). There is no unique set of variables which can be used to structure an inclusive classification sequence from simple to complex. And at least one example of every possible combination of characteristics is likely to be found somewhere, whether or not such a combination is deductively logical.

This chapter and Chapter 9 deal with two different systems of analysis, using organizational characteristics, and program characteristics, both of which are significant for describing the total set of human service production organizations, and for identifying similarities and differences. There are overlaps between the two analytic systems, yet they cannot be collapsed into a single system, given the complexity of reality. The analytic system described in this chapter deals with "sponsorship," or "accountability structure," that is: (1) "auspice" which is based on the *legal status* or source of organizational legitimation, together with *the balance between nongovernmental and governmental funds as the source of core funding;* and (2) the *proportion of service-generated fee income* in the total operating budget. The analytic system described in Chapter 9 deals with the societal function of the services produced by the organization.

These two elements involved in "accountability structure" are directly linked to the pattern of the original establishment of the service organization. In turn, they are critical elements in organizational continuity. Taken together, they define the ultimate sources to which the the organization is operationally accountable, and therefore they define the relation of the organization to the larger society. The unit of analysis for "accountability structure" is the legal entity identified as the service production organization, or agency, since this is the basic unit of legitimation and of accountability for financial resources.

Traditional organizational analyses of human service organizations assume that there are two basic forms of sponsorship in the United States.[1]

One is the free-standing, self-perpetuating, voluntary nonprofit corporation with funding for core production activities from its own fundraising, or endowment, limited income from service fees, and no governmental funding. It is linked to the larger society through the "public trustee" role of the members of the corporate Board of Directors and through public support expressed through voluntary contributions (Powell 1987).

The second traditional form of sponsorship is the governmental bureau, or service organization, which is an administrative component of a general purpose government, with funding for core production activities through the appropriation of tax funds by a single legislative body, and with only limited income, if any, from service fees. This organization is linked to the larger society through the political decision to levy taxes to provide funding support, and through the ultimate accountability of the agency administrator to a politically accountable legislative body.

These two forms of sponsorship, or "accountability structure," have been viewed as distinctly different, and as representing very different historical traditions, as described in Chapters 6 and 7. However, they are fundamentally similar in that, in both instances, the formation and continuation of such organizations is justified on the basis of "public purpose," or "collective benefit," rather than on the basis of "private benefits" to the initiators or organizers. Moreover, both legitimation, and core funding, are connected to sources in the larger society, rather than to the service user. Therefore, accountability is ultimately to those interest elements in the larger society which control legitimation and funding rather than to the immediate service users.

Differences in the characteristics of the accountability structure are also at the heart of traditional distinctions made between voluntary nonprofit and governmental organizations, and for-profit human service firms. The for-profit organization is legitimated by incorporation as a for-profit firm under the laws of a particular state. This legal status, however, assumes that the basic legitimation lies in the ownership of the corporation by its stockholders; the legitimation rests upon the basic concept of private property "ownership."

The *primary* purpose for the existence of a for-profit organization is to provide benefits to the "private" owners. It is viewed as being linked to the larger society through the legally defined, and protected, structure of the free-standing corporation in which the board of directors is accountable to the investing stockholders, as well as through participation in marketplace exchange processes with service users. Income from the sale of organizational products is the dominant source of funding for for-profit organizations. In the discussion that follows the relationship of for-profit organizations to the analytic system is examined following the examination of voluntary nonprofit and governmental organizations.

As already noted, the actual pattern of organizational sponsorship currently existing among human service organizations is considerably more complex than that suggested by traditional distinctions between governmental organizations and voluntary nonprofit organizations (Starr 1985). Some voluntary nonprofit organizations are dependent for core funding on governmental funding through contracts rather than on contributions, with accountability being discharged primarily through contract management channels, rather than through the board of directors. Some nonprofit corporations are created by governmental units at one level of government, but receive their core funding from a government unit at another level, with a board of directors appointed by and accountable to one or more legislative bodies.

There are many voluntary nonprofit organizations which do not depend on their own fundraising activities for core funding. Instead they share in a joint fundraising activity like the United Way, which systematically solicits contributions from the same inclusive community constituency from which local government collects taxes. And, as in the case of individual taxpayers whose preferences are mediated by a representative legislative body, the connection between individual United Way contributors and any one specific nonprofit service organization is mediated by a "representative" body of citizens who determine the actual allocations from the annual fundraising campaign to particular service organizations.

Moreover, there are both nonprofit organizations and governmental organizations, particularly in the health care field, which depend for funding primarily on service user fees, sometimes collected directly but more often paid through third-party insurance mechanisms. These "nonprofit" health care organizations actively participate in a competitive supply-and-demand marketplace. Indeed, in a number of instances, they compete directly with for-profit organizations providing similar services. An analytic system for accountability structures must deal with all of these organizational variations which are characteristic of the contemporary "mixed economy" of human service industries (Bendick 1985; Gilbert 1983; Gilbert 1985; Kramer 1985; Starr 1985).

The two elements in this analytic system as indicated at the beginning of this chapter are: first, the *auspices,* and second, the *proportion of service-generated fee income* in the total operating budget.

AUSPICE

Organizational auspice is determined by: (1) the source of organizational legitimation, or the *legal structure* of the organization; and (2) by the balance between *nongovernmental and governmental sources of core funding.* The range of auspices, from the self-supporting philanthropic organization with a self-perpetuating board of directors who personally fund the organization, to the tax-supported governmental service organization accountable to all citizens reflects the distinctions between nongovernmental and governmental action set forth by Weisbrod (1977).

Legal Structure

The variations in accountability built into the legal structure of human service organizations are part of a pattern that ranges from organizational accountability to a very narrowly defined self-appointed, self-perpetuating board of directors to organizational accountability to a broadly inclusive political constituency (see Figure 8-1). Examples include:

1. A nonprofit corporation established under state law as an autonomous structure with a Board of Directors which has full authority to adopt by-laws, to appoint future members of the Board, to appoint an administrator, and to

Figure 8-1. Auspice

	Narrowly Defined Private Constituency		Broadly Defined Political Constituency		
Legal Structure	1. Self-perpetuating Autonomous Nonprofit Corporation	3. Nonprofit Corporation as Instrument of Inclusive Organization	5. Independent Nonprofit Corporation Established by Governmental Body	7. Joint Powers Governmental Agency	9. Governmental Agency Accountable to Legislative Body
Core Funds	1. Single Source Grant or Contribution	3. Contributions from Agency Fundraising Campaign	6. Allocation from Community-wide Fund-raising Campaign	7. Governmental Grant for on-going Service Operations	9. Purchase-of-service Contract from Governmental Body	11. Legislative Appropriation for Agency Operations
Combined Categories	1. Self-perpetuating Nonprofit Corporation/ Single Source or Limited Number of Contributions	2. Nonprofit Corporation Controlled by Inclusive Organization/ Allocation from Community-wide Fundraising	3. Voluntary Nonprofit Corporation/ Governmental Grant or Purchase-of-Service	4. Governmental Nonprofit Corporation/ Governmental Grant or Purchase-of-Service	5. Governmental Agency/ Legislative Appropriation

control the resources and assets of the corporation (The Jefferson County Family Service Association).

2. A nonprofit corporation established under state law as an autonomous organization, but which is under the programmatic control of a larger organization which is accountable to an extensive membership constituency. The larger organization has the power to grant, or withdraw the "charter" of the local organization, and may have authority over ultimate disposal of organizational assets (Smithville YMCA).

3. A nonprofit corporation established by another nonprofit organization to carry out specialized functions as defined by the parent organization. The parent organization has the authority to appoint the Board of Directors, to establish the policies under which the organization functions, and to control the assets of the corporation (The Children's Home of the Northern Diocese of Iowa).

4. A nonprofit corporation established as the corporate instrument of an unincorporated association with the members of the association directly selecting the members of the Corporate Board and having ultimate authority over all corporate assets (The Woodland Community Development Corporation of the Woodland Neighborhood Association).

5. A nonprofit corporation established under the laws of a particular state at the initiative of a unit of government with an autonomous policy Board that has direct control of an operating budget and appoints an administrator, with the Board often being appointed under procedures established by the initiating governmental body to ensure representation of specific constituencies (Jones City Community Action Agency, Mid-Valley Senior Citizens Center).

6. A public authority or commission, with an autonomous policy body which controls a budget and appoints an administrator, with the policy body directly appointed by a governmental body or public official (State Youth Authority, Smithville Municipal Hospital Board).

7. A joint powers authority established by two or more governmental bodies to carry out activities on behalf of all of them with appointments of the policy board and the administrator subject to approval by the participating bodies (City-County Park Board, Mountain Top Special Education Cooperative).

8. A special purpose authority, or district with independent taxing authority and an independently elected Board, with authority to appoint an administrator (Ridgeway Independent School District).

9. An administrative unit of general purpose government with an administrator directly accountable to an elected public official or to a legislative body, and with limited control over the level of its own budget (Jones County Public Health Department, River City Recreation Department).

Sources of Core Funding: Nongovernmental or Governmental

The other major element in the definition of auspices is the source of *core funding*, other than fees for service. Core funding is the source of funding for those core administrative functions which are most essential for organizational continuity. Core funding, therefore, represents an ultimate source of organizational control. Core funding is not necessarily the largest element of funding, but it is that element of funding which is most directly linked to legitimation and accountability. A loss of core funding may be linked to a loss of legitimation, in comparison to *program funding*, the loss of which primarily involves a cut-back in the scope of program activities. The loss of core funding may require that the organization develop a new structure of legitimation, in addition to replacement of the lost funds.

Core funding that is not primarily fee-for-service payments consists of either contributions or tax funds. Both are forms of one-way transfers, or "grants," one voluntary, the other mandated by governmental decision (Boulding 1973). Even though both contributions and tax payments for support of human service programs are defined as one-way transfers, rather than as a form of economic exchange, they are normally conditioned by an expectation that there will be some form of collective benefit to the general public, including contributors and taxpayers, as well as private benefits to individual service users. That is, there is an expectation that both *public goods* and *private goods* will be produced as a result of the use of resources in the operation of the organization (see Chapter 9).

The traditional image of both contributions and tax funding for human services is that of funds raised in a local community that are used to finance services in the same community. The reality in both instances is more complex. Taxes are increasingly collected at one level of government and allocated for use at another level. Similarly many voluntary fundraising campaigns raise funds on a nationwide basis, for example through telethons, or through a nationally organized system of simultaneous campaigns in every local community, but the percent of the funds raised in a local community that remains in that community is determined at a national level. Thus there may be a substantial degree of geographic redistribution in the allocation of either tax funds or voluntary contributions, that is, funds raised in one community may be spent in a different community.

The variations in funding patterns also involve differences in the pattern of linkage between the funder (contributor or taxpayer) and the activity being funded. At one end of the continuum are specific contributions by a small group of individuals which are designated to be used for a very specific purpose defined by the contributors. At the other end of the continuum are general tax revenues which come from the entire community and are designated for very general purposes with very diffuse accountability.

The continuum of patterns of core funding, other than fee-for-service payments, which parallels the variations in legal structure, as indicated in Figure 8-1, includes the following:

1. Core funding through voluntary contributions from a single individual, corporation or association.
2. Core funding through grants or contributions from a single foundation.
3. Core funding from endowment representing past contributions from a limited number of donors.
4. Core funding from a small number of individuals or corporations directly solicited by the organization.
5. Core funding from a community-wide fundraising activity carried out by the service producing organization.
6. Core funding from participation in a community-wide fundraising campaign carried out by a separate fundraising organization (United Way).
7. Core funding by an unrestricted grant of funds from a governmental body.
8. Core funding by operating grants or demonstration grants designated for a specific purpose from a governmental body.
9. Core funding through a purchase of service contract from a governmental body.
10. Core funding through taxes levied by a special purpose district or authority for its own general operational purposes.
11. Core funding through allocations from a single general purpose legislative body.
12. Core funding of a local governmental agency through legislated allocations, or entitlements, from a general purpose government at another level of government.

The two elements of legal structure, and source of core funding, can be combined into a single continuum of accountability structures (Figure 8-1). This continuum ranges from organizations in which the policy unit, and, at least indirectly, the administrator, is accountable only to a small, self-defined constituency of direct contributors, to organizations in which the policy unit, and the administrator, are accountable through legal structure and funding mechanisms to very broad and inclusive political constituencies.

In theory the traditional governmental organization is more "political" in its pattern of accountability than the independent nonprofit corporation. In actual practice, however, governmental service organizations may be strongly buffered against direct political control by a variety of legislative provisions. On the other hand, the voluntary nonprofit organization may be subject to manipulative control by dominant political forces in the community through the direct participation of politically active persons on the board of directors, or through their influence on individuals who are on the board.

While the two ends of the continuum represent traditional organizations with distinctly different accountability structures, it is the *mixed types* involving a combination of the legal form of the nonprofit corporation and various forms and degrees of governmental funding which have become increasingly prevalent (Bendick 1985; Gilbert 1983; Kramer 1985; Starr 1985). In the instance of mixed type organizations there are often multiple, and frequently conflicting, patterns of accountability, based on differences between legal structure and core funding source. In these situations a key function of strategic management may be to deal with, or to develop procedures to resolve, such conflicting pressures.

SERVICE-GENERATED FEE INCOME

Income from service fees has traditionally been a minor element in the funding of either voluntary nonprofit or governmental service organizations. In general, it has been held that activities that show the potential of being economically self-supporting through payments for service should be in the private marketplace sector. Two developments, however, have resulted in the growth of service generated income in both voluntary nonprofit and governmental organizations. This process can be described as the "commercialization" of public service organizations (Gilbert 1985; Reichert 1977). First, organizations with established facilities and a reputation of professional competence have expanded their services into middle-income markets that had previously been underserved by private market provision. Among others these include nonprofit hospitals, family and individual counseling agencies, home nursing services and adoption agencies. When funding through contribution sources was too limited to support such expanded services, organizational income was often increased by establishing a sliding scale system of service fees. Similar patterns have emerged in charges for certain types of recreational activities in park and recreation departments under local governments. Having developed significant fee income, the design of the services produced by these organizations, and the marketing methods used to promote their use, have been modified to take advantage of these potential sources of income.

Second, the establishment of group insurance programs, prepayment systems or capitation programs, and other forms of third party or indirect reimbursement, has made it possible for many voluntary nonprofit and governmental service organizations, particularly in the health services field, to shift from contributions or governmental allocations as the source of core funding to a predominantly fee-for-service income pattern.[2]

One consequence of the group insurance arrangements and third party payment provisions is that the level of organizational income then tracks the level of service production, rather than service production levels being adjusted to a fixed level of contributions or of tax fund allocations.

The ratio of fee-for-service payments, both direct and from third party sources, to production costs in either nonprofit organizations or governmental organizations may become high enough to indicate the possibility of an entrepreneurial level of return from aggressive expansion of service production. These organizations may then find themselves in a position of actively competing with private market producers, for example in the hospital, home health, recreation and day care fields.

The role of the service users in defining the content of the service produced may be strengthened when a substantial part of the total organizational budget comes from service related income. Individuals paying a direct fee may be able to negotiate specific service conditions, complain when service does not meet required or desired standards, and may be able to take their business to a competing organization. The third-party, fee-paying organization may also serve as an advocate for consumers, on its own initiative through regular inspections, or through follow-up on specific complaints. However, the degree to which this is likely to occur is affected by the degree to which the third-party payment mechanism is controlled by interest groups other than users, as for example in the dominant role of hospital board members in the control of Blue Cross organizations, or the control by legislative bodies over the Medicare and Medicaid systems.

The over-all effect of an increase in the role of fee-for-service payments in the total budget is a shift of organizational accountability in the direction of user constituencies, and away from the special interests of funding contributors, or the "public interest" concerns of a legislative body. This, in turn, creates an additionally complex accountability situation for the administrator, who is subject both to "policy" inputs from traditional funding sources, voluntary or governmental, and to "marketplace" pressures from users, or organized user constituencies, such as the Grey Panthers.

ANALYSIS BY AUSPICE AND LEVEL OF FEE-FOR-SERVICE FUNDING

Figure 8-2 combines the auspice pattern with the level of fee-for-service income dimension to create an analytic matrix of alternative accountability structures. There are certain "pure" types of organizations which fall outside the matrix at each corner. The pure *voluntary supported-by-contributions organization* is the unincorporated membership association in which the members voluntarily contribute funds which are then used in their entirety to provide benefits for the members. The pure *voluntary income-from-payments* organization is the cooperative in which the organization is supported by

Figure 8-2. Accountability Structure

		Auspice				*Federal National Level Activity Only*
Service Payments as Proportion of Core Funding	*Unincorporated Private Association*	Narrowly Defined Private Constituency	Voluntary Nonprofit Government Grant	Government Nonprofit	General Purpose Government	
Low		Southside Community Center funded by B.J. Smith Machinery, Inc.	Lutheran Social Services with AOA Grant for Elderly Information and Referral and Day Care	Garcia County Community Action Agency	Owens County Social Services	
Third Party Payments Medium to High		St. Theresa Hospital funded by Catholic Diocese, Medicaid, Medicare and Blue Cross payments	Valley City Visiting Nurse Association funded by Title XX Contract, United Way and Medicaid	River County Community Mental Health Center	City of Lakeview Municipal Hospital	
Direct Payments Medium to High		Mount City Adoption Agency	Smithville Community Day Care Services with 20% Title XX slots and the balance sliding scale fees	Oak Hill Community College	Westview Municipal Golf Course	
Producer Cooperative with Services for Members Only					Municipal Water System (fees pay costs and capital investment)	

payments from the members for services provided to them, with the members also being the governing constituency.

The pure *governmental tax-supported service organization* is one, like the military, that provides an indivisible public good on a nationwide basis, supported by taxes which are assessed on a nationwide basis. A pure *governmental income-from-services organization* is the municipal water system which pays for capital and operating costs from consumer fees but is accountable to all the members of the community through the structure of local government.

While these four pure types represent relatively clear-cut administrative contexts, the other cells reflect to varying degrees the mix of legal auspice and funding patterns that actually exist within human services industries. Each cell in the matrix represents a different configuration of accountability imperatives and therefore a different set of political economy pressures with which an administrator must cope.

This analytic system does not deal with the dimension of regulatory authority, which can introduce an additional element of complexity in the political economy environment of "mixed economy" human services industries. Regulatory authority can involve a governmental body at one level of government exercising regulatory control over human service production activities in other governmental agencies at the same level, or at other governmental levels, as well as regulatory control over voluntary nonprofit and for-profit organizations. It can also involve industry level regulation through "voluntary" accreditation or certification bodies which may exercise varying degrees of quality control over governmental and voluntary nonprofit organizations, as well as over for-profit production organizations.

FOR-PROFIT CORPORATIONS

There has been an increasing diversity of for-profit corporations producing human services during the past two decades (Gilbert 1985). The pattern varies markedly among human service industries with for-profit firms having a very small role in service production in elementary and secondary education, but an increasingly large role in health care and mental health services. Moreover, for-profit organizations have very large roles as suppliers in all human service programs, for example text-books in elementary and secondary education. For-profit organizations are, therefore, significant participants at the industry level in every type of human service industry.

The proper role of for-profit organizations in human services industries has been argued extensively on normative and ideological grounds (Brooks, Liebman and Schelling 1984). However, it is important to examine the position of such organizations within human service industries analytically. It is possible to identify organizational patterns among for-profit human service production organizations that parallel the accountability structure patterns described above for voluntary nonprofit and governmental organizations. On one hand there are for-profit corporations accountable to a small, self-defined "owner" constituency, including small, family owned corporations and group professional practices in which the corporate officers are also the major stockholders. These organizations have a number of similarities to the small free-standing voluntary nonprofit corporation in which members of the board are also the major financial contributors.[3]

At the other extreme are for-profit corporate giants, particularly in the health care field, with a large, and dispersed, stockholder group in which the executives are employees who often own little or no stock. These for-profit firms have a number of similarities to the large governmental agency with a large and highly dispersed taxpayer constituency.

Also consistent with the accountability structure analysis presented in Figure 8-2, there are for-profit human service firms that are funded largely by lump-sum grants or contracts from governmental bodies and, on the other hand, for-profit organizations in which core funding comes primarily from either third-party reimbursements or from direct payments by service consumers. Every type of voluntary nonprofit or governmental organization structure has a counterpart structure among for-profit firms. Thus, the external political economy patterns with which the for-profit administrator may have to deal are similar in many ways to those faced by administrators in voluntary nonprofit and governmental organizations.

Technically any human service which can be produced by a nonprofit organization or a governmental agency can be produced by a for-profit organization. The technologies involved in such production, whether they are related to education, health care or social services, can be implemented under all possible types of organizational structures. However, there are important differences between the for-profit firm and voluntary, nonprofit organizations and governmental organizations, specifically in the *governance structure and the internal political economy*. These differences exist in some degree in connection with every type of for-profit corporation, but they are likely to be most pronounced in the instance of the large, conglomerate for-profit firm which has multiple operating components, receives most of its income from fee-for-service payments, and has a highly dispersed stockholder constitutency. These differences, while they may not have a direct impact on production technology, may have important consequences for both program management and strategic planning in the for-profit firm.

One critical difference lies in the nature of the relationship of the service production organization to the stockholder/owner constituency. Under the concept of private property "ownership" the stockholders collectively have a legally enforceable right to ultimate authority over the corporation and all of its assets. Moreover, the stockholder relation to the for-profit firm is defined as being legitimately motivated by individual economic self-interest. The stockholder's primary interest is focused on the level of financial return received for a financial investment. The degree of influence in the corporation of any one stockholder is expected to be roughly proportional to the size of the ownership share, so that large stockholders have a right to have a large voice in policy decisions.

This is distinctly different from the relation of individual contributors to the nonprofit organization or the individual taxpayer to the governmental human service agency. In both types of organizations neither contributors nor taxpayers have individual ownership rights, and the level of their financial participation has no direct relationship to their official influence within the service production organization.

The unique elements in the relation of the stockholder constituency to the for-profit firm have distinctive consequences for the accountability demands on the administrator. First, the expectation of "profit" or entrepreneurial return to the individual stockholders on their investment has no specific limits. More profit is better. In the instance of both voluntary nonprofit and governmental organizations there is a "break-even" "balance-the-budget" financial management expectation, which under conditions of reduced resources can lead to reductions in both quality and quantity of service production and/or reductions in the financial benefits to staff personnel. However, the authorized budget provides an explicit target for the financial management of the organization. There is not normally an expectation of, nor reward for, year-end surpluses at the expense of service production in the nonprofit organization, or "turned-back" funds with reduced services in the instance of the governmental agency. Service production goals drive the organization, rather than level-of-profit goals.

In the instance of the for-profit firm the stockholders are the only constituency explicitly represented on the board of directors, and the formal definition of accountability of the board of directors is to the stockholders above any other constituency. In turn, the executive is considered to be directly and exclusively accountable to the board. Under these conditions stockholder dividends, or long term appreciation of stock values, may be defined as the major criteria of successful administration, and any use of resources which would have a negative effect on stockholder return, therefore, would require explicit policy authorization.

Moreover, given the primary accountability of the executive for the level of return to stockholders, the power of the executive is most likely to be greater than the power of professional specialists in the production activities of the organization. When the criteria for defining the quality of outcomes are "soft," as in the instance of many human service programs (Hasenfeld 1983), or the evaluation of true outcomes is possible only after a substantial period of time, program evaluation or service user "feedback" may have little impact on corporate policymaking.

This pattern of limited accountability either to the general public or to service users may have limited impact on either the quality or quantity of services produced, under conditions of ample resources when a significant level of profit is available for the stockholders, comparable to the return available from other investments. Under such circumstances the for-profit firm may provide direct services, or "private goods," to the service user which are similar in quality and quantity to those provided by voluntary nonprofit or governmental service organizations, or even better. However, under conditions of stringent resources when an effort is made to maintain, or increase, the level of financial returns to stockholders in spite of a decrease in service-generated income, there may be a substantial impact on both quality and quantity of services in the for-profit firm.

The most fundamental distinction between the for-profit organization and voluntary nonprofit and governmental organizations is the absence of any official rationale for corporate policies in support of organizational activities which are intended to produce "public goods" rather than "private goods." In the instance of voluntary nonprofit and governmental service organizations there is an explicit expectation that the interests of contributors and taxpayers include the production of a collective or "public good" benefit in addition to any direct personal benefits which may accrue to either an individual contributor or individual taxpayer because a particular service is available. In the instance of the voluntary nonprofit organization the organizational charter or by-laws normally identifies benefits that are intended to be realized from the work of the organization that will help the whole community. The legitimacy of these objectives is recognized in federal law in the special tax status of "charitable" nonprofit organizations. In the instance of governmental agencies the enabling legislation normally sets forth a similar statement of purpose.

Thus the governing body of the voluntary nonprofit or governmental hospital is considered to be acting legitimately if it establishes a "redistributive" policy which provides for members of the medical staff to contribute certain levels of voluntary service to meet the medical needs of children and expectant mothers in medically-indigent families, and provides for the use of organizational personnel and resources to support such volunteered services. In addition to the "private goods" benefits to the individuals receiving the medical services such a policy may be viewed as contributing to the general level of health among all children in the community, and a reduction in community costs from contagious disease and from long term disabilities resulting from premature birth. It may also be justified as contributing to the perceived "quality-of-life" in the community as a whole. Such a policy may, in the long run, also have positive financial benefits for the hospital in that it may result in an increase in the level of voluntary contributions, or in the level of tax support provided for the hospital operation, although that is not the reason for undertaking the program.

On the other hand, the governing body of the for-profit hospital has no rationale for adopting such a policy, or for authorizing an administrator to implement such a policy, even if the out-of-pocket costs are limited, if the net effect is to reduce the return to stockholders. Where such a policy decision might, in fact, be made if stockholder/owners are members of the local community, it is particularly unlikely to be made if the same hospital is part of a large conglomerate in which neither the administrative staff nor any sizeable part of the thousands of stockholders have any "communal" linkages to the community of service. Similarly there is no rationale for the for-profit firm to use organizational resources for the education of technical and professional personnel over-and-beyond those who may be trainee employees of the organization, for providing for the participation of organizational personnel in the development of a communitywide preventive public education project or in the organization of a social policy advocacy coalition, or for the use of organizational resources in support of basic research.

In the production of direct services there is no rationale for the for-profit firm which might justify costs that would be involved in production of services which might have long-term community benefits over and beyond the benefits to the immediate service user. This would apply to the inclusion of human relations content in for-profit day care programs with the long-term objective of reducing ethnic group hostilities in the community, or the provision of staff support for the organization of volunteer service projects among residents in a congregate housing development.

Emphasis has been placed on the potential ability of the for-profit firm to provide specific services at a lower cost than public service organizations. In some instances this may be related to a more effective management of financial resources and to unit cost savings resulting from the efficiencies of a large scale operation. But it is also possible that the reduced costs are primarily a result of eliminating, as far as possible, any costs associated with the production of public good benefits, either as a specific corporate policy, or through the absence of policies that would support such activities.

Moreover, in using a "closed system" model of the firm expenditures associated with interorganizational linkage and network activities which may be important for continuity of service for all service users, but which cannot be assigned as a cost to any single individual service consumer, may be eliminated. Similar responses may also take place in nonprofit organizations when very explicit cost constraints are imposed, as in the instance of the use of Diagnostic Related Groups (DRG's) to define cost reimbursement to hospitals.

One further characteristic related to the role of stockholder owners distinguishes for-profit firms from voluntary nonprofit organizations. The legal existence of the for-profit firm and the ownership rights of the stockholders are independent of any specific service production activity. It is legitimate, and expected, that the for-profit firm will withdraw its assets from "unprofitable" activities if these activities have a consistently negative impact on return to stockholders, and that, in turn, the assets of the firm will be applied to an entirely different type of activity which is more profitable.

Financial manipulations, or "paper entrepreneurship" involving corporate assets (Reich 1983), which have positive financial outcomes for stockholders and / or executives, are considered legitimate business activities even if they have negative consequences for service production activities in a given location. The indirect or "external" consequences of closing a service facility on the service users, their families or the local community, are not a relevant consideration in making such a policy decision. That is, the corporate firm, *as a legal entity,* would not experience the effects of such external consequences, even though individual executives and other employees may have negative experiences. On the other hand, the legitimation of voluntary nonprofit organizations and government service organizations is normally linked directly to the production of a particular type of service and to the impact of its availability in a particular location. There might well be direct consequences for the continued existence of the organization if services are withdrawn in a particular location.

Within any specific field of service, the rational action of individual for-profit firms is to concentrate in those areas of service production in which there is the most consistent and substantial financial return, and to avoid those areas in which there is minimal or uncertain return. The large-scale corporate conglomerate has the greatest flexibility in shifting resources consistent with such objectives. If for-profit firms are part of a mix of organizational types, the industry wide consequences of such a concentration may be limited. However, if a human service industry is dominated by large-scale for-profit firms, then substantial gaps in the pattern of service provision may result even when the overall level of service production is relatively high.

For example, in the community with a mix of hospital auspices, including one for-profit hospital, and with a limited number of medically indigent families, voluntary and flexible arrangements as part of a "communal" system of informal redistribution may be sufficient to meet the needs of such families for hospital services, even if the for-profit hospital does not participate. In such a community where the only hospital facilities available are part of large for-profit conglomerates, it may be necessary to create a formal medical assistance program with detailed policies and an administrative staff to insure the provision of essential hospital care services for even a very few families.

SUMMARY

Contemporary human service industries include a wide diversity of for-profit firms, governmental service organizations and voluntary nonprofit corporations. Mixed auspice organizational structures are very prevalent.

Differences among these organizations can be analyzed along a series of structural dimensions. Among voluntary nonprofit and governmental organizations one dimension involves the combination of legal auspice and source of core funding. A second dimension among such organizations involves the proportion of fee-for-service payments in the total budget.

A similar pattern of variations can be identified among for-profit human service firms. However, there are also significant differences between voluntary nonprofit and governmental organizations of all types, and for-profit firms. These differences are primarily related to the role of the stockholder/owner constituency in the governance of the for-profit firm which, in turn, affects the policy decisions within the firm dealing with the production of "public goods" benefits as well as "private good" benefits. In the production of services for the individual consumer the for-profit firm may be as effective as any nonprofit corporation or governmental service organization, and under some circumstances it may be more efficient. However, there is no clear-cut organizational rationale for the for-profit firm to adopt policies which support the production of "public goods" in conjunction with its production of "private goods."

The most important consequences of the differences between voluntary nonprofit and governmental organizations, and for-profit firms, may be related to the role of for-profit firms within an industry structure. In a human service industry in which a limited number of small for-profit firms exist as a part of a diverse mix of service organizations, the characteristics of the political economy of policymaking in the for-profit firms may be quite similar to that of other organizations in the industry. The industry as a whole may be involved in the production of public good benefits as well as private goods. However, if a human services industry is dominated by large-scale for-profit firms which, in turn, control industry level structures, the political economy context may be very different with much less emphasis on the production of public good benefits, unless explicit provision is made for governmental funding to for-profit firms to produce such public good benefits, for example, the development and maintenance of a nationwide network for matching organ donors and organ recipients.

NOTES

1. Some economic analyses view the existence of both voluntary nonprofit and governmental service organizations as problematic exceptions in a marketplace capitalist economy (Rose-Ackerman 1986).

2. Annual family membership payments in organizations like the YMCA, YWCA and Jewish Community Centers are, in effect, a prepayment system similar to the prepaid Health Maintenance Organization.

3. There are also in the for-profit production sector of human service industries single person private practitioners with a single person functioning as owner, administrator, and professional specialist, with which this analysis does not deal.

Chapter 9

Comparative Analysis of Human Service Programs by Societal Function

PUBLIC GOODS, PRIVATE GOODS AND MIXED GOODS

A second analytic system is based on the societal function of the program outputs of voluntary nonprofit and governmental service organizations. These organizations are based on collective initiation of action, either as a voluntary activity by a group of individuals, or as a collective decision made through the legislative processes of government. The personal motivations reflected in the initiation of such collective action may be described variously as religious conviction, philanthrophy, altruism, charity, enlightened individual self-interest or social consciousness. But in each instance in which there is collective action to initiate the production of services there is an expectation that there will be some form of "social profit," or collective benefit, in addition to the direct benefits for the service users (Boulding 1973).

The collective benefits, or "public goods," that are expected to result from such services are available to all members of the social unit, not just to the individual contributors or taxpayers who provide the actual financial support for the production of the human service output (Olson 1968).[1] The "public good" consequences of such collective action may have an impact on persons who disapprove of such action, as well as on those who support it.

Economists, in general, restrict the term "public good" to those goods which are universally available and nonexcludable (Musgrave 1959; Olson 1968). When the benefits from the good are available to one person they are available to everyone, and the use or enjoyment of the good by one person does not decrease the availability of the good for others, for example the availability of unpolluted air to breath. Since such a public good cannot be divided into separate portions, and it is not possible to exclude anyone from enjoyment of the good, it is impossible to charge individuals a fee for utilization of the good, once it is available. From the perspective of most traditional economic analyses collective, or non-marketplace, production is logical only in the instance of such "pure" public goods (Olson 1968). From this perspective marketplace supply and demand exhange transactions are the logical form of production and distribution of all other economic goods. Collective action to produce any product other than a "pure" public good through either voluntary nonprofit organizations or governmental organizations, is viewed as problematic, requiring special explanations (Rose-Ackerman 1986).

However, in the discussion which follows it is assumed that collective production of a service, through either a voluntary organization or a governmental organization, may take place whenever there is a mixture of benefits which result from the production of a particular service, that is a combination of both "private goods" or discrete benefits to individuals, and "public goods," and there is a community of interest or constituency which identifies with and seeks the public good element in such "mixed goods"(Austin 1981). The choice to use a collective, or cooperative, form of action, rather than the marketplace, to produce such "mixed goods" is rooted in the nature of non-marketplace communal social structures, in particular the family, the friendship group, the communal neighborhood and the village (Hillery 1968). Within these social structures cooperative action is as common as marketplace exchanges. Such cooperative action is used to produce goods and services which both benefit particular individuals and strengthen communal bonds.

For example, given the strong conviction in most American communities about the common or collective benefits to be realized from an educated citizenry and a literate and skilled labor force, the production of elementary and secondary educational services through governmental action at a community level, rather than reliance on a system of privately purchased education, is not problematic. In communities where such convictions are not strong, local support for public education is likely to be minimal. In fact, public schools may only exist in such communities because there are convictions on a state-wide basis about the potential public good benefits, together with a recognition within the state-wide community that the absence of education in one community may have important future consequences or spill-over effects for other communities. Similar motivations support cooperative action in various forms to insure the provision of hospital care and to provide substitute care for children who have lost their biological parents.

The nature of the public good element in the production of any particular human service is related to the nature of actual program outputs, rather than to formal statements of program goals. The program goals identified with the process of original program creation, for example the statement of goals embodied in the preamble to enabling legislation, is often a documentation of the ambiguous compromises which have resulted from efforts to resolve conflicts among the interest groups and constituencies that supported the establishment of the program. Characteristics of actual program outputs are more explicit and consistent than program goal statements, and are therefore more relevant for analysis of the societal function of particular forms of service production.

The collective benefits resulting from program outputs can take several different forms. These differences have important consequences because it is the nature of the "public good" benefits which primarily determines the criteria on which program performance is judged by those who legitimate and fund a particular form of service production. These collective benefit criteria exist over and beyond the criteria used to judge the technical quality of the specific benefits provided to the service users or the degree of satisfaction experienced by service users. Since these public good criteria are linked to the original motivations for collective action to initiate the service, they are likely to be significant factors in the public assessment of administrative performance, and in determining the continuation of legitimation and funding.

These public good criteria are particularly significant when there is a direct and immediate linkage between the sources of sponsorship and funding, and program operation, for example when the initiators of a service are also the major voluntary contributors to the program and sit on the policy board. Or when the initiators of a governmental program include members of the legislative body that has oversight responsibility for a particular service program for which tax funding is specifically earmarked. The public good criteria are less controlling when financial support is part of a general appropriation and comes from general and diffuse sources, and the initiators are not part of the oversight and accountability structure. The public good criteria are of least significance when core funding comes primarily from direct payments by service consumers for the service they have received, whether that service is provided by a voluntary nonprofit organization or a governmental organization.

In this analysis of program function the unit of analysis is the program component (Hjern and Porter 1981). Most human service organizations produce a number of different service packages. The program component is that part of the organizational structure through which a particular service is produced. The nature of the public good benefits, and therefore the nature of the societal function, may vary as among the several program components within a single organization. A community mental health center may include such program components as an out-patient clinic open to the general public, a crisis center which provides services to individuals with chronic mental illness conditions, an alcoholism counseling program and a drug-addiction methadone program. A governmental child welfare agency may include separate program components for investigative services, follow-up services to natural families, foster-home placement and on-going supervision, and adoption services.

Each program component will normally have a unit or component administrator, a program unit budget, specialized staff personnel, a distinctive technology, and a specific work area within the physical facilities of the administrative organization. Program components will often have a specialized source of funding and deal with a particular service constitutency.

The societal function analysis deals with the nature of the public good benefits which result from the production of services by individual program components in both voluntary nonprofit organizations and governmental organizations. In principle, any of the various forms of human service production, including health care, education and social services, could be provided under either voluntary nonprofit auspices, or governmental auspices. In practice some types of services are more likely to be provided under governmental auspices than under voluntary auspices. But examples of both voluntary nonprofit and governmental sponsorship can be found of each type of program dealt with in this analytic system.

The production of services by for-profit firms may also have public good characteristics, in particular where the funding for such services comes through a contract from a governmental agency underwriting the total annual operation of a specialized program component. However, as indicated in the preceding chapter, for-profit firms will normally seek to minimize the use of resources for public good production unless the costs involved can be recovered through add-on charges to individual service consumers or through third party payment systems. For example, hospitals have traditionally met the costs of providing redistributive free or low-cost care for low income patients by adding to the charges for higher income patients.

There are three major distinctions in this analytic system. First, there is a distinction between those services which result in benefits that fit the traditional economic definition of public goods, the benefits are *indivisible* and available to everyone, in contrast to those "mixed good" services which result in benefits that are *divisible*, that is that have discrete benefits for specific service consumers, as well as public good benefits.

Second, there is a distinction between divisible services which are, in principle, *universal*, available to everyone, in contrast to those divisible services which are selective, or *categorical*, available only to particular categories of individuals or households, although sponsorship and funding comes from the community or society at large.

Third, there is a distinction between those categorical service programs which result in a public good benefit through the provision of *basic necessities* (income, food, housing or medical care), those service programs which result in a public good benefit through the provision of *remedial, rehabilitative,*

Figure 9-1. Functional Classification of Human Service
Program Components

I. Indivisible Services
  A. Protection Services
  B. Emergency and Hazard Services
  C. Common Facilities

II. Universal Divisble Services
  A. Intellectual, Religious, Cultural, Skill Development Services
  B. Standard of Living Services
  C. Quality of Life Services
  D. Primary Prevention-Health/ Mental Health Services
  E. Conflict Resolution Services
  F. Economic Development Services

III. Categorical Divisible Services
  A. Basic Necessity Services
    1. Income Provision
    2. Food Provision
    3. Housing Provision
    4. Medical Care Provision
  B. Remedial, Rehabilitative, Curative, Social Care, Deviance Control Services
  C. Employment Support Services

IV. Facilitative and Support Services
  A. Facilitative Services
  B. Secondary Support Services
  C. Tertiary Support Services
  D. Industry Level Services

---

curative, social care or deviance control services, and those service programs which result in a public good benefit through the provision of *employment support services.*

The combination of these three levels of analysis, together with a category of *facilitative and support services* results in the societal function analytic framework set forth in Figure 9-1. This chapter deals with *indivisible services*, and with *universal, divisible services.* Chapter 10, in turn, deals with *categorical, divisible services,* as well as *facilitative* and *support services.* In the following sections major concepts associated with each program category are identified which have distinctive implications for the political economy context of voluntary nonprofit and governmental service organizations. Specific attention is given to the pattern of *auspices, legitimation,* and the criteria for *evaluation,* for each major category.

INDIVISIBLE SERVICES

The collective, or public good, benefits provided by *indivisible services* most nearly fit the limited definition of "public good" generally used by economists. This is a benefit which, if produced for one individual will be wholly available to all other members of the social unit. If only a single individual, or small group of individuals, meets the costs for such benefits, for example, police patrol services, there is a high likelihood of "free-loaders" who may receive the collective benefits of the services without sharing in the cost because of spillover, or externalization of benefits (Olson 1968). Since there is little economic incentive for individuals to pay voluntarily for benefits they would receive anyway as a member of society, it is necessary to assess the costs of producing indivisible public goods across the entire community, with community sanctions used, if necessary, to compel universal participation in the payment of those costs. This is the basic rationale for systems of taxation. The basic structure of democratic government originally emerged around the process of collective decisionmaking required to impose taxes, with "the consent of the governed," to support the production of indivisible, collectively consumed public goods. Although some of these services do not fit within traditional definitions of "human services" they are included to illustrate the full dimensions of the analytic framework. Moreover, many of these services are important elements of the social environment, and therefore of the "standard of living" available to individuals and families.

Services

Three major types of service programs which result in indivisible public goods can be identified. To varying degrees there may also be some direct individual benefits from these services, but the primary rationale for creating the service is the indivisible public good.

Protection Services. The most fundamental indivisible public goods are those services which are part of the concept of "common protection." These services include: provisions for national defense; the maintenance of internal law and order, including the police patrol services and the criminal courts; public health protection against the spread of disease; mental health primary prevention initiatives directed against societal conditions which may result in mental illness; fire prevention services; the creation of, and protection of, a system of currency (which is a form of universal protection of the value of economic assets); weather reporting services; protection of air quality; and protection of water quality in large bodies of water.

Among the more controversial areas of common protection services are those related to the "protection" of a "healthy economy," such as the Federal Reserve Board and the Securities and Exchange Commission, with arguments, on one hand, that such services are an appropriate and explicit function of government, and arguments, on the other hand, that a healthy economy is a function of "natural processes" which should not be the object of any deliberate interventive action.

Since the measure of protection is the nonoccurrence of events and conditions, a result which in general cannot be measured, the actual form of public good benefit which is shared by all members of the community is the feeling of reassurance and personal security which results from the existence of the system of protection, and the general benefit which results if the protective service is actually needed. Single individuals, or families, are not the objects of specific service activities—the purity of the air is not protected by protecting the air in individual homes, fire departments do not provide fire prevention materials to individual homes, and national defense does not provide anti-aircraft guns for individual neighborhoods. However, since some forms of protection services may involve constraints on the actions of particular individuals, or business firms, for example restrictions on smoking in public areas, they may be resisted on the grounds that the service is actually a form of social control imposed by one group of citizens on another group of citizens, rather than an indivisible "public good."

Emergency and Hazard Services. Another form of indivisible, collectively consumed services involves the availability of assistance in the case of emergencies or the existence of hazardous conditions. Examples of such services include the fire fighting services, emergency medical services, child welfare protective service investigations of child abuse or neglect, adult protective service investigations of abuse or neglect of older adults, police responses to a specific attack against an individual or against property, epidemic immunization programs and civil defense/catastrophe services.

These services are different from the general protection services in that some beneficial services are provided directly to particular individuals. But the indivisible public good benefit which results from the security of having dependable services available to all persons, at all times, without regard to the costs of such assistance in a specific situation is the basis for the collective action creating and supporting such services. The existence of universal emergency services, for example firefighting services, may be regarded as a "right" which is part of the benefits associated with owning property in, or living in, a given community.

Common Facilities. A third form of indivisible services involves the provision of those common facilities which are available for use by everyone, or which provide common benefits, without payment of fees and without distinction as to the residential location or taxpayer status of the individual user. These facilities available for general use include local streets, sidewalks, bridges, urban parks, and public meeting halls. While individuals benefit directly by their use of a particular facility, there is a shared public good benefit for all persons in a given area resulting from the availability of these facilities for their potential use.

Political Economy Characteristics

The political economy context of the program components through which these indivisible, collective benefit services are produced have certain characteristics in common.

Auspices. Indivisible public goods are most often provided by organizations established under governmental auspices in order to be able to invoke the coercive power of government, if necessary, to compel participation in the costs of such services through taxation by everyone who shares in the benefits. Similarly, the coercive powers of government may be used to enforce controls required as part of a protection services program. Many *protection services* are established, and funded, at a broad and inclusive level of government because of the spill-over effects if a smaller geographic unit is used. National defense is organized as a national activity rather than state-by-state. If one state bears the full cost of protecting water quality in the Great Lakes, residents in other states bordering on the lakes benefit without paying. Other protection services like routine police patrols and fire protection activities which do not substantially benefit persons outside of the immediate service area are more often organized and funded on a smaller area basis (Ostrom, Parks and Whitaker 1978).

The establishment of any particular type of *emergency service* through governmental action is a deliberate political choice. In many societies such services are available only through individual or family action. However, in an urbanized, high technology society, the level of potential hazard, the high cost of not having emergency services—death, and relatively low per capita cost of having such services universally available, have led to a wide-spread pattern of public *provision* of such services. In some instances the actual *production* of such services, for example, emergency medical services, may be contracted for from a nonprofit organization or for-profit firm (Ostrom and Ostrom 1978).

Some emergency services, on the other hand, are produced through a community volunteer organization—emergency medical services and fire-fighting, for example. This is likely to occur when: (1) the costs are low because of infrequent emergencies and the availability of volunteers; (2) there is a broadly based pattern of financial contributions from the community; and (3) those who may not contribute either time or money, but receive the benefit of services anyway, are defined as part of the community, that is as part of "us." When a substantial number of persons who receive the benefits from such volunteer services do not contribute either money or time, and are not viewed as traditional members of the community, the volunteer service is likely to disappear or to be changed to a governmental, tax-supported program with a geographic taxing base large enough to include all households expecting to benefit from the services.

The third type of universal, indivisible services, those provided through *common facilities* are also likely to be built through governmental action and to be operated and maintained by a governmental agency. But again there are, for example, community center facilities which are built and maintained on a volunteer basis.

In the case of those protection services which are organized on a small area basis, as well as most emergency services and common facilities, there are significant variations among local communities. These variations reflect different estimates of the degree of risk, or of the need for facilities, and differing judgements about the acceptable level of taxation for support of such services (Parks and Ostrom 1981). Differences in the level of indivisible services and the level of taxes required to support them are often factors in the choice of residential location by individual households, particularly within metropolitan areas.

Legitimation. The decision that there is a public good purpose which requires collective action through government is a political judgement by the members of the political constituency, or *polity*. There must be a broad consensus that there is a common benefit to be achieved, and that organizational action is essential to achieve it. Implicit in the action to create a protection service, or emergency service, or to build a common facility, is the levying of taxes to meet the costs. Since compliance with tax laws must be largely voluntary to be effective in a democracy, the decision to levy taxes for a particular public good purpose must reflect a substantial degree of consensus among the members of the polity. *Indeed, it is a broadly-based consensus about the compelling importance of the production of protection and emergency services, and public facilities, which sustains the largely voluntary pattern of tax payments for the support of all governmental activities.*

Evaluation. The evaluation of indivisible *protection services* is essentially a subjective evaluation by individuals as to whether the level of protection provided is consistent with their estimate of the level of risk. Since individuals cannot determine the actual extent to which they have been protected against cholera by a public health quarantine at the border, or that their business has been protected against a burglary by a routine police car patrol, such judgements are necessarily subjective.

In the instance of *emergency and harzard services* there can be both objective and subjective evaluations of the performance of the service personnel. Since the response of emergency services usually takes place under highly visible conditions, the evaluations are made both by the persons directly assisted and by everyone else who has an opportunity to observe.

However, the organizational components which produce protection services, emergency services and common facility services are not, in general, significantly accountable to the evaluation of individual users. In the instance of protection services and common use facilities the subjective judgements of a majority of the members of the polity expressed through the political system constitute the evaluation, particularly since most such services are funded primarily by a single level of government. In the instance of emergency services the individual receiving direct services cannot enforce personal accountability under conditions of emergency or hazard, so that for these services also the enforcement of accountability is through majority opinion, which includes, at most, only a few individuals who have actually received services.

However, recent Supreme Court decisions have supported the right of individuals to sue governmental bodies over the consequences of failures in the provision of adequate and safe services, for example in the maintenance of sidewalks and roads, as well as explicitly harmful actions. These decisions have significantly changed the political economy context of those governmental organizations producing indivisible, "public good" services.

The expression of public evaluations of particular services through the political process is, at best, a slow and indirect process (Porter and Warner 1973). The impact of negative evaluations may be diluted by the positive impact of other aspects of these activities including the provision of employment for local residents, and the letting of contracts for construction and for equipment. The service organizations involved in the production of indivisible "public good" services may also provide a variety of other valued services, over and above their core functions, for example, the sponsorship of youth athletic activities by police departments, the collection and repair of toys by fire departments, and the participation of military units in parades and civic festivals. Police patrol activities may be valued because they enforce, in addition to specific laws and ordinances, local social norms for the behavior of adolescents, the presence of strangers in residential areas, and acceptable limits on public intoxication.

The political expression of the evaluations of service quality may often be more responsive to judgements about these secondary activities than to judgements about the core functions. It is the pattern of judgements by the majority of citizens which is crucial in determining the level of funding for a particular service. The evaluations of members of nonmajority groups in the community, for example about the quality of police patrol services, may have little impact on the performance of the police organization, unless such evaluations can be reinforced through such instruments as the press, advocacy groups, or the courts. Administrators of these indivisible public good services are, in general, expected to be responsive to the criteria used by the community majority in evaluating these services. The use of other criteria by nonmajority interest groups whose power is reinforced by the press or the courts, may create a major conflict situation.

Summary

Protection services, emergency services and common use facilities are established primarily to provide indivisible collective benefits. Although individuals may receive certain direct benefits, the public good, and therefore the justification for collective action to create and maintain the service, derives from the commonality of availability for usage by all individuals in the social unit. These activities are almost always under the auspice of a particular unit of government, and, indeed, these services constitute the core functions of government. Such service activities, therefore, are likely to have a high priority for governmental funding if there is public consensus about "need," even when economic resources are scarce, regardless of whether there is objective evidence of their effectiveness. The steady increase in the size and number of jails and prisons, in spite of consistent evidence of their ineffectiveness in changing individual behavior and reducing the level of crime, is one example of the political economy dynamics of protection services.

UNIVERSAL, DIVISIBLE SERVICES

There are also collectively established services which produce goods which can be divided into a discrete number of separate units which are used, or consumed, by particular individuals or households. These *divisible services* result in a mixture of private benefits and collective or public good benefits, and therefore constitute a form of "mixed" economic goods. Similar services, which are not intended to have any explicit public benefit, are often available through the marketplace, or through membership associations which limit the access to such services to association members. The following discussion, however, deals with those services which are provided through some type of collective sponsorship, either voluntary or governmental, and are available to members of the general public.

Consistent with the mixed goods character of divisible services the financial costs of production may be met by varying combinations of fee-for-service payments, contributions and tax funds. Within the total range of human services which have this divisible "mixed goods" characteristic there are two major subcategories: (1) those that are *universal*, that is they are available, in principle, without restrictive eligibility requirements, although the quantity of services in any one location may be limited; and (2) those that are *categorical,* that is they are selectively targeted to particular categories of indivdiuals, households or communities, based on either redistribution objectives, or behavior change/social control objectives.

The collective, or public good, benefits which result from *universal, divisible* services take two forms. First, there is a collective benefit from the ready availability, or accessibility, of a particular service for everyone who might ever need such a service. The availability of the public school system means that families with children are relieved of the responsiblity of planning individually for the education of their children and for meeting the associated costs. In some instances the use of a divisible service by any one person may be only on an occasional or infrequent basis, for example, the use of the reference and research collection of a public library system. But there is a collective benefit from such a collection being available when it is needed.

Second, there is a collective benefit which is a spill-over from the utilization of these services by large numbers of individuals that occurs because they are universally available. For example, it has long been assumed that a democratic society functions best as an organized society, with increased benefits for all citizens, if all voters have a high level of education and personal development, and that a universally available public education system contributes to the creation of this public good. Universal divisible services include a wide range of different types of services produced by both voluntary nonprofit and governmental organizations. It is often difficult to make an arbitrary distinction among all of the different types of universal divisible services between "human services" and other types of services. To a substantial degree the diversity and quantity of universal divisible services is a measure of the standard of living generally available within a given community, or society, for all individuals and families.

Services

Intellectual, Religious, Cultural, Skill Development Services. These services include elementary and secondary education (which also has some of the characteristics of a behavior change/social control service because of the compulsory nature of participation), early childhood education including nursery schools, youth membership and character development organizations and a wide variety of other formal and informal education programs and personal development programs for all age groups. This category also includes religious worship services which are open to members of the general public who choose to participate (in contrast to those worship services which are explicitly limited to the membership of a particular religious body). It also includes developmental service programs for individuals with handicaps where these are open to any person with a handicap at the initiative of that person without restrictive eligibility requirements.

Standard of Living Services. These services include individually utilized services provided on a community-wide basis which are considered part of the standard infrastructure, or expected amenities of a modern, urbanized society. These include some services which are provided directly through collective action and some services which are provided through franchised and regulated for-profit utilities. Examples include water and wastewater services, electrical services, intercity highways, railroad systems, local telephone facilities, garbage and trash collection and public transit systems.

Quality of Life Services. These are services that are utilized individually on a voluntary, private initiative basis, primarily on a personal enjoyment basis. These include fiction/non-fiction library collections and circulation services, recreational sports facilities, craft and hobby facilities, museums, orchestras and other forms of nonprofit musical and dramatic performances, public radio and television broadcasts, community center social activities and public festivals and fairs.

Primary Prevention Health/Mental Health Services. These are services which directly affect the health of particular individuals, in contrast to those protection/prevention services described earlier which deal with the general environment. They include such services as: universally available preventive immunization; health screening, health education in mental health and nutrition; stress management training; parenting effectiveness education; support groups for persons with specific illnesses, and peer support groups for persons experiencing stress (Parents without Partners, support groups for widows or widowers).

Conflict Resolution Services. These are services which deal with conflicts among individuals, households and business firms, in contrast to conflicts between individuals and society involving violations of criminal law. These services include: the civil courts, family reconciliation services, arbitration and mediation services, human rights commissions, regulatory appeal boards, and ombudsmen.

Economic Development Services. These services are intended to enhance the general functioning of the economy through the availability of particular services for individuals. While many of these services when produced by a voluntary nonprofit or governmental service organization are redistributional, and are discussed below, some are available on a community-wide basis. These include employment information and placement services, small business loans and development assistance services, tourist information services, industry oriented technical training programs, and land use development projects which support general business and industrial development.

Political Economy Characteristics

While the external political economy of the program components within each of these subcategories has distinctive characteristics, there are political economy characteristics which are similar across all the categories of *universal, divisible service* program components.

Auspices. Collective provision of these services may be under either governmental or voluntary nonprofit auspices. Similar services may also be available through for-profit organizations. In any given community universal divisible services may be provided only by governmental and nonprofit organizations, or only by for-profit organizations, or by a combination of all three. This reflects differing evaluations of the potential for economic profit from the production of a particular service, or of the importance of the public good benefit resulting from the universal availability of such services. Many similar services are also provided, on a non-organizational basis, within families or within neighborhoods, particularly by parents for their children or by grown children for their parents.

The establishment of many of these services, for example, a community water system, requires a substantial initial capital investment in facilities and/or a major entrepreneurial development effort with the benefits to be realized only over a long period of time. Such an initial investment is unlikely to be undertaken as a for-profit marketplace activity because of the uncertainty of the long run level of economic return. The initial developmental effort required to create the service is, therefore, undertaken as a collective activity without entrepreneurial profits for any single indivdiual. In addition, the risk that results from uncertainty about the total level of benefits to be realized over a long period of time is carried by the collective group which initiates the project, and their successors.

Regardless of the form of collective provision there may be a variety of fee charges for these universal, divisible services. The fees are usually set at a level to cover some portion of operating costs without substantially restricting utilization, since restricted utilization, below the level of the available service production capacity, would reduce the potential collective benefits.[2] However, fee charges may be used to ration the limited supply of a particular service, for example, increasing charges for water services in an area with limited water resources.

To the extent that the use of these divisible services is primarily by residents in a given locality, and the collective benefits resulting from the availability and accessibility of the services and their utilization is a localized benefit, such services are likely to operate under local auspices, with local funding for core functions. However, some services, such as national parks, serve a nationwide constituency and are therefore organized on a nationwide basis. The debates about the break-up of the Bell Telephone system involved the issue as to whether the public good benefits of the availability of a single system of universal telephone services were primarily national or primarily local. The current policy outcome assumes that the public good benefits from a single system of telephone services are primarily local, and that a single uniform nationwide system did not provide significant public good benefits.

There has been a traditional assumption that when governmental auspices are established for the *provision* of universal, divisible services, that a governmental organization is the appropriate *producer* of those services. For example, governmental provision for universal elementary and secondary education has meant that the educational services are produced by a public elementary and secondary school system.

Recently, however, there have been a variety of proposals to separate governmental provision from governmental production (Ostrom and Ostrom 1978; Savas 1982). These include proposals to provide universal day care through publicly funded vouchers which would permit the user to choose among a number of different day care producers, as well as for publicly funded vouchers for the payment of tuition at both public and private elementary and secondary schools.

The issue is whether the public good benefits depend substantially on the uniform production of the services by a single organization that is accountable to the community at large. Or, conversely, whether the universal availability of the services is sufficient to provide the public good even if the characteristics of services produced by separate organizations differ substantially.

Legitimation. A decision to provide universal, divisible services under collective auspices, rather than to rely on households or the marketplace, requires some form of group action. The most frequent sequence is for a small group of citizens to band together to provide such services which are supported initially through some combination of volunteer services, voluntary contributions and payments for services. The public good rationale which is persuasive to the group of individuals initiating the service may be either that of benefit to the members of the community at large, including themselves, from utilization, or the ready availability/accessibility of such services for persons who are particularly interested (Weisbrod 1977).

The actual production of the service may make it possible to expand the base of voluntary support so that it includes a majority of the community residents (or a majority of the community power structure). At that point action may be initiated to establish the service under some form of governmental auspice with tax funding, based on the argument that the public good benefits are significant and accrue to all citizens, that potential access to the private benefits for individuals should be universally available, for example, museum educational programs for all school children, and that at least a part of the costs should therefore be supported by all taxpayers.

Some decisions to provide tax support result from the lobbying of special interest groups such as hobby groups who would like to have hobby facilities in public recreation facilities, thereby reducing the costs of such facilities for individual users, or potential users. Professional associations that are interested in expanding employment opportunities and professional domain, may lobby for the establishment of new services under governmental auspices, for example the inclusion of pre-school nursery programs on a universal basis as part of the public elementary/secondary school system.

Decisions about which services should be collectively provided, what proportion of the costs should be met by user fees, and whether the services should be supported by voluntary contributions or through governmental funding, may change from time to time. The changes may come as a result of demographic and life style changes at the local level, shifts in the political balance of power, or changes in economic conditions. Many universal services may be viewed as desirable, but not essential, by many taxpayers, and therefore as programs to be eliminated from governmental funding in periods of economic austerity.

Particularly during the past two decades there have been a number of successful efforts by special interest groups to use state and federal legislatures to mandate the establishment of universally available services at the local level, for example mandates for the universal accessibility of publicly supported services and facilities to persons with handicaps (Section 504, Rehabilitation Act of 1973) and the mandate for provision of "appropriate" and free education for all children with disabilities (Public Law 94-142 (1975) Education for All Handicapped Children Act). Some of these mandates have been accompanied by substantial financial assistance from state and federal levels. But increasingly these state and federal mandates have included only limited assistance or no assistance, on the implicit assumption that the public good benefits of such universal services as well as private benefits for individuals accrue to the local community.

Federal courts have also played a role in supporting the requirements for such universal services, for example in supporting a mandate for the availability of athletic sports programs for women in educational institutions receiving federal funds, if there are such sports programs for men. Thus a small group of intensely concerned citizens who previously might have used their own time and money to create a voluntary nonprofit corporation and to raise the funds through contributions to provide a service for which there was not majority support in a local community, may now use the same resources, in combination with similar groups from other communities, to seek to have such services mandated through the courts or through legislative action at other levels of government.

By the early 1980s the legitimacy of these mandated universal divisible services had become a major domestic policy issue in the United States. Individuals concerned with the cumulative tax costs of these universal service programs, as well as the costs of other redistributive and behavior change/ social control programs, sought to weaken the legislative mandates and to eliminate federal funding for such programs (Gilder 1981). Their argument was that the public good benefits, if in fact there are such benefits, as well as the private benefits, are primarily local and therefore funding decisions about such services should be made at a local level.

Evaluation. With the exception of cognitive and skill development it is difficult to evaluate the outputs of many of these universal, divisible services beyond the level of user satisfaction. Even in the area of education co-production and normal maturation are such significant factors that it is difficult to assess the role of specific educational services in achieving individual outcomes. Similarly individual motivation and external economic factors are often the determining factors in job placements and in economic development, rather than the content of specific manpower training and economic development services. In the absence of definitive evaluations of the individual outputs, service performance evaluation is frequently based on quantitative measures of activity: the number of books circulated by a library; the number of visitors to a museum; the quantity of water delivered; the number of cases handled by the probate court; or the number of students enrolled in school.

Accountability of program administrators is primarily controlled through the evaluations of the majority of service users. The preferences of this majority are likely to shape the characteristics of the services. Individual consumers evaluate the services on the basis of regularity, dependability, access to their "fair share" of benefits, and the quality of the service as compared to their own standards of quality. If unit program costs or per capita tax costs are available they may play a part in the collective evaluation of the services, but the public availability of such information tends to be limited.

The impact of user satisfaction, or dissatisfaction, evaluations is likely to reflect political and economic power relationships within the community. The preferences, opinions and service experiences of individuals who have an active role in local decisionmaking, either in government or in voluntary nonprofit activities, are likely to be influential in shaping the characteristics of particular service programs. This may include the quality of staff personnel and facilities provided for particular neighborhoods, or the quality of staff assigned to particular responsibilities, for example, teaching mathematics to college-bound high school students. Local residents with little political or economic power may have difficulty in obtaining access to universal services which are comparable in quality to those in other parts of the community, unless their power is reinforced by external resources, such as well-organized advocacy organizations or rulings by state or federal courts, although they may pay a proportional share of costs through local taxation or through their contributions.

Positive evaluations of universal services are seldom gathered systematically. Negative evaluations are often expressed as individual criticisms of organizational management rather than of individual service workers. It is only when consumers band together to express negative evaluations that such evaluations become a public issue. Otherwise there is an explicit assumption that once there has been collective action to establish a universally available service it will continue indefinitely. The use of such procedures as zero-based budgetting and sunset reviews represent, in part, an effort to force periodic review of the legitimacy of such universal service programs, as well as of their actual production costs.

SUMMARY

Universal, divisible services may be provided through either voluntary or governmental action. Governmental sponsorship is most likely when a majority of the community is convinced of the public good benefits to be realized. The rationale for collective action, and for the balance between fee-for-service funding and collective funding for any particular service, is that there are collective benefits from the universal character of the provision, in addition to the private benefits to individuals.

The specific characteristics of the services in any single program are likely to reflect the preferences of the majority of the active users, both as to program content and relative level of program expenditures. When those preferences change, support of the service program may change, regardless of the technical quality of the existing service provision. When the preferences of the majority of users conflict with the preferences of smaller, or weaker, groups in the community who have equal right of access to the services, administrators are often faced by a conflict between principle and political realities. A similar conflict may exist when the preferences of powerful interest groups conflict with preferences of the majority of the users.

However, when the preferences of powerful interest groups and a broad majority of the users are similar, administration may be relatively easy, primarily guided by technical or professional criteria. Such a condition often exists in small, upper-income suburban communities, and in traditional culturally homogeneous middle-income rural communities and small towns. It is least likely to exist in central cities of industrial metropolises in which the preferences of the majority of the diverse population of local service users and of powerful economic interests are frequently in conflict.

NOTES

1.   The collective benefit can also be described as an *externality*, or as a *spill-over consequence* that is outside, or over and beyond, the interaction between the service producer and the immediate service user. However, in this instance such an externality is an essential element in the objectives sought through collective action.

2.   The question as to whether that principle should be applied to local telephone services is the basis for current debates about whether telephone companies should be required to make available below cost "life-line" services so that all households in a community can afford to have basic telephone services.

Chapter 10

Comparative Analysis
by Societal Function
Continued-Categorical
Divisible Services

CATEGORICAL DIVISIBLE SERVICES

The most complex policy and administrative issues in human service programs emerge around divisible services which are categorically, or selectively, targeted. These categorical services fall into three broad classifications (see Figure 9-1). The first classification includes those categorically targeted service programs that provide for the *transfer of basic necessities* needed for physical survival directly to individuals or households. These include income transfer programs in the form of collectively supported social insurance programs, pensions, means-tested public assistance, and private charity, and alternatively the direct provision of food, housing (including utilities) or medical care.

The second classification includes categorically targeted services which are *remedial, rehabilitative, curative, or involve social care or deviance control*. These include many types of personal social services, education services, counseling services, health care services, rehabilitation services, correction services, mental health services, substance abuse treatment services, and so forth.

The third classification includes categorically targeted *employment support* services that reinforce entrance into and continued participation in employment. These include job training and placement services, employment related day care and similar employment support services, unemployment insurance, and economic development activities that are targeted to economically depressed areas and population groups.

Like universal divisible services *categorical divisible* services involve the production of public good benefits as well as private benefits for individual service users. However, in categorical divisible service programs the public good functions are quite different than those for universal divisible services, creating a very different political economy context.

There are two basic public good functions which are applicable to categorical divisible services: (1) a redistribution function, and (2) a behavior change or social control function. Many categorical service programs involve a mixture of redistribution and social control functions. However, *basic necessity services* are primarily designed to fulfill a redistribution function, while *remedial, rehabilitative, curative, social care, deviance control services* are primarily designed to fulfill a behavior change/social control function. *Employment support services* are designed to fulfill a combination of redistribution and behavior change/social control functions.

Basic Necessity Services

Services. The establishment of basic necessity service programs which fulfill a redistribution function involves a collective decision to provide income, food, housing, or medical care to selective categories of individuals, households, and in some instances neighborhoods. In a market economy most households obtain these basic necessities through the marketplace. In redistributional basic necessity service programs one set of individuals and households with economic resources makes voluntary contributions, or agrees through the political process to pay taxes, in order to provide or transfer economic resources to other individuals and households that are judged to have inadequate economic resources.[1]

In a basic necessity service which has a "pure" redistribution function, for example, Social Security retirement benefits for individuals over 72 years-of-age, the benefits are provided to individuals without any expectation of a change in the behavior of the recipients as a direct consequence of such assistance. However, many basic necessity services are "conditioned" by behavior change expectations, for example, the expectation that the adult caretaker recipients of AFDC benefits will actively seek employment.

The individual motivations which support collective decisions to provide redistributional basic necessity assistance have been variously described as charity, philanthropy, altruism, enlightened self-interest, and also as a response to the fear of the consequences of social disorder (Boulding 1973). A variety of explanations have been suggested to account for these motivations, and for the existence of systematically organized redistributional basic necessity services (in contrast to the occasional idiosyncratic acts of charity by individuals). These include theological theories, religious beliefs, theories of the societal social order (Titmuss 1970), humanistic values (Morris 1986), the genetic protection and transmission theories of sociobiology (Wilson 1978), theories of class conflict (Gough 1979; Piven and Cloward 1971), and economic cost-benefit theories dealing with the development of and protection of human capital.

However, the theoretical explanations for such collective actions, which run counter to narrowly defined economic self-interest, must take into account not only the general existence of redistributional basic necessity service programs but also the dynamics of the public policy decisions which are reflected in the specific characteristics of actual basic necessity redistributional programs.[2]

One rationale for redistributional basic necessity services which fits this requirement is based on the concept of *communal mutual assistance obligations.* As described in Chapter 1, the family and other communal groups (Hillery 1968) are an arena of social behavior which is equal in importance to the marketplace. The rules governing relationships and exchanges within communal groups are different from the rules of the marketplace. Within communal groups behavior is governed largely by role definitions and role expectations, rather than by economic self-interest. Membership in communal units—families, friendship groups, neighborhoods, locality communities, or ethnic or cultural communities, national societies—involves affective relationships and normative relationships, rather than marketplace or contractual relationships. Most communal groups, such as the nuclear family, involve primary relationships among all members, that is face-to-face relationships on an individual basis. However, individuals also identify themselves with "secondary" communal units, such as the locality community, or the "national society," which are not based on face-to-face relationships among all members.

Among the role expectations involved in these communal relationships is a *noncontractual* mutual obligation among members of the unit to come to the assistance of each other under certain conditions. Without some degree of mutual assistance obligation, there is no communal group. This is the difference between a *primary neighborhood*, in which there is a shared sense of mutual obligation among households to come to the assistance of each other if needed, and a *geographic neighborhood* with a similar number of households among whom there is no sense of mutual obligation.[3]

These mutual assistance obligations, between husband and wife, between parents and children, among friends, among communal neighbors, among residents in a locality community, or among the citizens of a national society, include the sharing of economic resources to ensure at least minimum access to those basic necessities essential for physical survival: food, shelter and medical care.

Few individuals are completely free of some degree of awareness of a mutual assistance obligation to other members of some communal group. Indeed, affiliation with communal groups, including an acknowledgement of the mutual assistance obligation, provides a critical element of self identity. The acknowledgement of obligations to other members is essential to mutual acknowledgement of that individual as a participant in that communal group. If mutual assistance communal obligations are not fulfilled, recognition as a member of the communal group may be threatened. A parent who abandons a child, or a family member who does not provide assistance to an elderly parent in need, is not meeting the societal expectations attached to such roles, and thus may be viewed by others as not a "true" member of the family. To the extent that an important element of an individual's self identity is linked to acknowledgement as a communal group member, such self identity may be seriously threatened by a failure to fulfill obligations of mutual assistance.

The degree of commitment by any one person at any one time to help other members of a communal group, including the obligation to provide assistance with basic necessities, may vary widely. It may be affected by the loyalty which the individual had to the communal group, the role of the person needing assistance, the degree of vulnerability, that is the degree to which the individual needing assistance is dependent upon the actions of a particular individual for assistance (Goodin 1985), and the extent to which the individual believes that he or she may have a similar need for assistance from other members of the group at some future time. However, the commitment to mutual assistance among members of a family, or among friends, or even among members of the cultural group, is a very powerful dynamic in the lives of most individuals, overriding economic self-interest in many instances. It is primarily the claims of mutual assistance obligation, rather than economic self-interest, that are involved in those instances in which individuals risk their lives for other persons.

In many instances the mutual assistance obligation is fullfilled through the provision of direct and immediate asssistance by one individual to another within the framework of a primary relationship, for example, when a parent provides temporary financial assistance to a son or daughter who has lost a job, or a daughter or son gives up a job to provide personal care for an elderly parent, or a neighbor provides temporary shelter to a family that has lost a home in a fire. However, such acts of direct personal assistance are often not sufficient to fulfill mutual assistance obligations within the communal unit. Members of immediate families are often separated and unable to give immediate assistance. Substantial numbers of older parents, and children, need long-term assistance beyond the resources of immmediate family members.

Moreover, many abandoned children or older adults, within contemporary urban societies, have no family or communal group members immediately available to whom they can turn for assistance. The impersonality of relationships in densely populated apartment housing neighborhoods prevents the development of a neighborhood sense of mutual assistance obligation. Differences in ethnic identity, religion, nationality and language in a neighborhood may also interfere with the development of an inclusive pattern of mutual assistance. In all of these instances particular individuals, or households, may have no primary communal group network to turn to when assistance is needed.

In a mobile urban society in which there are large numbers of persons who, at a time of need, do not have direct access to assistance through a primary communal group the fulfillment of mutual assistance obligations among members of a communal unit often requires that the responsibilities for providing such assistance be shared among the members of larger, more inclusive communal units such as the locality community, religious and fraternal associations, ethnic culture societies and the national society. The collective discharge of the responsibility for mutual assistance among the members of these larger, "secondary" communal groups requires an organizational structure through which resources are collected, and distributed. Among the early forms of such organizational structures in the United States were the New England town meetings which administered "poor relief," and the cooperative burial societies organized by immigrant nationality groups. Some of these burial societies have later become national *mutual* insurance companies.

Membership identification with a larger, "secondary" communal group, such as locality community, a state civil society, or the national society, results in a less intensive feeling of individual obligation to provide mutual assistance to other members of the same group, but it can lead to a more extensive pattern of coverage in the provision of assistance. The public good benefit which is created through a formally organized inclusive redistribution service is the common satisfaction which is shared by members of such communal groups when the recognized obligation to assist other members of the group is fulfilled, even though the fulfillment of that obligation is not directly from one individual to another. For example, there is a shared satisfaction among members of a locality community when a local Red Cross or Salvation Army emergency service, supported by local contributions, provides temporary housing assistance to the victims of a fire. There is a similar shared satisfaction from general recognition that individuals over 65 within the national society have protection from the costs of medical care as a result of legislative provisions under the Social Security Act.

The acknowledgement of a public good benefit may not be universal. The minimum requirement is that a sufficient number of persons acknowledge a public good benefit to provide the political majority required to enact a governmental redistribution program. However, there may be a discrepancy between a broad-based public acknowledgement of a public good benefit resulting from the existence of a basic necessity redistribution program, and public endorsement of a tax plan for financing such a program. The reaction to a tax plan involves, among other things, public evaluation of governmental officials, of the purposes for which present taxes are being used, and the fairness of the proposed tax procedures. Thus individual citizens may endorse a series of specific service programs that provide redistributional benefits to particular groups of people, and simultaneously, react negatively to "government" as being "too big," and to taxes as being "too high."

In order for those individuals who are motivated by a sense of communal obligation to provide assistance willingly, either through contributions or through taxes, for a basic necessity service in which there is not a direct, face-to-face, or primary group relationship among those providing and those receiving assistance, two criteria must be met. First, the persons providing the economic resources for assistance must perceive the persons receiving assistance as being fellow members in some communal group, at some level of society— members of the same locality community, of the same religious or fraternal association, of the same national society, or of the same ethnic culture, for example. Second, the individuals receiving assistance must be perceived, in general, as being "worthy" or "deserving." That is, they must be perceived as having made a special contribution to the group, for example, military veterans, or workers who retire after long years of employment during which they produced goods and services used by other members of the group. Or, *at a minimum* they must be perceived as not having violated communal norms in a way that would cancel their claim to be considered a member of the communal group, thus forfeiting their right to assistance from other members of the group.

If these two criteria are met, all the members of the group which legitimate the redistribution service, and provide financial support, can share in the collective benefit of knowing that assistance has been provided to persons who are "one of us" and who also "deserve" help. To the degree that communal group membership is ambiguous, as in the instance of undocumented aliens, provision of assistance is likely to be a source of argument. To the degree that the second criteria, that is "deservedness" is not fully met in the perception of those providing assistance, a redistributional basic necessities service program is particularly likely to include behavior change/social control characteristics, that is that recipients of assistance should behave in particular ways. If neither criteria is fulfilled, that is the persons needing assistance are perceived as not "one of us" and as not "deserving," then collective action to support a redistribution service is unlikely.

The categorical, or selective, pattern of redistributional basic necessity services, and the differences in actual practice as to the amount of assistance which is provided to different categories of persons needing assistance, reflect consistent variations in the evaluations which individuals make of the degree to which there is a mutually shared communal obligation to provide assistance. This may be very different from an objective determination of the degree of relative need as among different categories. However, within a given category an objective definition of need may be used as the criteria for the amount of assistance to be provided to particular individuals. There are also consistent distinctions made between providing one-time assistance in an emergency situation to a particular individual, and providing long-term assistance on a regular basis to a category of similar individuals.

In a highly homogenous society the persons who are perceived as being in need of basic necessity assistance may fall into a few, very inclusive categories around which there is broad consensus as their "right" to receive assistance and as to the general level of assistance which is to be provided. In a very heterogenous society, such as the United States, the persons perceived as being in need of assistance fall into a large number of narrowly defined categories around which there is only limited consensus about who has a "right" to assistance and at what level assistance is to be provided.

Redistributional basic necessity services, including income assistance, food, housing and medical care, in general are more substantial for persons over 65 than for those under 65, an arbitrary definition of the expected age of retirement built into the Social Security system. They are more substantial for children, than for single adults in their working years. They are more extensive for mothers of young children, and particularly for widows, in single parent households, than they are for fathers in two parent households. Benefits for veterans, and their families, are more generous than those for nonveterans. The benefits provided through redistribution basic necessity programs are more substantial for individuals with a record of wage or salary employment, than for those without such a record. State expenditures for redistribution benefits are more extensive for residents within a state, than for temporary nonresidents. National provisions for redistribution benefits for national citizens, taken all together, are more extensive than national expenditures for international assistance to individuals in need in other nations.

Political Economy Characteristics

Auspices. The primary provider of basic necessity redistributional services in the United States is now the federal government, particularly if provisions for retirement benefits for military personnel and federal employees are included. Even programs that require substantial state and local financial participation, such as Medicaid, have been initiated by the federal government and are largely controlled by federal legislation and regulations. Social insurance programs, such as Social Security, rely on federal authority to compel universal participation. Moreover, federal legislation, rather than actuarial analyses, determines the actual level and pattern of benefits from Social Security. Federal regulations also control and underwrite retirement income provisions of corporate pension systems.

In part, this pattern of federal auspices reflects the ability of the federal government to impose uniform taxes on both corporate and individual incomes on a nationwide basis. It also reflects the fact that individuals and households who require basic necessity assistance are unevenly distributed among the states, particularly in relation to the location of economic resources. The current pattern of federal auspices has emerged as a result of a series of changes in basic necessity redistributional services over the past century, as described in Chapters 6 and 7.

A key question surrounding redistributional basic necessity services in the 1980s is whether the federal role in such services should be curtailed, rather than being expanded. It has become evident that it is only possible to insure a significant degree of uniform provision, and an inclusive sharing of economic responsibility for redistributional basic necessity services, if the operational definition of mutual assistance obligations is on a nationwide basis, on a "we are all citizens of one nation" basis.

However, a commitment to the concept of universal citizenship in a national society, and a commitment to the concept of mutual assistance obligation inclusive of all members of the national society who are in need of such assistance, is only partially accepted by many members of this society. Distinctions in policy and in practice are made between individuals who are "more deserving" of organized assistance, including veterans, retired workers, and individuals with permanent disabilities, and those who are "not so deserving," primarily unemployed able-bodied adults below the age of retirement. Distinctions among redistributional basic necessity service programs also reflect varying judgements about the extent to which, in a composite, multi-cultural society, members of particular ethnic and cultural groups are perceived as being, in fact, "one of us."

One consequence of these distinctions is that those categories that are most universally regarded as "one of us" and "deserving" receive the most consistent and dependable assistance, provided on a single nationwide basis through such programs as veterans benefits, Social Security insurance and means-tested Supplementary Security Income, that is the "categorical transfer" programs dealt with in Chapter 4. On the other hand, current policy provides for federal control but *state administration* of benefits in the food stamp program, state control of unemployment insurance eligibility, together with state control of benefit levels in AFDC. General Assistance operates under state/local funding and control with no federal involvement, and in some states with no significant state involvement. These latter programs, AFDC and General Assistance, provide assistance to many individuals and households about which there is the greatest ambivalence both as to whether they are "one of us" and whether they are "deserving."[4]

This latter pattern of state and local controls, primarily affecting programs serving able-bodied adults (the *labor force transfers* dealt with in Chapter 4), and young children in families headed by such adults, implies that although the United States is a single economic system, the primary responsibility for the "welfare" of nonelderly, nondisabled citizens rests on a collection of fifty separate and distinct civil societies. This concept is reinforced by policies which provide for nationwide portability of benefits under veterans pensions, Social Security insurance and SSI, but no automatic transfer of eligibility across state lines for food stamps, AFDC, general assistance, or for unemployment insurance.

This policy approach to labor force transfer programs allows for the political processes within each state to determine the degree of perceived mutual obligation and the definitions of eligibility to be applied to that obligation, and to determine the relationship of the level of assistance to the economic status of individual taxpayers, as they themselves view it. It also intensifies the political conflict between the normative implications of mutual assistance obligations among the citizens of a particular state and economic competition among the states seeking to attract, and retain, businesses that can move freely within a single national (and increasingly international) economy.

Although the basic auspices for the provision of redistribution services are largely federal and state governments, the actual *producers* of such services are highly varied. As indicated above, the producers of income transfers for older adults and the severely disabled are federal agencies. Other redistributional basic necessity services are produced by state, county, and city governments, and by independent authorities (housing authorities and hospital districts). Recently voluntary nonprofit "food pantries" and "food banks" have become important sources of food assistance. Voluntary nonprofit organizations, such as the Salvation Army and St. Vincent de Paul, also produce basic necessity services, in particular for those individuals and families about whom there is the least agreement in the general community about "deservedness." These include individuals with chronic alcoholism, and "street people." The existence of these organizations reflects the convictions of particular groups of individuals that the mutual assistance obligation goes beyond the criteria defined by the community majority.

Other organizations which provide basic necessity assistance to individuals in other nations reflect a conviction that the boundaries of mutual obligation are, in fact, world-wide. Federal policy in the United States has varied between regarding governmental international assistance as a redistribution service to be administered by international bodies, and regarding it as primarily a tool of national self-interest to be provided only on the basis of a self-interest exchange relationship which provides explicit political, economic and military benefits to the United States.

Legitimation. Legitimation for any single redistributional basic necessity service rests on the collective decision of a group of individuals to share the costs of providing some form of assistance to persons other than themselves. This may range from a neighborhood collection to help a family in trouble to the action of the United States Congress, acting in a representative capacity for all citizens, in establishing broadly inclusive redistributional programs such as the Social Security system. In voluntary associations the decision to provide such assistance must essentially be unanimous since any individual who does not agree is free not to contribute. In a formal sense governmental action requires a decision by only a bare majority of elected representatives. However, in reality a political consensus representing substantially more than a bare majority is usually necessary to establish the legitimacy of a new redistributional basic necessities program, or to make major changes in an existing program. Changes in the Social Security retirement system in the early 1980s, for example, were based on a consensus negotiated within a bi-partisan Congressional task-force before legislation was introduced.

Within any group of individuals there will be a range of attitudes about the degree to which there is a particular mutual assistance obligation, just as there is within any one family, or within a neighborhood. Some individuals feel no real obligation to provide economic assistance to anyone, even within their own family, even if this is inconsistent with the role-related expectations of other persons. Any political decision to provide tax-financing for redistributional basic necessity services will compel financial support from some individuals who may not feel any obligation to assist the individuals who may receive benefits from such services, as well as support from persons who have actively lobbied in favor of such a program. Political decisions involve an averaging out of these attitudes both among individual citizens, and among the public officials involved in making the actual policy decision.

The political process becomes increasingly complex when the recipients of the redistribution benefits are also a substantial part of the polity involved in the decision, as in the case of retired workers and veterans (Janowitz 1978). These groups may strongly support the concept of mutual assistance obligation as it applies to themselves. However, the members of such groups may also feel that there is little obligation for them to provide assistance to individuals in any other category of need.

The actual pattern of redistributional basic necessity services within any one society may be affected by factors other than the perceptions of mutual assistance obligation. These include the fear of social or political disruption by persons in need, which may lead to at least a temporary expansion of basic necessity services (Piven and Cloward 1971). In the United States there have also been federal court decisions, based on constitutional principles, which have restricted the extent to which a political majority can unilaterally exclude members of a minority constituency, defined by ethnic background or citizenship, from access to redistributional basic necessity services.

The Constitutional definition of the mutual assistance obligation of residents of the United States to each other, as interpreted by the federal courts, is more inclusive than the majority controlled political definition that is likely to be supported at any given time. For example, the courts have extended *eligibility* for redistributional basic necessity services to resident noncitizens who were not explicitly covered in the basic legislation. On the other hand, the federal courts have ruled that the *level of assistance* to be provided in a governmental redistributional basic necessity service is a legislative, and therefore a political, decision. While there is a constitutional "due process" right to have access to a program for which one is economically eligible, there is not a constitutional "right" to a particular level of assistance.

Since the basis of redistributional basic necessity services involves individual judgements about the nature of the mutual obligation to provide assistance and about the "deservedness" of potential recipients, the demographic characteristics of the eligible group can affect the perceived legitimacy of a particular service. The issue of including migrant farmworkers in state unemployment insurance coverage is affected in part by the economic dynamics of the agricultural industry; but the political decision primarily involves the question as to whether migrant farmworkers are really "one of us," or, alternatively, temporary visitors from a different culture, for whom "we" have no systematic responsibility. The changes that occurred between the 1930s and the 1970s in the characteristics of AFDC recipients from a small group of predominantly white widows with several children to a relatively large group of divorced, separated, and never-married women, many of whom are from an ethnic minority background, with a smaller number of children in each household, changed the political economy context of that redistribution program (Wilson 1985).

The effective level of redistributional basic necessity benefits, including direct income provision, for any particular category of recipients, is likely to be *at the minimum level* at which the feeling of mutual assistance obligation is fulfilled for the majority of those involved in providing, or legitimating, the assistance. This judgement will reflect perceptions by individuals of their own current and potential future economic condition, as well as the extent of their responsibilities to individuals for whom they may feel a stronger personal sense of obligation, for example, members of their own immediate family. Individuals are unlikely to support the concept of a level of redistribution assistance, for a category of persons with whom they have little or no direct contact, which is higher than their own standard of living, or higher than the level of assistance which they would be willing, or able, to provide for similar individuals within their own family.

Extended periods of economic slowdown usually bring changes in the characteristics of basic necessity programs. These include the narrowing of eligibility definitions to include only those persons around whom there is the broadest consensus about mutual assistance obligation, for example, those that President Reagan defined as being covered by the social "safety net." Restrictive eligibility requirements are enforced more rigorously, and they may include informal tests of "worthiness" over and beyond the formal eligibility criteria. The level of benefits may be reduced and behavior change/ social control expectations may be added. While these changes often have the overt objective of reducing program costs, they are more fundamentally a restructuring of the program to fit politically redefined concepts of program legitimacy.

The legitimation, and the political economy context, of redistributional basic necessity services depends largely on the perceptions and judgements of those providing the economic resources for the program rather than on objective measures of need among potential recipients. There are only a few critics of the provision of Social Security retirement benefits for middle-income widows who come from an ethnic majority background and who have other substantial sources of retirement income. However, there are widespread objections to systematic provision of redistributional financial assistance to "employable" single young adults from an ethnic minority background who have grown up in very deprived households and who are chronically unemployed under conditions of high unemployment.

Evaluation. The evaluation of redistributional basic necessity services involves two distinctive elements: evaluation by those legitimating and funding the program, and evaluation by those receiving the services. Evaluation of the program as a whole by those legitimating and financing the services focuses on questions dealing with the administrative parameters of the program. Since the degree of public good motivation which supports a redistribution service, that is the fulfillment of mutual assistance obligations based on common membership in a communal group, is linked to categorical definitions of eligibility, the evaluation of any program is highly dependent on evidence that the benefits are, in fact, going to the persons for whom the program is intended.

There is constant demand by critics of redistributional basic necessity programs for confirmation that the assistance is given only to "those for whom the program is really intended." Thus the constant emphasis on fraud and error control in AFDC and food stamp programs, as well as local media exposes about eligibility abuses in general assistance programs. Similarly there have been large administrative expenditures, frequent policy adjustments, and reevaluations of individual situations in the SSI Disability program in an effort to determine who is, in fact, legitimately to be considered "disabled" (Stone 1985).

There is also a concern in such programs about *horizontal equity*, and about *vertical equity*. Horizontal equity requires that individuals, and households, in comparable situations receive comparable benefits. This requirement applies within programs so that two households of an adult and two children in different parts of the country, all other income elements being the same, receive, for instance, the same level of food stamp benefits. Horizontal equity also applies to the relationship between redistributional benefits and earned income, requiring, in principle, that individuals receiving redistributional benefits do not receive greater economic benefits than comparable individuals can earn through full-time employment.

Vertical equity requires that households which have different characteristics receive redistributional benefits consistent with those differences; large families receive more benefits than small families, individuals with a higher wage rate receive a higher level of unemployment benefits, individuals with supplementary employment have a higher over-all level of total income, including redistributional benefits, than families in which no one is employed. The effort to achieve a no-error rate on eligibility, minimize the opportunities for recipient fraud, and achieve both horizontal and vertical equity requires a very complex, and everchanging, system of rules and enforcement procedures. This, in turn, requires a large administrative organization. All of these complexities lead to a continuous, and frequently contentious, oversight process by legislative bodies, as well as by the courts.

The program may also be assessed, at least informally, by the extent to which recipients respond in ways that are viewed as consistent with mutual assistance obligations within a communal framework, in contrast to the expectations of a contractual obligation. That is the recipients are expected to show appreciation and a pattern of behavior generally consistent with social norms. For example, families living in public housing are expected, in general, to meet community expectations in housekeeping, where a similar family renting a privately owned home is not expected to be accountable to the community as to its standard of housekeeping. It is accountable to the landlord only to the extent that such standards are part of the contract lease agreement.

There may be specific evaluations of individual programs to determine if the actual receipt of the basic necessity benefits has a beneficial impact on the individual recipients of such benefits. But since the objective of basic necessity services is the physical survival of the individual, evidence of such survival is generally taken as evidence of the beneficial impact of the service. Criteria which deal with the impact on specific individuals are, in any case, likely to be considered less important than the administrative performance criteria described above.

Evaluation of the basic necessity services from the perspective of the service recipients involves very different criteria. The key criterion for a redistributional basic necessity program from the point of view of the recipient is "adequacy," a concept which can be defined in several ways: *minimal subsistence* which is support at a level expected to prevent imminent illness and death; *minimal adequacy* which currently in the United States could be defined as the "poverty line;" and *full participation adequacy* which might be defined as roughly equal to the median income level in the society. Program sponsors, recipients, and recipient advocates, usually disagree as to which of these criteria should be used in a particular program. There is likely to be some greater degree of agreement, however, about the level at which a particular program is actually operating.

Redistributional basic necessity services are defined within a public policy framework as one way discretionary transfers, or grants, to the recipients (Boulding 1973). The level of benefits and terms of eligibility can be changed unilaterally by the sponsors of the program, but not by the recipients of the benefits. This view of the benefits conflicts with the view of recipients, and of recipient advocates, who prefer to define them as a constitutionally, or legislatively defined, and legally assertable "right" or "claim" (Rein 1983b).

Disagreements over the definition of the program may result in conflicts between direct service staff who support the organizational definition of the benefits, and recipients asserting a "right" to more adequate benefits. Or, if direct service workers identify closely with recipients, the conflict may be between the front-line workers and supervisors and administrators (Withorn 1984). The existence of two different sets of evaluation criteria, and different assertions as to whom the program is primarily accountable frequently result in both policy and personal conflicts within redistributional basic necessity programs.

Summary. Marketplace processes are relatively ineffective in distributing the economic benefits from a highly productive industrial system so as to provide, at a minimum, the basic necessities of life for eveyone, including those persons who are not part of the employed labor force. This is particularly the case in terms of the two ends of the age continuum—very young and very old persons—and those with severe handicapping conditions, as changes take place in family structures, and in the ability of the nuclear family to provide long-term assistance for anyone except immediate family members.

The limitations of the marketplace as a comprehensive income distribution mechanism are also, in part, a consequence of adaptations in the economic system to rapid changes in production technologies and consumer demands. These adaptations result in frequent disruptions in employment for many workers, and geographic shifts in economic activity which may leave some workers unemployed for long periods of time. Historic patterns of educational and employment discrimination contribute substantially to the distributive ineffectiveness of marketplace processes. The result has been a requirement for alternatives to the marketplace for providing income, or the basic necessities of food, shelter and medical care, to a large number of households.

This situation has led to the creation of a number of large categorical programs, primarily under federal and state governmental auspices, replacing earlier provisions in the form of local almshouses, local public poor relief and private charity. The definitions of the recipient categories, and the differences in the level of provision for different categories, reflect variations in the perceptions of mutual assistance obligation among individuals who share a common communal group membership.

The organization of large categorical programs provides a substantial degree of assurance that some assistance will be provided to those toward whom some sense of obligation is felt. However, the intensity of commitment by individuals as contributors, or as taxpayers, to such large programs is, in turn, very limited. Where the feelings of mutal assistance obligation are weak, the provision of assistance may be provided only at a minimum survival level, and significant behavior change/social control requirements may be added to the program.

The effort to maintain vertical and horizontal equity within particular categorical programs, and between the recipients of assistance and other members of the society, has led to the creation of large, hierarchial, multilevel, rule-controlled, "people-processing" (Hasenfeld 1983) eligibility determination and monitoring systems, often involving federal, state, county and city components. One consequence is the variety of administrative problems which are common to such organizations, including problems of effective management control, continuous elaboration of rules and procedures, psychological burn-out and high turn-over of direct service staff, and antagonism between direct service personnel and recipients.

Such redistributional basic necessity programs are also subject to severely conflicting pressures from service recipients for more adequate benefits, and from governmental sponsors and taxpayers for control of costs and rigorous enforcement of categorical eligibility definitions. There is an intensification of the conflicts in the political economy environment of these services as changes in the society result in a steady growth in the proportion of households that "need" basic necessity services and in the total expenditures for such services, while the public perceives a decrease in the rate of economic growth and an increase in the general level of taxation.

Remedial, Rehabilitative, Curative, Social Care, and Deviance Control Services

Services. This analytic category includes the widest diversity of human service programs. These person-to-person services are generally similar to services which may be provided within the framework of the family, friendship group, or other primary communal groups. Examples include: advice-giving; personal counseling; rehabilitation treatments after illness or in the instance of chronic disability; remedial assistance with educational assignments; treatment of illnesses including mental and emotional illnesses; nursing care during illness; serving as a supportive advocate; relieving distress in times of personal crisis; helping a group of children in resolving a quarrel; substitute child care; homemaking and personal assistance for an older member of the family with disabilities; and the use of punishments, and rewards, to encourage certain behaviors and to discourage others.

All of these services are also produced by voluntary nonprofit and governmental human service agencies, although not all types of such organizational services are available in every geographic area. Moreover, many similar types of services are also available through the marketplace from individual professionals or from for-profit organizations. In some instances the service provided through voluntary nonprofit or governmental organizations bears marked similarity to that which might be provided within a family. In other instances the service involves technically specialized assistance not generally available within a family or between friends. In many instances the service is provided through an organizational program because it is required over a longer period of time than a family or friends can sustain.

When produced by voluntary nonprofit or governmental organizations, these services are, in nearly all instances, selectively targeted to categorical groups of consumers. The categorical definitions used often include economic criteria as well as other forms of eligibility criteria. Therefore, these services usually have some of the characteristics of a redistributional service. However, the major societal function of these organizationally produced services is to *change*, or to *control*, the behavior of particular individuals, families, groups or communities. This includes changes which result in an increase in socially desired behavior, and controls which lead to a decrease in behavior which is considered socially undesirable (Rochefort 1981).

These organizationally produced services cover all types of conditions which are considered problematic by some group in the society. And for every type of problem there are specialized program components for every different age group, provided under the auspices of a variety of human service professional disciplines. As an example of the diversity of service programs which have a behavior change/social control function, services which deal with aggressive behavior range from programs for young children (hyperactive behavior), to programs for adolescents (delinquency), and programs dealing with adults (criminal behavior). Included in this range of service programs are medically based services which may involve prescription of medication and/or psychoanalytic treatment, psychologically based programs involving behavior modification, social work based programs involving resocialization activities with teen-age gang groups, social work based programs involving person-environment changes through employment training and the creation of employment opportunities, education based remediation programs, and criminal justice programs using judicially ordered restitution by the delinquent or criminal offender. Scott and Black (1986) provide an overview of the range and complexity of services produced in the field of mental health.

Remedial, rehabilitative, curative, social care and deviance control services produced by voluntary nonprofit and governmental organizations are seldom available on a community wide universal use basis. Both the need for, and the demand for, any one type of service is likely to be distributed very unevenly throughout the community. There is a high degree of variation among households and individuals as to their preferences for services produced within the family, for services purchased in the marketplace, or for services produced by either a voluntary nonprofit organization or a governmental organization. For example, there may be a strong preference by some individuals or families for maintaining personal privacy by providing helping services within the family, even if voluntary nonprofit or governmental services are readily available.

On a community wide basis the benefits of many of these services may be viewed as primarily private benefits, with the expectation that they will be provided either within a family or through the marketplace. There is, in fact, little support in the society at large for a concept that every possible form of such personal services should be provided for every type of family, in every geographic area, on a nonmarketplace universal use basis through voluntary nonprofit or governmental organizations.

In some limited instances the provision of a specific service may be based only on a "pure" redistribution rationale. For example, a nonprofit voluntary Visiting Nurse Association may provide temporary personal care and home-maker services to an older adult who cannot pay the costs for such services, without any specific behavior change objectives. However, in most instances, the collective provision of remedial, rehabilitative, curative, social care or deviance control services through voluntary nonprofit or governmental organizations is based on a community interest in either developing and supporting individual behaviors which are collectively viewed as desirable, or modifying or restricting behaviors which are viewed as undesirable (Rochefort 1981).[5]

Such collectively provided behavior change/social control services, also called "people changing services" (Hasenfeld 1983), are, therefore, selectively directed to categories of individuals, households and communities viewed as "high need" or "high risk" situations having the potential of creating negative consequences for the members of the social unit which is sponsoring the service.

The behavior change/social control rationale for collective provision of services to particular individuals is based on the concept that in an organized society there is a common body of values, rules, and norms which serve as guides to those aspects of personal and interpersonal behavior that support and enhance the functioning and continuity of the society. Common assumptions about behavior that underlie the orderly functioning of the society are embodied in laws, in widely accepted value preferences, and in social norms, or expectations. Some of these assumptions may represent only the behavior preferences of the social majority. Others, like the prohibition against murder, are fundamental elements of social order. When individual, or group, behaviors do not conform to these laws, values or norms, such behaviors are viewed as a threat to the orderly functioning of the society and a threat to the security and well-being of the members of the society.

This system of laws, values and norms includes among others such widely supported concepts as: the responsibility to protect both one's own life and the lives of other human beings; personal resistance to discrimination and exploitation; the protection and nurture of children; obedience to laws and official authority; participation as a "citizen" in democratic political processes; the "good Samaritan" responsibility to offer assistance to persons at risk of injury or death; conformance of private behavior to public norms in public places; respect for and protection of private property; volunteer self-help and cooperation among members of local communities to deal with local problems; reduction of intergroup conflict within the community or within the society; maximizing individual independence, self-care, and self-realization; and the responsibility to contribute to the general welfare through work to produce goods and services. On the other hand, a variety of other rules, values and norms that are strongly supported by particular religious groups, or distinctive nationality or ethnic groups, as expectations for their own members, may not be an immediate concern of the community majority.

These normative elements of organized society are supported, reinforced and protected through the socialization of children within families and through organized education. They are also supported through the communication and reinforcement of values and norms by the public media and by civic and political leaders, and through the reaffirmation of values and norms within voluntary associations, including religious and fraternal groups. In addition, as indicated above, these rules, values and norms may be supported and protected through a wide variety of person-to-person behavior change/social control service activities which are directed towards high need or high risk situations.

Categorical services with behavior change/social control objectives have been developed, in part, as an alternative to coercive methods of behavior change, for example, psychiatric counseling and medication as an alternative to strait jackets and padded cells to deal with psychotic outbursts and probation services for juveniles in place of serving time in the county jail. In substantial part this shift from coercion to behavior change services is a response to the fact that in a complex interdependent society most forms of socially preferred behavior require voluntary action on the part of the individual; the preferred behavior cannot be coerced. A current dramatic example involves educational efforts to persuade individuals to say "No" voluntarily to the use of addictive drugs, as an alternative to the application of the coercive punishments which are provided for in existing laws, but which have been largely ineffective in reducing the general level of drug usage.

An outreach *deviance control* program directed to adolescents in a particular neighborhood which has the program objective of reducing glue-snifting, or marijuana smoking, may have many normative objectives: to protect individuals from death or permanent disability; to curtail behavior which interferes with educational achievement and with the administration of educational programs; to encourage alternative ways of satisfying personal interests; to prevent delinquency and crime; and to limit public behavior which may influence the future behavior of younger children. Such programs may be supported by federal, state, or local government funds, by United Way funding, and/or by contributions and volunteer services from a group of concerned neighborhood residents.

Services which have a behavior change/social control function may appear in serveral different forms. There may be categorically targeted program components within a broader universal service, for example, intensified educational motivation programs in public schools, established originally under the provisions of Title I of the Elementary and Secondary Education Act, targeted to schools with low academic achievement. There may be specialized behavior change/social control components within a broader basic necessities redistributive program, for example, the nutrition education component in the Women, Infants, and Children (WIC) program which provides nutritional supplements for pregnant women and young children. And there are service organizations that have behavior change/social control as their major function, for example, juvenile probation departments and residential treatment centers for children.

The development of many types of organizationally based service professions has been strongly linked with service programs organized around a behavior change/social control rationale. The administration of such programs involves dealing, in varying degrees, with individual professional specialists and with their organized associations. The variety of organizational auspices for these programs, and the professional domain or "turf" dynamics within each of the human service professions, have resulted in a very complex pattern of services, which includes overlapping programs as well as service gaps for which there are few resources.

Categorical services, both voluntary nonprofit and governmental, which serve a behavior change/social control function are "mixed goods" services. The objective is to provide both private benefits to the service consumer, and also "public goods" benefits in the form of changed behavior among the total group of persons served in the direction of behavior which is consistent with the laws, values and norms of the society, or that is consistent with the values and norms of the members of a specific group of sponsors and funders.

The specific behavior change/social control objectives for a particular service program are established primarily by the legitimators and financial supporters of that service. *This process of establishing organizational program objectives*

is independent of the personal objectives or interests of individual service users.
In addition, professional specialists involved in the production of these services
often have professionally defined service objectives. These behavior change/
social control objectives not only affect the structure of the program
organization; they also affect the actual process of service production and the
characteristics of the specific service outputs. Thus the benefits produced by a
particular remedial, rehabilitative, curative, social care or social control program
are not only a "mixed good;" they are also a form of *merit good* (Austin 1981).[6]

In some instances the characteristics of the benefits to the user may be nearly
identical to those which the user would prefer, if the user had the full power
to define the content of the service. However, in most instances there are
significant differences between the specific preferences of the service user and
the characteristics of the service as produced by the service organization. These
differences may involve the nature of the actual benefits provided. It may also
involve the level of such nonmonetary costs for the service user as travel time
and cost, convenience of scheduling, and the attractiveness and social status
of the service location, for example, in the case of a nonprofit day care center
for children in low-income single parent households.

Because there are differences between the characteristics of the personal
benefits from the service, and the associated personal costs, and the specific
preferences of the service users, organizational program components with
behavior change/social control objectives depend on a mixture of incentives
and opportunities (carrots) and disincentives and restraints (sticks) in order
to secure the participation of the intended service consumers. Moreover, the
service production technology in behavior change/social control programs
requires, in nearly every instance, some form of *co-production* between the
service specialist and the service user to produce the actual service output. The
personal counselor and the person being counseled must interact in a verbal
exchange, and the accomplishment of the counseling objectives depends
ultimately on the self-determined behaviors of the person being counseled.
Learning reading or mathematics in a special education classroom requires an
interactive process between the teacher and the student with a disability, and
the accomplishment of the teaching objectives depends largely on the
willingness of the student to make an effort to learn. In recovery from surgery,
or from a serious illness, the personal care behavior of the patient, including
self-administration of medicine according to directions, is an essential part of
a successful outcome. The co-production motivation of the service user is a
critical factor in achieving program objectives in remedial, rehabilitative,
curative, social care and deviance control programs.

A major incentive for using the service and in participating actively in the
co-production process, in most instances, is the availability of the service at
no cost, or at a cost below that of a marketplace equivalent. In some instances,
however, restraints are the dominant factor in securing participation, for

example in the case of rehabilitative correctional services provided at a maximum security prison. Even here, "good time" rewards may also be added to encourage active co-production participation in such services. Economic necessity may be a powerful form of restraint, for example, in compelling the participation of certain AFDC recipients in workfare programs as a condition of receiving assistance payments. Positive incentives in form of supplementary food provision are used to promote participation in the nutrition education services of the WIC program.

In elementary and secondary education the formal structure of service production is based on the concept that it is a universal divisible service with voluntary participation, or, at least, that the incentives and disincentives which support individual attendance are applied by parents. However, the "merit good" characteristics of educational services for children and adolescents are reflected in the provisions for legal penalties in the case of persistent truancy. These penalties exist primarily to support the behavior change/social control objectives of the educational program in the instance of those children who would not attend voluntarily, or whose parents do not support attendance.

Truancy control programs use a combination of the threat of court action, and efforts to increase the saliency of the personal rewards to be gained from education, either by counseling with the student and family, or through making modifications in the student's educational program, or both. The potential public good benefit of such truancy services comes from improved academic achievement and, in turn employment-relevant capabilities, as a result of school attendance among the students who are the users of such services. Such public good benefits may be achieved to a limited degree, even if the student's personal preference, all things being equal, would still be to leave school. However, an increase in the power of positive motivations which results in a more active process of co-production participation may result in a greater level of intellectual achievement, and in the public good benefit which results.

In the instance of individual counseling services, including mental health counseling, the negative pressures supporting service utilization involve the potential persistence of an individually stressful, or life-threatening condition as well as the concerns expressed by other persons, including employers. The positive incentives for participation include the ready availability of a low-cost treatment service which can provide relief from personal stress. The public good benefit comes from an expected reduction in the general level of disruptive or destructive behaviors, or behaviors which may interfere with employment or other day-to-day forms of normal social participation by the individual.

The services which have a behavior change/social control function also include what are defined as "social care," or "people sustaining" (Hasenfeld 1983) services, such as foster care of children, services provided in a variety of organized residential settings and "care" services provided to persons living in their own home. These programs have some of the characteristics of redistributional basic necessity services, that is the provision of food, shelter and routine personal and medical care in order to sustain normal behaviors and prevent deterioriation in physical and social performance.

However, the collective provision of such services also involves behavioral objectives. Many residential social care settings involve significant social control elements. These involve, at a minimum, limits on personal freedom to move about in the community outside of the residential setting, and they may often involve limits on the pattern of personal association within the residential setting. The recent expansion of noninstitutional social care services, including *case management*, for individuals with a variety of disabilities—mental illness, mental retardation, and age-related functional limitations—has had the specific objective of encouraging and supporting self-sustaining behaviors of independent living. The public good from such social care services results, in part, from minimizing utilization of collectively provided, high-cost residential settings such as general hospitals, psychiatric hospitals, state schools.

Political Economy Characteristics

Auspices. Categorical remedial, rehabilitative, curative, social care, and deviance control services with a behavior change/social control function may be established under a wide variety of organizational auspices. Governmental auspices include all levels of government from federal (Headstart) to state and local governments. Voluntary nonprofit auspices may also range from national (Red Cross Home Services) to state and local organizations (family service agency). Such service programs may be established by a small group of individuals with a single objective, for example, providing shelter for women who have been abused by their husbands. They may also be established on a society-wide basis with very broad and diverse objectives, for example, the community action component of the Office of Economic Opportunity, or community mental health centers.

Services with behavior change/social control objectives have developed the most diverse pattern of separation between *provider auspices* and *producer auspices* (Bendick 1985; Kolderie 1986). This has occurred in the voluntary nonprofit sector in which provision organizations, such as foundations and community-wide fundraising bodies like the United Way, are organizationally separate from direct service production. This has also occurred in governmental service programs as tax-supported agencies have increasingly used contracting to produce specialized services (Poole 1985). Cities and counties may use local tax funds and revenue sharing funds for grants and contracts with independent nonprofit organizations to achieve the production of such services, rather than establishing new governmental operating departments.

The development of this pattern of separation between provider organizations and service producers has been a result of a number of factors.

The diversity of services potentially involved, and, therefore, the diversity of service technologies involved, is much greater than any single administrative structure can readily accommodate. In part this is a consequence of the complexities involved when more than one professional discipline is centrally involved in service production, as in the field of mental health services. Administrative decentralization of service production through contracting also increases the opportunity for flexibility in program structure. Financial support for a particular type of service can be increased or decreased, separate from decisions about the level of support for other programs, a process that is often more difficult when departments within a single organization are involved.

Through contracting organizational problems associated with long-term employment security commitments to service specialists are reduced, as is the risk that all types of service needs, regardless of their actual characteristics, will be redefined to fit the skills and interests of existing staff members. Some types of highly specialized services which are required only occasionally can be obtained on an "as needed" basis through a purchase of service procedure, rather than through the employment of a permanent full-time staff specialist.

Political support for appropriations for a particular type of service may be broadened through the use of a network of service producers (Massachusetts Taxpayers Foundation 1980). Board members and staff members of contract organizations are free to lobby for increased expenditures, including direct approaches to legislators and other policymaking officials; employees of a governmental agency cannot do so.

A more complex aspect of this pattern of system decentralization is the increased degree of buffering, or loose coupling, it introduces into the service delivery system. It creates a further separation between the *collectively defined public good objectives* of the provider organization, reflecting the interests of those individuals and groups legitimating and funding the over-all program, and the *objectives of direct service producers* responsible for specific program components. Under the broad behavior change/social control purposes involved in initial establishment of a major service program, grants and contracts may be used to fund a variety of program production components administered by a variety of organizations which have similar, but not necessarily identical, objectives. For example, a juvenile delinquency program in which the legislated program objectives emphasize the direct reduction of aggressive behavior among teen-age "gang" members may contract for services with a psychological counseling service whose operational approach to delinquency prevention involves counseling with pre-teens who are in conflict with school authorities.

Individual program component objectives may be shaped primarily by the policy board of the contract producer, by the agency executive who often interprets the expectations of the contracting agency, or by the staff of service specialists, all of whom may have their own version of the behavior change/

social control objectives. The "loosely-coupled" contract monitoring and accountability system which often exists in such situations may allow both the providing organization and the producing organizations to assert that program purposes are being fulfilled.

This separation of functions may reduce the external pressures on each organization by reducing the number of constituencies which must be responded to. However, it may also reduce the extent to which any single set of public good objectives is being consistently achieved, in particular the behavior change/social control objectives of the original funders and legitimators. As Potuchek suggests (1986), the quality of the working relationship between the provider and the producer may be more important in maintaining funding than evidence of compliance with the program objectives.

The concept of federal block grants for human service programs, such as mental health and alcoholism services, is an extension of the separation of provision and production, further reducing the probability that specific legislative objectives originally included in enabling federal legislation are likely to be achieved. However, the separation of functions involved in the block grant concept can also reduce conflicting political pressures on federal executive and legislative branches over the definition of detailed objectives for particular programs. Under block grants these political pressures are largely diverted to the state or local level.

The separation of provision from production also externalizes what could otherwise be interdepartmental competition for resources in an inclusive service organization, particularly in a period of resource scarcity. However, the rationing of limited resources for a decentralized network of producers may require that the provider organization develop a complex competitive bidding process, proposal screening and review procedures, due process rules for the choice of producer, and elaborate program and fiscal auditing procedures to assure compliance with contract terms.

The development of a large organized group of independent service producers may also result in the formation of a coalition with political leaders. This coalition, in turn, may have the objective of maximizing the level of financial support for service production, minimizing the accountability procedures administered by the governmental provider agency, and limiting the scope of the provider agency expenditures on such support services as planning and program evaluation (Massachusetts Taxpayer's Foundation 1980).

Legitimation. Legitimation of categorical services with behavior change/ social control objectives depends upon agreement on the nature of the objectives to be sought among a group of individuals who are prepared to secure core financial support either directly by soliciting contributions, or indirectly by advocating for governmental support. Such an agreement may reflect a systematic examination of those social and health conditions considered by the sponsors to be indicators of the empirical "need" for a particular service. Or the support for the establishment of a particular service may be based on personal convictions about the importance of the behavior changes to be sought.

A group of potential users, or their families, may form the core of an initiating group, as when parents of young children with developmental disabilities create a specialized day care service. Or services with behavior change/social control objectives may be established first, and users recruited to fit the service through the use of incentives and constraints, just as a market demand for a new product may be generated through advertising after an initial decision has been made to produce a product.

Legitimation of a service as one justifying broad community support either through community wide voluntary fundraising or through governmental funding requires that the behavioral change objectives of the program fit within the normative consensus of the community. It is often difficult to gain community wide sanction and support for a service which has nominal support from a majority of the community but is strongly opposed on normative grounds by a highly organized minority of community members. An existing program may find its legitimacy threatened if there is a marked change in the community consensus about the behavioral change/social control objectives or the appropriateness of the incentives and constraints in the program.

In such a situation an agency may change its support base, for example by withdrawing from a community-wide fund raising organization, and carrying out its own fundraising activities among those individuals who support the objectives of the program. This has occurred in a number of communities with Planned Parenthood organizations. The service organization, on the other hand, may adapt and change its behavioral objectives and the characteristics of a particular program component. Or it may choose to restate its objectives in language which is in keeping with changed attitudes, but make only limited modifications in the actual characteristics of its services.

Legitimation may also be tied to a requirement for recognition by an organized professional discipline, either through formal accreditation procedures controlled by the discipline, through the designation of the program as a training location for professional students, or through the personal endorsement of recognized professional specialists as reflected in their willingness to serve as staff members or to accept membership on a policy board or professional advisory committee. Withdrawal of legitimation may occur through withdrawal of any, or all, of these forms of recognition.

The criteria for professional legitimation, however, may conflict with the criteria for community, or political legitimation. Pressures by a professional association for increased professionalization of the staff may be viewed as a challenge to the importance assigned within the program to the objectives of the sponsors. The organized profession may not recognize or support the behavior change/social control objectives held by the community, or by the legislative program sponsors. The professional staff supported by the organized profession may also urge that the positive incentives for program participation be increased and disincentives or restraints be decreased on the basis that more persons will use the service, and that co-production of beneficial service outputs will be improved, with an over-all increase in community benefits.

However, this may also increase the unit costs of the program and increase the pressures on sponsors to raise additional funds. If additional financial support is sought through the introduction of service fees, or by increasing the level of existing fees, increased weight is likely to be given to the preferences of service users as a way of encouraging continued participation. This may result in a decrease in the attention given to the behavioral outcome objectives of other groups, such as the objectives of voluntary contributors or governmental sponsors, which may lead to the withdrawal of legitimation of the program as a collectively sponsored activity.

The legitimation of a service with behavior change/social control objectives may be directly affected by community or political conflicts over the definition of the behavior change objectives or over the balance of incentives and constraints within the structure of the service. It may also be affected by conflicts between the objectives of program sponsors, those of professional service personnel and the preferences of service users and organized user constituencies.

Evaluation. Program evaluation of services which have behavior change/social control objectives receives more attention than other categories of human services. Program objectives specify changes in behavior, and evidence of these changes in behavior is viewed as the justification for continued collective provision. Moreover, because they are labor intensive activities, the unit costs of such programs are relatively high. Therefore, program sponsors not only seek information that provides evidence of behavior changes but also evidence that they are attributable to the program. Is there a decrease in rates of delinquent behavior? Is this decrease a consequence of the work of the juvenile probation department, or of a decrease in the number of adolescents? Is there an increase in the number of job placements among AFDC recipients in employment programs? Is it a result of the job placement element in that program, or of an upturn in the economy?

However, the actual process of evaluation in such programs is unusually difficult. And the results are often relatively unsatisfactory from the perspective of the program sponsors. Since the formal behavior change objectives of the program differ, at least in degree, from the purposes and preferences of the service users, user satisfaction, by itself, is not a satisfactory base for evaluation of program outcomes. Systematic evaluation of the actual outcomes of the service program requires detailed specification of the original program objectives. In the course of developing a detailed statement of objectives, differences in the definition of such objectives as among sponsors, administrators, service staff, and service users are made explicit, creating difficulties for the evaluation process and potentially intensifying the level of conflict within the service organization. Many of the specific behavior changes being sought as program outcomes are often difficult, if not impossible, to observe directly without violation of personal privacy. User self-reports of behavior changes may be distorted in a variety of ways.

Measurement of attitude changes on the part of service users as an alternative approach involves indirect methods of measurement. These methods are often internally consistent but they have seldom been validated by systematic evidence of their relation to specific behavior changes. Where there are significant findings of persistent changes in the behavior of program participants, it is often difficult to prove a cause and effect relationship between the specific technology of the service program and the outcomes, in part because of the significant role of co-production. In co-production processes the personality of the service provider, and the potential role of that personality in motivating active participation and in determining the outcomes, independent of specific program content or technology, becomes a confounding factor. Other potentially confounding factors include differences in the initial motivations of service users, discrepancies between the officially specified pattern of service production activities and the "operative" pattern of such activities (Hasenfeld 1983), as well as significant variations in the application of service technology among service workers.

In the absence of clear-cut evaluation evidence of significant program outcomes, persons seeking information that will support the continued legitimation and funding of such service programs frequently rely on quantitative evidence of effort, that is the amount of service activity. Process evaluation that provides evidence that the service activities are being carried out as planned, or as prescribed by professional standards, may also be used. In many instances, information about outcomes in individual case situations and user testimonials are used to illustrate program validity. Testimony by individuals is also utilized to show continuing need for the services. These evaluation procedures are not only easier to carry out, but they also involve much lower costs than scientifically valid evaluation studies of program outcomes.

The accountability of these categorical service programs with behavior change/social control objectives, as expressed through the provisions for evaulation, is primarily to the sponsors who represent legitimating authority and funding sources. Because of the degree of imbalance in the power to enforce accountability through evaluation as between sponsors and users, specific procedures have been established in some instances to redress the imbalance. These procedures include formal provisions for joint approval of service plans by the service worker and the service user, official internal appeal procedures as well as peer review of professional procedures, detailed evaluations of service quality by service users at the end of a period of receiving services, independent individuals (ombudsmen) or groups (patient rights committees) to whom service participants can make complaints, and creation of independent "advocacy and protection" organizations in some service areas.

Summary. Categorically targeted services with behavior change/social control objectives involve the full range of complexities in human service programs in general. The range of organizational auspices reflects the diversity dealt with in Chapter 8. Some are administered nationwide by the federal government, for example the alcoholism counseling services for military veterans. Some are sponsored by a voluntary association in a single neighborhood, for example, the East Side Teen Center. Each service program is shaped by a potentially conflictual combination of the objectives of the sponsors, the objectives of the service specialists and the needs and preferences of the service users. They are "mixed goods" and "merit good" services.

Some service programs with behavior change/social control functions have very broad and inclusive objectives—to improve the mental health of the people of the United States. Some have very narrowly defined objectives—to reduce the incidence of truancy among junior high students in the Greenwood School District. Legitimation of the service program may depend more on a consensus about the objectives to be sought than on evidence of either need or of results. The service producing technologies are imprecise. And since the service outcomes are co-produced, the results may depend as much on the motivational abilities of the service specialists, the unique personality characteristics of the service user, and the pattern of interaction between the two, as on technical skills. Evaluations of the results are often confounded by the uniqueness of the individual service situation and the lack of precise guidelines for assessing actual outcomes.

The scope and justification for such service programs, the definition of program objectives, and the choice of incentives and restraints to support participation are directly linked to fundamental issues of purpose and goals within the American society as a whole. It is therefore not surprising that these issues are often hotly contested. Funders and legitimators, professional disciplines, and service users and their advocates often take very different positions about the purposes of a service program which all parties agree is needed in some form.

Employment Support Services

Categorical employment support services have the specific objective of assisting individuals in gaining access to employment, in maintaining employment, and in achieving promotions and career advancement. Employment support services have a particular importance in the structure of human services in the United States because of the central significance of employment in American society. Income is distributed primarily through employment channels. Occupational status and employment are critical elements in defining personal identity and status for all adults and employment patterns among specific population groups are directly related to the relative political and economic power of those groups. Employment support services include technical training, job readiness, personal and vocational counseling, work experience programs, placement services, affirmative action advocacy, employment-related day care provision and job-related assertiveness training. These services also include unemployment insurance, which is explicitly designed not only to provide temporary income for basic necessities but also to encourage continuing attachment to the labor force during periods of personal unemployment.

The categorical employment support services produced by voluntary non-profit and governmental organizations have both redistributive characteristics and behavior change/social control characteristics. They are primarily targeted on a redistributional basis to socially and economically disadvantaged groups, the members of which face barriers in access to employment and in promotion after employment. These include members of ethnic minority populations, individuals with physical and developmental handicaps, school leavers, unemployed recipients of income assistance, residents in areas which are economically depressed or in which major industrial closures have taken place. Employment support services also have specific behavior change/social control objectives involving the fit between an individual's occupational skills and work-related behavior and the requirements of the job market. The political economy characteristics of employment support service programs are similar to the political economy characteristics of both categorical basic necessity services and categorical remedial, rehabilitative, curative, social care and deviance control services.

FACILITATIVE AND SUPPORT SERVICES

This chapter has dealt with an analysis of the social functions of primary services produced through voluntary nonprofit and governmental organizations. Other types of program activities are often found in close association with these primary services, often as critical elements of the interorganizational service delivery system (Hjern and Porter 1981). These facilitative and support activities, which are included in Figure 9-1, although part of the human services industries, have operational characteristics which are generally much like those of similar activities in other industries.

Facilitative Services

These are linkage or ancillary services which are often an essential element in service delivery. They include special purpose transportation, information and referral services, outreach services, translators and consumer advocacy services. They may be organized as the core activities of a free-standing organization, or as a facilitating program component within a larger service agency. Where the facilitative services are part of a larger organization these program components may involve policy and administrative procedure issues similar to those involved in the direct service components of the larger service agency of which they are a part.

Secondary Support Services

These services include technical, or "staff" services that are part of the administrative infrastructure including personnel administration, financial management, management information and program data systems, program evaluation, resource mobilization and other similar activities. These technical services often require individuals, either as staff members or on a consultant basis, who have specialized knowledge and competencies different from those of the direct service staff. The evaluation of the quality and effectiveness of these components is often a major responsiblity of the organizational executive.

Tertiary Support Services

These include separately organized activities that support the general service delivery structure such as combined fundraising activities, which includes both the solicitation of and collection of voluntary contributions, and the authorization of and collection of taxes, together with the planning and fund-allocating components which are often part of fundraising organizations. The headquarters component of large state and national governmental agencies performs similar functions. Also included are educational programs for technical and professional personnel, local or specialized foundations, accreditation organizations, free-standing research and testing organizations, associations of service users and user advocates, lobbying and advocacy organizations, publishers of specialized materials, and producers of specialized technical services, materials and equipment. While the substantive content of the activities within these tertiary support services is distinctive to the human services, most of the administrative and technical procedures involved are similar to those of organizations in other fields.

Industry Level Organizations

An additional level of organizational structures can be identified at the industry level. These include state, national and international trade associations of organizations, industry-wide conferences, professional membership associations, general purpose national foundations which often provide both funding and technical assistance, industry relevant research institutes and standard setting research, and industry level lobbying and public education organizations. Cabinet level offices, including Health and Human Services, Education, Labor, Agriculture, and Transportation also perform industry wide functions. Again while the substantive content of the activities of these organizations has a distinctive relation to particular types of human services, the administrative and staff activities of the organizations are, in general, like those in similar organizations in other industries.

NOTES

1. There are also public policies and service programs that have a positive distribution effect; they result in an increase in the effective economic resources of persons whose earned income is already above the median. Many of these take the form of "tax shelter" provisions in the tax code but they also include such things as farm production subsidies for "gentlemen" farmers and special benefits for retired military officers.

2. Many of the analyses of this issue deal primarily with normative arguments about why individuals "should" provide assistance to others, rather than dealing with the behavioral dynamics that underlie the actual redistributional pattern of basic necessity programs that exist.

3. In some instances employees in a particular organization may develop a communal pattern of mutual assistance obligations which is separate from the pattern of role relationships involved in normal production activities within the organization, but this is the exception rather than the rule.

4. The Earned Income Tax Credit, a modest version of a negative income tax, directly administered at a federal level, is the only program which provides assistance to low-income households without elaborate categorical eligibility determination procedures. However, by being limited to households with children it also includes a "deservedness" criteria.

5. There are some types of behavior change services that are primarily intended to support desired behavior in "high potential" situations, for example specialized educational programs for "gifted and talented" students.

6. The term "merit good" is used to describe a service which is produced in response to the preferences of persons other than the service user, which Musgrave (1959) describes as a "merit want." The character of the private good benefit obtained by the service user is defined, at least in part, not by the user but by the providers and the producers, that is those who have established the program and by the professional staff involved in producing the service.

Chapter 11

Implications of the Political Economy Perspective for Executives and Researchers

This book has been addressed in particular to executives in human service programs in all of the varied forms of voluntary nonprofit and governmental organizations. It is an effort to explore forces that actually shape the environment with which executives deal every day. The executive role in human service programs includes a complex mix of policymaking and management responsibilities; these responsibilities are also shared with other organizational participants such as board members, elected public officials, and professional specialists. Yet it is the executive role, in particular, that carries continuous responsibility and ultimate accountability for strategic planning and contingency management and that carries responsibilty for the effectiveness of internal production activities in achieving the public good objectives which are the primary basis for the funding and legitimation of the service organization.

To deal successfully with these inherent responsibilities the executive must have an understanding of the political economy environment of human service programs in general and an understanding of the specific political economy environment of a particular organization, as well as the ability to function effectively in that environment. While the characteristics of the political economy environment are important for everyone involved in a human service organization, these characteristics are particularly important for the executive. This chapter summarizes critical concepts from the political economy analysis presented in this volume that have particular significance for executives in human service programs, and for researchers who are interested in exploring issues in the functioning of human service programs.

THE STRUCTURE OF HUMAN SERVICE PROGRAMS

The complex structure of human service programs is of central importance to the human services executive. Specific service production activities take place as person-to-person transactions within *program components*, which are distinctive units of activity within an organization in which a defined group of staff personnel using specific technologies interact with a particular group of service users to co-produce a specific type of human service—the care of a child outside of the natural family, teaching/learning arithmetic, health maintenance of a woman who is pregnant, the treatment of an eating disorder, the resolution of family conflicts, the maintenance of self-care by an older adult with disabilities who is living alone, the economic maintenance of a family without personal income.

These program components, in turn, are elements in two types of more complex social structures. First, the vertically organized *service organization*, which is the basic budgetary and financial management structure, and the structure with which employed staff personnel are identified, and second, the horizontally organized local *interorganizational service delivery network*, or *implementation structure* (Hjern and Porter 1981).

Both service organizations and service delivery networks are elements of *human service industries* in social services, health care, mental health treatment, elementary and secondary education and rehabilitation. Human service industries are, in turn, embedded in the *societal political economy environment*, an environment which increasingly has not only national characterstics, but also international world-wide characteristics. That political economy environment, in turn, determines the conditions of legitimation and the characteristics of the resource flow for human service industries in general, and for individual human service organizations in particular.

The policymaking and management activities of the executive in human service organizations are largely reactive. They are primarily responses to developments in this political economy environment, developments over which neither the executive nor any other member of the organization has control. However, in an interactive fashion, executives and other members of human service organizations are also dynamic factors in the political economy. They lobby aggressively for the needs of service users as well as for program funding for their own ogranization. They also participate in special interest coalitions at local, state and national levels which have impacts on public policy decisions. Moreover, the perceived effectiveness, or ineffectiveness, of the services produced by human service organizations in achieving public good objectives often has a significant long-term impact on the political economy environment.

THE BEHAVIORAL BASE OF THE POLITICAL ECONOMY

Both the political power patterns and the economic distribution patterns which together consititute the political economy environment are shaped by the combined actions of all of the individuals in a given society (Chapter 1). There has been a major emphasis in contemporary political economy analyses on "self-interest," and in particular on *economic self-interest,* as the dominant source of motivation for the actions of individuals, not only in marketplace exchanges, but also in the enactment of political participation roles and organizational position roles (Buchanan and Tullock 1962; Tullock 1965). Therefore, it is argued, economic self-interest motivations are the dominant dynamic in collective or societal processes as well as in marketplace exchanges. In turn, economic analyses become the dominant form of policy analysis and assessment.

Collective, or societal, behavior is, indeed, ultimately based on individual choices and actions. There is no "collective will" or "public interest" which exists apart from the aggregated pattern of choices made, and actions taken, by individuals, past and present. Moreover, economic self-interest, rooted in the need to procure the basic necessities required for individual physical survival, and other forms of explicitly personal self-interest, are extremely important in the dynamics of collective action, including the collective action involved in the creation and maintenance of the voluntary nonprofit and governmental organizations involved in human service programs.

However, in addition to economic self-interest motivations there is a second set of important motivational forces that underlie many of the individual choices and actions involved in collective behavior. These are *communal relationship* motivations based on perceptions by individuals of the mutual interdependencies involved in relationships among individuals within a family, and within other communal structures, including the extended family, friendship groups, primary neighborhoods, locality communities, ethnic and cultural communities and national societies (Chapter 1).

Communal structures, in particular the family, are marked by the importance of culturally defined role-related behavioral expectations—the behavior expected of a parent, a sibling, a relative, a friend, a neighbor. These expectations include the obligations of mutual assistance, sharing and compassion. The power of these communal behavioral motivations, like the power of economic self-interest motivations, varies markedly among individuals and is affected by differences in cultural traditions, as described in *Habits of the Heart* (Bellah, Madsen, Swidler, Sullivan and Tipton 1985).

These communal behavioral expectations, *which are often not consistent with economic self-interest,* are different from marketplace exchange behavioral expectations. Exchanges based on communal relationships are not mediated by monetary transactions and are not contractual. Where economic marketplace relationships are defined, in principle, as universalistic and impersonal, communal relationships are particularistic and value laden.

The motivational dynamics involved in the enactment of family roles and other communal roles are particularly important in the political economy of human service programs. As described in Chapter 1, human service programs are analogs of activities within families and other communal groups. In many ways both the staff personnel involved in the production of human services and the users of human services are enacting communal roles.

In nearly all instances the production of human services involves person-to-person relationships in which, even for brief periods of time, the individuals involved become significant persons to each other. Indeed, the ethical prescriptions of human service professions fundamentally embody the concept that the professional service relationship involves a *moral* obligation of the professional specialist—teacher, social worker, physician, nurse—to the service user as a particular individual, or as in the instance of the public administrator or the city planner, to a particular communal group of individuals.

Voluntary nonprofit and governmental human service organizations are forms of collective activity which lie between communal groups and the marketplace. Some form of monetary exchange is involved in most contemporary forms of human services production. However, the basis for the specific monetary valuation of these exchanges is always problematic, reflecting their similarity to non-monetary exchanges within communal groups. What is the basis for determining the true economic value of: the parenting provided by a foster-parent; the intensive care provided by nurses after an organ transplant in which the patient is a seven-year-old child; the career counseling provided by an experienced high school teacher; the prenatal care which prevents a premature birth, extensive neonatal care and possibly life-long mental retardation; the income assistance to a family with adolescents which prevents school dropouts; or family therapy which maintains the integrity of a family that includes young children?

The activities of voluntary nonprofit and governmental human service organizations include a wide variety of marketplace exchanges in day-to-day operations—in the purchase of supplies and equipment. in the payment of personnel, in the investment of endowments, in the sale of a variety of products to service users. But the production and distribution of services in these organizations always involves, in varying degrees, the "sharing," or "redistribution," of valued and sometimes scarce resources. Such sharing is not consistent with the contractual expectations of marketplace relationships, but it is consistent with the obligations involved in communal relationships.

The actions taken by individuals both in their private lives and through their participation in politics and other collective activities in response to communal motivations involve important distinctions about who is "one of us" and who is "deserving" (Chapter 9). These motivations, therefore, do not lead directly to support for universal and equal sharing with everyone in need, a goal sought by many social philosophers, and by many workers in human service programs (Morris 1986). It is, however, the motivational dynamics rooted in the complex patterns of communal relationships, as well as those which are rooted in patterns of economic exchange relationships, that must be taken into account in understanding, and dealing with, the real political economy of human service programs.

THE ROLE OF IDEOLOGIES IN THE POLITICAL ECONOMY OF HUMAN SERVICE PROGRAMS

Much of the contemporary analysis of policy issues in human service programs, and in particular the debate over the "future of the welfare state," is based on ideological concepts developed at the beginning of the period of industrialization in Europe and the United States (Chapter 2). Indeed, the term "political economy" has most often been associated with analyses based on the ideologies of traditional marketplace capitalism or traditional state socialism.

However, both traditional marketplace capitalism and traditional state socialism paradigms make assumptions about the political economy dynamics of postindustrial society which are no longer valid. Changes which have taken place render these traditional ideologies largely irrelevant to the analysis of the role of human service programs within such societies (Chapter 3).

- The blurring of distinctions between the governmental/political sector and the business/economic sector leading to the development of a "mixed economy" society in which there is an interpenetration of "public" government and "private" business, including, but not limited to, human service industries.
- Blurring of class definitions involving both "the working-class" and "upper-class capitalists," and the absence of cohesive "class consciousness" within both social status categories.
- The replacement of "class conflict" by a variety of conflicts between the institutional maintenance interests of powerful corporate organizations in both business and government, and the individual interests of consumers and citizens at all social status levels.
- Changes in the role of labor unions within the labor force and a decrease in the power of labor unions in the structure of political parties, as the proportion of industrial "blue-collar" employees decreases.
- The expansion of the "middle-class" as a broadly inclusive self-defined social status which includes individuals who support both the provision of "public good" benefits through collective action *and* "private good" benefits through the marketplace. The large-scale participation of

women in the labor force has been the important factor in the increased number of two-income "middle-class" households.

• A recognition of the inherent limitations of centralized authority and of large-scale production organizations which are logical outcomes from the unrestricted application of both traditional marketplace capitalism and state socialism paradigms (Chapter 5). These limitations include difficulties in institutional adaptation to changes in the environment, destructive consequences for individuals who work in large-scale organizations, and difficulties in maintaining quality and enforcing accountability in production activities, particularly in the instance of human service production.

• The demonstrated inability in the 1980s of politically successful ideological movements explicitly committed to traditional capitalism (Great Britian and the United States) or traditional socialism (France) to restructure their societies consistent with their ideological models (Carny and Schain 1985).

The irrelevance of traditional ideological models based on early industrialism suggests a need for more pragmatically grounded conceptual frameworks for analyzing contemporary human service policy issues, and for identifying alternative directions for future development. Welfare capitalism and social democracy represent two alternative ideological frameworks. Both serve, to a limited degree, as frameworks for criticizing existing societies. However, neither has yet gained the status of being a broadly accepted base for political mobilization, or for prophetic definition of the future. The effort to develop a forward looking ideology of democratic socialism has advanced further in Europe than in the United States (Himmelstrand, Ahrne, Lundberg and Lundberg 1981; Offe 1984).

THE MEANING OF REDISTRIBUTION

A central issue in ideological analyses of the political economy is the role of government in economic redistribution (Chapter 4). The traditional focus of social welfare analyses has been a single inclusive model of redistribution, which deals both the philosophical and moral rationales for a universal pattern of redistribution and the mechanisms of such redistribution. The objective set forth is to develop an approach which will create a substantial degree of economic equality across the entire society, off-setting inequalities which result from marketplace processes (Morris 1986). However, postindustrial societies involve a number of distinctive economic sectors each with distinctive redistributional issues, including the definition of equality, and involving different mechanisms. A single redistributional model is not applicable to all categories of persons and households in postindustrial societies.

Traditional social welfare analyses have focused primarily on the policy issues involving low-income *labor force related* households, that is households in which one or more persons has a labor force attachment, or is potentially a labor force participant. Existing labor force related redistributional programs involve a number of unresolved policy issues, and widespread inequities, in part a consequence of the limitations of communal relationship motivations in a mobile, culturally diverse society like the United States. However, the major concerns about redistributional policies and their impact on national economies now involve *categorical redistribution*, namely the redistribution of economic resources to persons without a presumptive labor force attachment. Because marketplace processes are unable to deal with systematic long-term redistribution to persons without a labor-force attachment, the role of governmental programs is of primary significance as the number of such persons increases steadily.

Categorical redistribution programs include individuals beyond retirement age and younger individuals with a variety of disabilities. They benefit individuals from both low-income and middle-income backgrounds and therefore do not fit into traditional class conflict analyses of welfare state issues. Moreover, since there is no explicit economic criterion for defining an appropriate level for categorical redistributions, recipient groups, and their advocacy supporters, are necessarily drawn into active participation in the political arena, contributing directly to the competition for resources and the politicalization of human service policy issues (Janowitz 1978).

Another factor in the growing economic and political importance of categorical redistributional programs is the increase in the scope and costs of medical, rehabilitation and social care services; it is difficult to establish an economically rational pattern of reimbursement because of the large role of professional service costs. In turn, such categorical redistributional programs as Medicare, Medicaid and Supplemental Security Income have become major funding sources for the human service industries producing such services. This is coupled with scientific advancements in medical technology which has increased the number of medical care specialists whose livelihood is dependent upon such categorical funding. As the scope of categorical redistribution programs increases, the political economy dynamics, which affect not only the level of funding but also the administrative requirements applied to service organizations, are shaped less by the perception of mutual communal obligations than they are by political power bargaining, not unlike the pattern in categorical redistributional programs for military veterans.

THE CHARACTERISTICS OF HUMAN SERVICE INDUSTRIES

One of the important characteristics of human service industries in the United States has been the parallel development of both voluntary nonprofit and governmental service organizations, particularly in health care and social services (Chapters 6 and 7). Until the 1940s these two sectors conceptually, and operationally, developed on a parallel and frequently antagonistic basis. Attitudes towards these two sectors reflected different ideological perspectives. Advocates of traditional capitalism primarily supported "voluntarism." Advocates of socialist alternatives to capitalism primarily supported the expansion of governmental services. Supporters of welfare capitalism advocated for the simultaneous development of both voluntary nonprofit and governmental services.

Major expansion in governmental human service programs began in the 1930s, while the high point of the development of the voluntary nonprofit sector as a nationwide "system" came in the 1950s. Since the 1950s there has been a steady growth in the scope of both voluntary nonprofit and governmental human service sectors, an increasingly "mixed economy" melding of these two sectors, and a significant decrease in the distinctive "system" characteristics of the voluntary nonprofit sector. While the concept of the nonprofit sector has been expanded through the formation of Independent Sector, the linkages of local nonprofit organizations with governmental programs in particular service areas has taken precedence over their identification with the nonprofit sector as a distinctive social force.

The melding of major segments of the voluntary nonprofit sector and the governmental sector has increased the diversity of organizational auspices so that mixed auspices, primarily involving various combinations of nonprofit legal structure with a variety of governmental funding sources, are the most prevalent pattern (Chapter 8). The commercialization of many human service programs has also resulted in some voluntary nonprofit organizations, and some governmental organizations, becoming very similar to marketplace for-profit firms. Each of these varied forms of auspice has a different pattern of accountability linkages with key elements in the political economy environment.

There has also been a steady growth in the number and scope of for-profit firms in human service industries, as well as an increase in the number and variety of private practitioners (Chapter 8). These developments reflect: ideological ascendancy of marketplace theories in the 1980s; changes in funding mechanisms, in particular in commercial and governmental insurance mechanisms, covering mental health services as well as general health care services; a competitive edge for for-profit firms resulting, in part, from their access to the capital resources required for organizational development; the preference of professionally educated women for the autonomy and flexibility involved in private practice as compared to the conditions of employment in large-scale human service organizations; and a movement of entreprenurial business executives into service industries.

For-profit firms have the technical capability to produce any type of human service which is produced by either voluntary nonprofit or governmental service organizations. However, there are important differences between voluntary nonprofit and governmental organizations and for-profit firms in the organizational governance structure which controls organizational assets, with only stockholder interests being consistently represented at the policymaking level in for-profit firms. The political economy significance of these differences is primarily related to the relative size of the for-profit sector within any one human service industry.

The increasing complexity of human service industries reflects the diverse characteristics of the services being produced. Unlike industrial firms or retail stores whose products are evaluated solely by the purchasers who seek "private good" benefits from them, voluntary nonprofit and governmental human service organizations produce services which provide "private good" benefits to users, and "public good" benefits to other members of the local community or the society at large. The "mixed good" character of human service products means that such organizations have dual accountability both to users, and to those persons who control legitimation and funding of the organization.

Moreover, different types of services—universal; basic necessities; remedial, rehabilitative, curative, social care, deviance control; and employment support—necessarily involve different types of "public good," so that a single model of accountability, or evaluation, is not appropriate. Remedial, rehabilitative, curative, social care, deviance control services which are organized around a behavior change/social control rationale are, in particular, shaped as much by the preferences of policymakers and professionals as by the preferences of service users. The "merit good" characteristics of such services requires a mix of incentives and constraints to attract and maintain user participation. The balance between incentives and constraints must ultimately be acceptable to those who legitimate and fund the organization, as well as being beneficial to the users. Changes in the relative influence of any of these groups, for example by providing funds to service users to be used for the direct purchase of services, leads to changes in the characteristics of the services and the evaluation standards applied to them.

Another important characteristic of human service industries is the increasing importance of a network of organized professions. Organized professions, rather than employing organizations, largely control both admission to and the content of professional education. To the extent that the completion of professional education is a prerequisite to professional certification or licensing, a combination of the organized profession and educators in professional schools controls access to professional status, and therefore determines the size and characteristics of the labor force supply of professional specialists. Professional membership associations advocate for the restriction of key organizational staff positions to professionally credentialed individuals, further restricting personnel options. Informal linkages among professional colleagues, however, may often be an essential element in the functioning of interorganizational service delivery systems, and be a source of advance information on technological developments, funding for program services or research, and critical legislative and administrative policy developments.

Professional colleague networks often serve as a counterforce to the authority of policymakers and executives in particular organizations, sometimes in support of the concerns of service users, and, on other occasions, in support of professional standards or the self-interests of professional practitioners. Efforts by professional specialists and professional associations to protect the concept of professional autonomy in making critical judgements in diagnosis, prescription, treatment and evaluation also limit the discretion of the executive. They contribute directly to the pattern of "loose coupling" within human service organizations.

The power of organized professions within human service industries has been constrained by competition among professions over conflicting domain definitions, sometimes with overtones of male-female competition (nurses vs. doctors, social workers vs. psychologists). However, recent moves to establish collaborative relationships among a number of mental health professional associations may substantially increase the power of organized professions in human service industries in general. Such a development becomes increasingly important as the organizational structure of human service industries becomes more decentralized.

Most human service industries are undergoing a general process of service production decentralization with the downshifting of federal administrative controls attached to federal categorical funding to state and local levels under block grant funding; the appearance of numerous new "alternative" service organizations; the development of new types of specialized services to meet the needs of specialized segments of the user market; the increasing use of contracting with a number of different service producers by governmental service organizations; the growth of private practice in such fields as social work; the emergence of for-profit firms; and the growth of human service activities within business firms.

Among the consequences of this general pattern of decentralization there has been an increase in the number of executive positions. Competition among organizations for resources has increased and there has been a marked increase in the complexity of interorganizational service delivery systems together with problems of accountability and control. However, the competitive development of service organizations also increases the service options available to potential service users in some situations. There is a greater level of instability within industries as some organizations become larger in particular market "niches," while other organizations disappear, or are restructured to serve a new market. In turn, fewer professional specialists have life-long careers in a single employing organization.

IMPLICATIONS FOR HUMAN SERVICE EXECUTIVES

Human service industries are a major economic and political force in postindustrial societies. The societal move towards greater individualism has increased both the range of opportunities for personal expression and development, and the risks of personal difficulty and disaster. The extension of life has extended the potential range of situations in which help is needed. While members of communal groups—family members, friends, neighbors and fellow community members—continue to be the largest source of all types of services in the society as a whole, the demand (expressed both through the marketplace and through the political arena) for organized services providing for temporary financial assistance, the education and socialization of children, or the care of an elderly parent with severe disabilities, has increased steadily. An even greater rate of increase in such demand can be anticipated in the forseeable future.

Human service executives, as well as governmental and voluntary policymakers and professional specialists of all types, have a critical set of responsibilities within these humans service industries. Among the most important of these responsibilities is an understanding of both the constraints and opportunities which exist within the everchanging political economy environment. Understanding these factors is essential for the development and maintenance of the service organization. Another important responsibility is an understanding of the relation of a particular service organization to the network of organizations involved in particular service delivery systems. It is the quality of the service delivery system, rather than the quality of service production in any single organization, that ultimately determines the benefits which a particular individual or household receives.

One of the important leadership functions of the human service executive is to assist other personnel within the service organization to understand the characteristics of the environment within which the organization is operating. It is essential to understand the nature of the diverse "stakeholder" interests which shape that environment. However, it is also a major responsibility of the executive to "buffer the production technology" so that direct service personnel can increase their effectiveness by focusing primarily on the immediate service situations for which they are responsible. This requires "political," "negotiating," "boundary-spanning," "interpretative," "environmental scanning," "strategic management," and "entrepreneurial" or "opportunity seizing" skills. The executive function has become increasingly complex as these environmental interaction and leadership functions are combined with control over financial, legal, and accountability procedures, program policy development and the maintenance of quality service production.

IMPLICATIONS FOR RESEARCH

The political economy analysis of human service programs raises a number of issues which need detailed study. The research suggestions which follow primarily address policy and operational concerns rather than theory building concerns. Parts of this research agenda have been addressed, but the results are published piecemeal in a variety of professional and discipline journals, so that the information is not generally available to policymakers and executives in usable form, that takes into account the distinctive operational characteristics of specific human service programs. It is recognized that many types of potential research involving human service programs are very difficult to carry out, given the impreciseness of the technology in nearly all human service fields, and the difficulties involved in gaining agreement about an appropriate definition of the outcomes to be studied and the criteria for judging effectiveness.

Studies of Human Service Industries. The concept of human service industries suggests the appropriateness of detailed system mapping studies of specific human service industries at local, state and national levels, including for-profit firms. Such studies should also include an analysis of the political economy environment of the industry; linkages of that environment to societal patterns of power and resource distribution; opportunities and constraints created by the political economy; and the processes of change within that environment.

Of particular importance would be studies of resource availability and resource flows within the industry; the impact of specific forms of legislation on the industry; the impacts of labor force changes; patterns of utilization substitution between families, voluntary nonprofit, governmental and for-profit producers; the role of professional networks in the control system of the industry; and the impacts of demographic changes on industry structure. Longitudinal studies of a representative panel of service organizations within an industry, using several different criteria of effectiveness, and "success," would provide an opportunity to monitor the impact of these factors at an operational level.

Labor Force Studies. Human service industries are labor intensive activities, and are therefore highly dependent on personnel resources. There is a need for studies which identify societal patterns of change which may affect the availability of personnel resources. Changes in patterns of career preferences and choices, established as early as high school, may have long term consequences, particularly for those service programs dependent on technically and professionally trained personnel. For example, changes in occupational preferences among women and in patterns of financial support for students in higher education may contribute directly to future changes in the organizational structure of particular human service industries. These patterns of change point to the importance of labor force studies within particular human service industries, as well as comparative studies across different types of human service programs. Studies are also needed of the impact of shortages of specialized personnel on the relative influence of professional staff constituencies on the establishment of program objectives and procedures.

Human service programs have traditionally been a channel for upward occupational mobility for individuals from ethnic minority backgrounds. Studies are needed of the effects of changes in occupational patterns in other segments of the society on the pattern of recruitment of such individuals into particular human service programs. Other types of studies which are needed include personnel utilization studies, cohort studies of career patterns among professional specialists, patterns of recruitment into professional specializations and patterns of withdrawal, and patterns of personnel substitution when preferred specialists are not available.

Studies of Public Attitudes. This political economy analysis has pointed to the importance of communal relationship motivations in collective action. There is relatively little information, however, about the dynamics of communal motivations, as compared to economic self-interest motivations, in the support of collective action. Studies are needed of the ways in which individuals define the boundaries of their communal responsibilities, and the relative weighting which they give to different communal relationships. The studies of these issues should include different age groups, controlling for differences in gender, ethnic background, family role and pattern of childhood experience. There is also a need for detailed studies of public attitudes towards specific redistributional programs controlling for personal ideological orientations.

Studies of Service Co-production. Very little is actually known about the specific processes of service co-production as they take place in individual human service organizations. Many of the existing studies of service production methods are primarily focused on efforts to prove, or disprove, the effectiveness of specific theoretical orientations, or technologies. These studies often use quantifiable outcome measures, and take for granted the consistency of the actions of service workers with their espoused practice theories. For the purposes of policymaking and administration the greatest need is for objective qualitative field studies of specific types of service production activities. These studies need to be essentially exploratory, rather than quantitative, experimental model outcome testing studies, in which the intervention activity is not clearly specified in detail. In particular, there is a need for comparative studies across professions of similarities and differences in actual service production technologies used by different professional specialists, for example in outpatient mental health services.

There is also a need for additional information about the extent to which service production is driven by theoretical perspectives, or is primarily interactive, being adapted by service practitioners, on an ad hoc basis, to the unique characteristics and situations of individual service users. Linked to this is the need for information about the importance of supportive and motivational behaviors on the part of service staff in the effective production of various forms of human services. This is particularly important in services organized around a behavior change/social control rationale in which service staff often have a wide range of choices in the use of incentives and constraints that are intended to reinforce the motivational content of person-to-person communication.

Information is needed about similarities and differences in the perceptions which service specialists, and service users, have of the service production process and the relation between those perceptions and the degree of follow-up compliance by service users with prescriptions for behavior. This could include comparative studies involving both large-scale service organizations and decentralized service networks of small and medium-sized organizations.

Community Resource Studies. Community resource studies, including needs assessment studies, have traditionally been built around inventories of service organizations which make few distinctions as to auspice or social function. Such inventories seldom make distinctions between self-contained program components, and service components which are a specialized element within a complex service delivery system. For-profit firms, and informally organized volunteer activities, are usually not included either as part of the existing inventory of services or as a potential part of future developments.

Community surveys often ask respondents to identify "needs," without the consideration of the characteristics of alternative auspices, or other factors that may directly affect the actual "demand" by these persons for specific services. Alternatively, community leaders may be asked to assign priority ratings among a set of service organizations, ignoring the diversity of program components that are often included in a single organization.

This analysis suggests that a more relevant approach would begin with a mapping of major service delivery systems, identification of existing organizational resources by auspice including for-profit firms, and by functional category of service for each program component, followed by a market analysis which uses information from existing service organizations to identify which segments of the community are being served by which service components. The result could be a more useful mapping of gaps in the current service production pattern, and a framework for explicitly targeting survey instruments to particular user constituencies. Such studies might indicate that the priority "need" in a particular service delivery system, for example, recognized by potential users but not by the public at large, is for a facilitating service, like transportation, rather than for additional service production capacity.

These suggested approaches to community studies could produce a relevant set of policy and program alternatives for priority evaluation by a variety of stakeholder groups, such as policymakers and persons in community leadership positions, persons who control funding resources, potential user constituencies, executives and professional specialists, and community members-at-large.

Evaluation Studies. Program evaluation studies have traditionally focused on single organizations, their production processes and their outputs. However, service effectiveness *outcomes* for the service user are often dependent on a series of related services provided by program components in different organizations. In these instances it is the interorganizational service delivery system which is the relevant unit of investigation (Hjern and Porter 1981). Service delivery system evaluation, in turn, requires the ability to monitor service users through the system over time, making use of common diagnostic definitions and common definitions of service units.

Meaningful evaluation studies of human service programs require recognition of the diversity of "stakeholders" involved in any given service program, each with a different view of program objectives. The outcome of "stakeholder" evaluation studies may thus be a series of assessments, reflecting very different perspectives. Among the important distinctions to be included in such studies are those between the "public good" objectives of persons who control legitimation and funding, the "public good" objectives of professional staff personnel, and the "private good" objectives of service users. Given the pattern of co-production in service production and the informal nature of many of the service-facilitating linkages in service delivery systems, such systemic evaluation studies would require access to service users, as well as substantial degrees of support and cooperation from both executives and direct service workers in the key service organizations.

Studies of Human Service Executives. At the organization level considerable attention has been given recently to the behavioral patterns of executives in "successful" for-profit corporations. However, there has been little systematic study of the behavioral patterns of "successful" executives in human service organizations, or of persons in other critical organizational positions, such as program unit directors, or board chairpersons in successful voluntary nonprofit organizations. In particular, studies are needed of the patterns of involvement of such persons in the political economy environment, and their working relationships with professional specialists, studies that include both executives from a human services professional background, and those without such a background, as well as studies that cut across traditional fields of service and professional domains.

SUMMARY

During the twentieth century the United States and other postindustrial societies have been shaped primarily by the elaboration of the economy and by the development of highly visible national and international industries in electronics, transportation, communications, military equipment, etc. However, only limited attention has been given to the industry characteristics of human service industries, including social services, education and health care, which are increasingly the dominant elements in the rapidly growing "service sector" of the economy. Most of the academic and professional attention within these industries has been directed to the service production, or "direct services" level within single organizations. This chapter, on the other hand, has suggested some possible consequences that an industry-level perspective could have for administrative practice and research in human service programs.

References

Aaron, H. J. (1978). *Politics and the Professors*. Washington, D.C.: The Brookings Institution.

Abbott, G. (1941). *From Relief to Social Security: The Development of the New Social Services*. Chicago: University of Chicago Press.

Abramson, A. J. and Salamon, L. M. (1986). *The Nonprofit Sector and the New Federal Budget*. Washington, D.C.: Urban Institute.

Adams, P. (1985). "Social Policy and the Working Class." *Social Service Review* 59 (3):387-401.

Adams, W. and Brock, J. W. (1986). *The Bigness Complex*.New York: Pantheon Books.

Addams, J. (1910). *Twenty Years at Hull House*. New York: The Macmillan Company.

Addams, J. (1965). "The Objective Value of a Social Settlement." Pp. 44-61 in *The Social Thought of Jane Addams,* edited by C. Lasch. Indianapolis: Bobbs-Merrill.

Agranoff, R. and Pattaos, A. (1970). *Dimensions of Service Integration: Service Delivery, Program Linkages, Policy Management, Organizational Structure*. Human Services Monograph Series 13, Washington, D.C.: Project SHARE.

Aldrich, H. (1978). "Centralization Versus Decentralization in the Design of Human Service Delivery Systems." Pp. 51-79 in *The Management of Human Services*, edited by R. Sarri and Y. Hasenfeld. New York: Columbia University Press.

Allen, R. and Allen, P. (1974). *Reluctant Reformers: The Impact of Racism on American Social Reform Movements*. Washington, D.C.: Howard University Press.

Altschuler, A. (1970). *Community Control: The Black Demand for Participation in Large American Cities*. New York: Western Publishing.

Anderson, M. (1978). *The Political Economy of Welfare Reform in the United States*. Stanford, CA: Hoover Institution Press.

Auclaire, P. A. (1984). "Public Attitudes Towards Social Welfare Expenditures." *Social Work* 29 (2):139-145.

Austin, D. M. (1972). "Resident Participation, Political Mobilization, Or Organizational Cooptation." *Public Administration Review*. 32 (Special):409-420.

Austin, D. M. (1978). "The Politics and Organization of Services: Consolidation and Integration." *Public Welfare* 36 (3):20-28.

Austin, D. M. (1981). "The Political Economy of Social Benefit Organizations: Redistributive Services and Merit Goods." Pp. 37-88 in *Organization and the Human Services: Cross-Disciplinary Reflections*, edited by H.D. Stein. Philadelphia: Temple University Press.

245

Austin, D. M. (1983a). "The Political Economy of Human Services." *Policy and Politics.* 11 (3):343-359.

Austin, D. M. (1983b). "The Flexner Myth and the History of Social Work." *Social Service Review* 57 (3):357-377.

Austin, D. M. (1986). *A History of Social Work Education.* Austin, TX: School of Social Work, University of Texas at Austin.

Austin, D. M. and Hasenfeld, Y. (1985). "A Prefatory Essay on the Future Administration of Human Services." *Journal of Applied Behavioral Science* 21 (4):351-364.

Baltzell, E. D. (1964). *The Protestant Establishment: Aristocracy and Caste in America.* New York: Random House.

Banfield, E.C. (1970). *The Unheavenly City: The Nature and Future of Our Urban Crisis.* Boston: Little, Brown and Company.

Barclay, P. M. (1982). *Social Workers and Their Tasks.* London: Bedford Square.

Beeson, P.G. (1983). "The Bureaucratic Context of Mental Health Care." Pp. 237-250 in *Bureaucracy as a Social Problem*, edited by W.B. Litrell, G. Sjoberg and L. Zurcher. Greenwich, Conn: JAI Press.

Bell, D. (1973). *The Coming of Post Industrial Society.* New York: Basic Books.

Bell, D. (1974). "The Public Household." *The Public Interest* (37):29-68.

Bell, D. (1988). *The End of Ideology.* Cambridge, MA: Harvard University Press.

Bellah, R.N., Madsen, R., Swidler, A., Sullivan, W.M., and Tipton, S.M., *Habits of the Heart: Individualism and Commitment in American Life.* Berkeley: University of California Press.

Bendick, Jr., M. (1985). "Privatizing the Delivery of Social Welfare Services." *Working Paper No. 6—Privatization.* Project on the Federal Social Role. Washington, D.C.: National Conference on Social Welfare.

Bendick, M., Jr. and Levinson, P.M. (1984). "Private Sector Initiatives or Public-Private Partnerships?" Pp. 455-479 in *The Reagan Presidency and the Governing of America*, edited by L.M. Salamon and M.S. Lund. Washington, D.C.: The Urban Institute.

Benson, J. K. (1975). "The Interorganizational Network as a Political Economy." *Administrative Science Quarterly* 20 (2):229-249.

Benson, J. K. (1981). "Networks and Policy Sectors: A Framework for Extending Interorganizational Analysis." Pp. 137-176 in *Interorganizational Coordination*, edited by D. Roger and D. Whitten. Ames, Iowa: Iowa State University.

Bentley, G. R. (1970). *A History of the Freedmen's Bureau.* New York: Octagon.

Berger, P. L. and Neuhaus, R.J. (1977). *To Empower People: The Role of Mediating Structures in Public Policy.* Washington, D.C.: American Enterprise Institute.

Berger, P. L. and Luckman, T. (1966). *The Social Construction of Reality.* New York: Doubleday.

Berkowitz, E. and McQuaid, K. (1980). *Creating the Welfare State: The Political Economy of Twentieth Century Reform.* New York: Praeger Publishers.

Bernstein, B. J. (1968). "The New Deal: The Conservative Achievement of Liberal Reform." Pp. 263-288 in *Towards a New Past: Dissenting Essays in American History*, edited by B.J. Bernstein. New York: Pantheon Books.

Bluestone, B. and Harrison, B. (1982). *The Deindustrialization of America.* New York: Basic Books.

Bluestone, B., Murphy, W.M., and Stevenson, M. (1973). *Low Wages and the Working Poor: Policy Papers in Human Resources and Industrial Relations 22.* Ann Arbor, MI: The Institute of Labor and Industrial Relations.

Boothby, D. W. (1984). *The Determinants of Earnings and Occupation for Young Women.* New York: Garland.

Boulding, K. E. (1973). *The Economy of Love and Fear: A Preface to Grants Economy.* Belmont, CA: Wadsworth Publishing.

Brace, C. L. (1872). *The Dangerous Classes of New York and Twenty Years Work Among Them.* New York: Wynkoop & Hallenbeck.

Brandt, L. (1942). *Growth and Development of the AICP and COS.* New York: Community Service Society of New York.

Breckinridge, S. (1927). *Public Welfare Administration.* Chicago: University of Chicago Press.

Bremmer, R. H. (1980). *The Public Good: Philanthropy and Welfare in the Civil War Era.* New York: Alfred A. Knopf.

Brewer, C. and Lait, J. (1980). *Can Social Work Survive?* London: Temple Smith.

Brooks, H., Liebman, L., and Schelling, C.S. (1984). *Public-Private Partnership: New Opportunities for Meeting Social Needs.* Cambridge, MA: Ballinger Publishing.

Brown, D. S. (1982). *Managing the Large Organization: Issues, Ideas, Precepts, Innovations.* Mt. Airy, MD: Lomond Books.

Bruno, F. J. (1957). *Trends in Social Work 1874-1956: A History Based on the Proceedings of the National Conference of Social Work, Second Edition.* New York: Columbia University Press.

Buchanan, J. M. and Tullock, G. (1962). *The Calculus of Consent: Logical Foundations of Constitutional Democracy.* Ann Arbor: University of Michigan Press.

Buell, B. and Associates. (1958). *Community Planning for Human Services.* New York: Columbia University Press.

Burt, M. R. and Pittman, K. J. (1985). *Testing the Social Safety Net.* Washington, D.C.: Urban Institute.

Caplan, R. (1969). *Psychiatry and the Community in Nineteenth Century America.* New York: Basic Books.

Cates, J. (1982). *Insuring Inequality: Administrative Leadership in Social Security.* Ann Arbor: University of Michigan Press.

Cerny, P.G. and Schain, M. A. (1985). *Socialism, the State and Public Policy in France.* New York: Methuen.

Chambers, C. A. (1963). *Seedtime of Reform: American Social Service and Social Action, 1918-1933.* Minneapolis: University of Minnesota Press.

Chambers, C. A and Hinching, A. (1968). "Charity Workers, The Settlements and the Poor." *Social Casework,* 49 (2) 96-101.

Cherniss, C. (1980). *Professional Burnout in Human Service Organizations.* New York: Praeger.

Christian, W. P. and Hannah, G. T. (1983). *Effective Management in Human Services.* Englewood Cliffs, NJ: Prentice-Hall.

Clark, K. B. (1965). *Dark Ghetto: Dilemmas of Social Power.* New York: Harper and Row.

Clark, K. B. and Hopkins, J. (1969). *A Relevant War Against Poverty: A Study of Community Action Programs and Observable Community Change.* New York: Harper and Row.

Cloward, R. and Epstein, I. (1965). "Private Welfare's Disengagement from the Poor: The Case of Family Adjustment Agencies." Pp. 623-643 in *Social Welfare Institutions,* edited by M.N. Zald. New York: Wiley.

Cohen, M. R. (1931). *Reason and Nature, An Essay on the Meaning of Scientific Method.* New York: Harcourt, Brace.

Coit, S. (1891). *Neighborhood Guilds: An Instrument of Social Reform.* London: S. Sonnenschein and Company.

Commager, H. S. (ed.) (1969). *Lester Ward and the Welfare State.* Indianapolis: Bobbs-Merrill.

Conference of Catholic Bishops, (1986). *U.S. Bishops Pastoral Letter on Catholic Social Teaching and the U.S. Economy.* Washington, D.C.

Coser, L. A. (1972). "Marxist Thought in the First Quarter of the 20th Century." *American Journal of Sociology* 78 (1):173-201.

Cross, R.D. (ed.) (1967). *The Church and the City, 1865-1910.* Indianapolis: Bobbs-Merrill.

Crossman, R. (ed.) (1952). *New Fabian Essays.* London: Turnstile Press.

Cutlip S.M. (1965). *Fund Raising in the United States: Its Role in American Philanthropy.* New Brunswick, NJ: Rutgers University Press.

Cyert, R. M. (1975). *The Management of Nonprofit Organizations.* Lexington, MA: D.C. Heath.

Dahlberg, J. S. (1966). *The New York Bureau of Municipal Research: Pioneer in Government Administration.* New York: New York University Press.

Davis H. and Scase, R. (1985). *Western Capitalism and State Socialism.* New York: Basil Blackwell.

Davis, A. (1967). *Spearheads for Reform: The Social Settlements and The Progressive Movement 1890-1914.* New York: Oxford University Press.

Davis, K. E. (1975). *Fund Raising in the Black Community: History, Feasibility and Conflict.* Metuchen, NJ: Scarecrow Press.

Dawson, W. H. (1912). *Social Insurance in Germany, 1882-1911.* London: Unwin.

deForest, R. and Veiller, L. (1962). "The Tenement House Problem." Pp. 98-132 in *The Progressive Years: The Spirit of Achievement of American Reform,* edited by O. Pease. New York: George Braziller.

Derthick, M. (1970). *The Influence of Federal Grants.* Cambridge, MA: Harvard University Press.

Derthick, M. (1975). *Uncontrolled Spending for Social Service Grants.* Washington, D.C.: Brookings Institution.

Dexter, W. F. (1932). *Herbert Hoover and American Individualism: A Modern Interpretation of a National Ideal.* New York: The Macmillan Company.

Diner, S. J. (1970). "Chicago Social Workers and Blacks in the Progressive Era." *Social Service Review* 44 (4):393-410.

Downs, A. (1957). *An Economic Theory of Democracy.* New York: Harpers.

Duncan, G. J. and Ponza, M. (1987). Public Attitudes Toward the Structure of Income Maintenance Programs. Ann Arbor, MI: University of Michigan Survey Research Center. Unpublished paper.

Ehrenreich, J. H. (1985). *The Altruistic Imagination: A History of Social Work and Social Policy in the United States.* Ithaca, NY: Cornell.

Feldstein, M. (1985). "The Social Security Explosion." *The Public Interest.* (81):94-106.

Ferman, L.A. (ed.) (1984). "The Future of American Unionism." *The Annals of the American Academy of Political and Social Science.* 473 (May).

Ferris, J. and Graddy E. (1986). "Contracting out: For What? With Whom?" *Public Administration Review,* 46 (4):332-344.

Fish, V. K. (1985). "Hull House: Pioneer in Urban Research During Its Creative Years." *History of Sociology* 61 (1):33-54.

Fisher, J. (1980). *The Response of Social Work to the Depression.* Cambridge, MA: Schenkman.

Fox, D. (1967). *The Discovery of Abundance: Simon N. Patten and the Transformation of Social Theory.* New York: Cornell University Press.

Frieden, B. J. and Kaplan, M. (1975). *The Politics of Neglect: Urban Aid from Model Cities to Revenue Sharing.* Cambridge, MA: MIT Press.

Frieden, B. J. and Morris M. (eds.) (1968). *Urban Planning and Social Policy.* New York: Basic Books.

Friedman, M. (1962). *Capitalism and Freedom.* Chicago: University of Chicago Press.

Fuchs, V. R. (1968). *The Service Economy.* New York: National Bureau of Economic Research.

Galbraith, J. K. (1960). *The Affluent Society.* Boston: Houghton Mifflin.

Galper, J. H. (1975). *The Politics of Social Services.* Englewood Cliffs, NJ: Prentice-Hall.

Garraty, J. (1978). *Unemployment in History: Economic Thought and Public Policy.* New York: Harper and Row.

Gerth, H. H. and Mills, C. W. (1958). *From Max Weber: Essays in Sociology.* New York: Oxford University Press.

Gil, D. G. (1976). *The Challenge of Social Equality: Essays on Social Policy, Social Development and Political Practice.* Cambridge, MA: Schenkman.

Gilbert, N. (1983). *Capitalism and the Welfare State: Dilemmas of Social Benevolence.* New Haven: Yale University Press.

Gilbert, N. (1985). "The Commercialization of Social Welfare." *Journal of Applied Behavioral Science* 21 (4):365-376.

Gilbert, N. (1986). "The Welfare State Adrift." *Social Work* 31 (4):251-256.

Gilder, G. (1981). *Wealth and Poverty.* New York: Basic Books.

Ginzberg, E. and Vojta, G. J. (1981). "The Service Sector of the U.S. Economy." *Scientific American* 244, 48-55.

Glazer, N. (1983). "Towards a Self-Service Society?" *The Public Interest* (70):66-90.

Glazer, N. (1984). "The Social Policy of the Reagan Administration: A Review." *The Public Interest* (75):76-98.

Glenn, J. M., Brandt, L. and Andrews, F. E. (1947). *Russell Sage Foundation, 1907-1946.* New York: Russell Sage Foundation.

Goodin, R. E. (1985). *Protecting the Vulnerable: A Re-analysis of our Social Responsibilities.* Chicago: University of Chicago Press.

Gottschalk, S. S. (1975). *Communities and Alternatives: An Exploration of the Limits of Planning.* Cambridge, MA: Schenkman.

Gough, I., (1979). *The Political Economy of the Welfare State.* London: The Macmillan Press.

Grantham, D. W. (1983). *Southern Progressivism: The Reconciliation of Progress and Tradition.* Knoxville, TN: University of Tennessee Press.

Greenslade, R. (1976). *Goodbye to the Working Class.* London: Open Forum.

Grob, G. N. (1973). *Mental Institutions in America, Social Policy to 1875.* New York: Free Press.

Grob, G. N. (1983). *Mental Illness and American Society, 1875-1940.* Princeton: Princeton University Press.

Gronberg, K. A. (1982). Private Welfare in the Welfare State: Recent U.S. Patterns. *Social Service Review* 56 (1): 1-26.

Haar, C.M. (1975). *Between the Idea and the Reality: A Study in the Origin, Fate and Legacy of the Model Cities Program.* Boston: Little, Brown and Company.

Habermas, J. (1975). *Legitimation Crisis.* Boston: Beacon Press.

Haddow, S. and Jones, M. A. (1981). *Sources of Voluntary Agency Income 1979-1980.* New York: Child Welfare League of America, Inc.

Hadley, R. and Hatch, S. (1981). *Social Welfare and the Failure of the State: Centralised Social Services and Participatory Alternatives.* London: George Allen and Unwin.

Hagebak, B.R. (1979). "Local Human Service Delivery: The Integration Imperative." *Public Administration Review* 39 (6):595-599.

Hagen, H. and Hansen, J.E. (1978). "The Politics and Organization of Services: How the States Put the Programs Together." *Public Welfare* 36 (3):43-47.

Hale, Jr., N. G. (1971). *Freud and the Americans: The Beginnings of Psychoanalysis in the United Staes, 1876-1917.* New York: Oxford University Press.

Hall, P. (1987). "A Historical Overview of the Private Nonprofit Sector." Pp. 3-26 in *The Nonprofit Sector: A Research Handbook*, edited by W.W. Powell. New Haven: Yale University Press.

Hamilton, G. (1940). *Theory and Practice of Social Casework.* New York: Columbia University Press.

Hanaford, P. A. (1875). *The Life of George Peabody.* Augusta, Maine: E.C. Allen.

Handler, J. F. and Sosin, M. (1983). *Last Resorts: Emergency Assistance and Special Needs Programs in Public Welfare.* New York: Academic Press.

Harlan, L.R. (ed.) (1972). *The Booker T. Washington Papers.* Urbana, IL: University of Illinois Press.

Harrington, M. (1968). *Towards a Democratic Left: A radical program for a new majority.* New York: MacMillan Press.

Harris, C. .S. (1984). "The Magnitude of Job Loss from Plant Closings and the Generation of Replacement Jobs: Some Recent Evidence." *The Annals of the American Academy of Political and Social Science.* 475:15-27.

Harrison, W. D. and Hoshino, G. (1984). "Britain's Barclay Report: Lessons for the United States." *Social Work* 29 (3):213-218.

Hasenfeld, Y. (1983). *Human Service Organizations.* Englewood Cliffs, NJ: Prentice-Hall.

Hasenfeld, Y. (1986). "Community Mental Health Centers as Human Service Organizations." In *The Organization of Mental Health Services: Societal and Community Systems,* edited by W.R. Scott and B.L. Black. Beverly Hills, CA: Sage.

Hatry, H. (1983). *A Review of Private Approaches for the Delivery of Public Services.* Washington, D.C.: The Urban Institute.

Haveman, R. H. (ed.) (1977). *A Decade of Federal Antipoverty Programs.* New York: Academic Press.

Haynes, K. S. and Sallee, A. L. (1975). *An Evaluative Framework for Comparison of Selected Social Service Taxonomies.* Austin, TX: School of Social Work, University of Texas at Austin.

Hillery, G. A. (1968). *Communal Organizations: A Study of Local Societies.* Chicago: University of Chicago Press.

Himmelstrand, U., Ahrne, G., Lundberg, L., and Lundberg, L. (1981). *Beyond Welfare Capitalism: Issues, Actors and Forces in Societal Change.* London: Heinemann.

Hirschman, A. O. (1980). "The Welfare State in Trouble: Systemic Crisis or Growing Pains?" *The American Economic Review* 70 (2):113.

Hjern, B. and Porter, D.O. (1981). "Implementation Structures: A New Unit of Analysis." *Organization Studies* 2 (3):211-228.

Hochschild, J. L. (1981). *What's Fair?* Cambridge, MA: Harvard University Press.

Hollingsworth, J. R. and Hanneman, R. (1984). *Centralization and Power in Social Service Delivery Systems.* Boston: Kluwer-Nijhoff Publishing.

Hopkins, H. L. (1936). *Spending to Save: The Complete Story of Relief.* New York: W.W. Norton.

Howe, I. (1985). *Socialism and America* New York: Harcourt Brace Jovanovich.

Huggins, N. I. (1971). *Protestants Against Poverty: Boston's Charities 1870-1900.* Westport, CT: Greenwood Publishing.

Human Services Coordination Alliance (1976). *Human Services Coordination Alliance, Partnership to Improve the Delivery of Service.* Louisville, KY: Human Services Coordination Alliance.

Hutchinson, W. R. (ed.) (1968). *American Protestant Thought: The Liberal Era.* New York: Harper & Row.

Hutchinson, W. R. (1976). *The Modernist Impulse in American Protestantism.* Cambridge, MA: Harvard University Press.

Illich, I. D. (1970). *DeSchooling Society.* New York: Harper and Row.

Immerschein, A. W., Polivka, L., Gordon-Girvin, S., Chackerian, R., and Martin, P. (1986). "Service Networks in Florida: An Analysis of Administrative Decentralizaton and Its Effects on Service Delivery." *Public Administration Review* 46 (2):161-169.

Janowitz, M. (1978). *The last Fifty Years: Societal Change and Politics in the United States.* Chicago: University of Chicago Press.

Judge, K. (1981). "State Pensions and the Growth of Social Welfare Expenditure." *Journal of Social Policy* 10 (4):503-530.

Kahn, A.J. (1969). *Theory and Practice of Social Planning.* New York: Russell Sage.

Kaplan, B. J. (1978). "Reformers and Charity: The Abolition of Public Outdoor Relief in New York City, 1870-1898." *Social Service Review* 52 (2):202-210.

Kellogg, C. D. (1893). "Charity Organization in the United States." *Proceedings of the National Conference of Charities and Correction, 1893.* Boston: George H. Ellis Press.

Kirschner, D. S. (1986). *The Paradox of Professionalism: Reform and Public Service in Urban America, 1900-1940.* Westport, CT: Greenwood Press.

Klein, P. (1968). *From Philanthrophy to Social Welfare.* San Francisco, CA: Jossey-Bass.

Knapp, D. and Polk, K. (1971). *Scouting the War on Poverty: Reform Policies in the Kennedy Administration.* Lexington, MA: D.C. Heath.

Knight, K. and McDaniel, R. (1979). *Organization Theory—An Information Systems Perspective.* Belmont, CA: Wadsworth.

Koldarie, T. (1986). "Two Different Concepts of Privatization." *Public Administration Review* 46 (4):285-291.

Kolko, G. (1963). *The Triumph of Conservatism: A Reinterpretation of American History, 1900-1916.* New York: The Free Press.

Kramer, R. M. (1985). "The Future of the Voluntary Agency in a Mixed Economy." *Journal of Applied Behavioral Science* 21 (4): 377-392.

Kramer, R. M. (1969). *Participation of the Poor: Comparative Community Case Studies in the War on Poverty.* Englewood Cliffs, NJ: Prentice-Hall.

Kurzman, P. (1974). *Harry Hopkins and the New Deal.* Fairlawn, NJ: Burdick.

Kuttner, R. (1984). *The Economic Illusion: False Choices between Prosperity and Social Justice.* Boston: Houghton Mifflin.

Lasch, C. (ed.) (1965). *The Social Thought of Jane Addams.* Indianapolis: Bobbs-Merrill.

Lee, P.R. (1937). *Social Work as Cause and Function, and Other Papers.* New York: Columbia University Press.

Leiby, J. (1978). *A History of Social Welfare and Social Work in the United States.* New York: Columbia University Press.

Leiby, J. (1984). "Charity Organization Reconsidered." *Social Service Review* 58 (4):523-538.

Leif, A. (ed.) (1948). *The Commonsense Psychiatry of Dr. Adolf Meyer: Fifty-Two Selected Papers.* New York: McGraw-Hill.

Leighninger, L. H. (1981). *The Development of Social Work as a Professison, 1930-1960.* Berkeley, CA: University of California, Berkeley, Dissertation.

Lens, S. (1966). *Radicalism in America.* New York: Thomas Y. Crowell.

Lens, S. (1969). *Poverty: America's Enduring Paradox, A History of the Richest Nation's Unwon War.* New York: Thomas Y. Crowell.

Levitan, S. (1969). *The Great Society's Poor Law: A New Approach to Poverty.* Baltimore: The Johns Hopkins Press.

Lippman, W. (1937). *An Inquiry into the Principles of the Good Society.* Boston: Little, Brown and Company.

Lipsky, M. (1980). *Street-Level Bureaucracy: Dilemmas of the Individual in Public Services.* New York: Russell Sage Foundation.

Lloyd, G. A. (1971). *Charities, Settlements and Social Work: An Inquiry into Philosophy and Method, 1890-1915.* New Orleans: Tulane University School of Social Welfare.

Lovell, C. and Tobin, C. (1981). "The Mandate Issue." *Public Administration Review* 41 (3):319-320.

Lowell, J.S. (1884). *Public Relief and Private Charity.* New York: G.P. Putnam's Sons.

Lowi, T. (1969). *The End of Liberalism.* New York: W.W. Norton.

Lubove, R. (1962). *The Progressives and the Slums: Tenement House Reform in New York City, 1890-1917.* Pittsburgh: University of Pittsburgh Press.

Lubove, R. (1965). *The Professional Altruist: The Emergence of Social Work as a Career, 1880-1930.* Cambridge, MA: Harvard University Press.

Lubove, R. (1968). *The Struggle for Social Security, 1900-1935.* Cambridge: Harvard University Press.

Lundberg, E. O. (1928). "Progress of Mothers' Aid Administration." *Social Service Review* 2 (3):435-458.

Macarov, D. (1970). *Incentives to Work*. San Francisco, CA: Jossey-Bass.

Malthus, T. (1958). *Essay on Population*. London: Dent.

Martin, P. Y. (1985). "Multiple Constituencies, Dominant Societal Values and the Human Service Administrator: Implications for Service Delivery." Pp. 72-84 in *Social Administration: The Management of the Social Services, Second Edition, Vol 1*. edited by S. Slavin. New York: Haworth Press.

Marty, M.E. (1980). "Social Services: Godly and Godless." *Social Service Review*. 54 (4):463-481.

Marx, K. (1968). *Theories of Surplus Value*. Moscow: Progress Publishers.

Marx, K. (1972). *Capital*. London: Lawrence & Wishart.

Masschusetts Taxpayers Foundation (1980). *Purchase of Service: Can State Government Gain Control?* Boston: Massachusetts Taxpayers Foundation, Inc.

Matusow, A. J. (1984). *The Unraveling of America: A History of Liberalism in the 1960s*. New York: Harper and Row.

Mayer, R. R. and Greenwood, E. (1980). *The Design of Social Policy Research*. Englewood Cliffs, NJ: Prentice-Hall.

Meier, E. (1954). *A History of the New York School of Social Work*. New York: Columbia University Press.

Mencher, S. (1967). *Poor Law to Poverty Program: Economic Security Policy in Britain and the United States*. Pittsburgh: Unviersity of Pittsburgh Press.

Milward, H. B. and Francisco, R. A. (1983). "Subsystem Politics and Corporatism in the United States." *Policy and Politics* 11:273-293.

Minton, M. H. with Block J. L. (1984). *What is a Wife Worth?* New York: Morrow.

Mintz, B. and Schwartz, M. (1986). *The Power Structure of American Business*, Chicago: University of Chicago Press.

Morris, Jr. J. A. and Ozawa, M. N. (1985). "Benefit-Cost Analysis and Social Service Agency: A Model for Decision Making." Pp. 80-93 in *Social Administration: The Managment of the Social Services. Second Edition, Vol II* edited by S. Slavin. New York: Haworth Press.

Morris, R. (1986). *Rethinking Social Welfare: Why Care for the Stranger?* New York: Longman.

Morris, R. and Rein, M. (1968). "Emerging Patterns in Community Planning." Pp. 23-38 *Urban Planning and Social Policy*, edited by B.J. Frieden and R. Morris. New York: Basic Books.

Moss, K. (1984). "Institutional Reform Through Litigation." *Social Service Review*, 58 (3):421-433.

Moynihan, D. P. (1969). *Maximum Feasible Misunderstanding*. New York: The Free Press.

Mullen, E. J. and Dumpson, J. R. (eds.) (1972). *Evaluation of Social Intervention*. San Francisco: Jossey-Bass.

Murray, C. A. (1984). *Losing Ground: American Social Policy 1950-1980*. New York: Basic Books.

Musgrave, R. A. (1959). *The Theory of Public Finance*. New York: McGraw-Hill.

Neugeboren, B. (1985). *Organization, Policy and Practice in the Human Services*. New York: Longman.

Novak, M. (1982). *The Spirit of Democratic Capitalism*. New York: Simon and Schuster.

Offe, C. (1984). *Contradictions of the Welfare State*. Cambridge, MA: MIT Press.

Olson, L. K. (1982). *The Political Economy of Aging: The State, Private Power, and Social Welfare*. New York: Columbia University Press.

Olson, M. ((1965). *The Logic of Collective Action*. Cambridge, MA: Harvard University Press.

Orfield, G. (1985). "Race and the Federal Agenda: The Loss of the Integrationist Dream, 1965-1974." *Working Paper No. 7-Race and Policy*. Project on the Federal Social Role. Washington, D.C.: National Conference on Social Welfare.

Ostrander, S. A. (1985). "Voluntary Social Service Agencies in the United States." *Social Service Review* 59 (3):435-454.

Ostrom, V. and Ostrom, E. (1978). "Public Goods and Public Choices." Pp. 7-49 in *Alternatives for Delivering Public Goods: Towards Improved Performance,* edited by E. S. Savas. Boulder, CO: Westview.

Ostrom, E., Parks, R. B. and Whitaker, G. P. (1978). *Patterns of Metropolitan Policing.* Cambridge, MA: Ballinger Publishing.

Ouchi, W. G. (1978). "Coupled versus Uncoupled Control in Organizational Hierarchies." Pp. 264-289 in *Environments and Organizations.* edited by M. W. Meyer and Associates. San Francisco: Jossey-Bass.

Palmer, J. L. and Sawhill, I. V. (1982). *The Reagan Experiment.* Washington, D.C.: Urban Institute.

Parks, R. B. and Ostrom, E. (1981). "Developing and Testing Complex Models of Urban Service Systems." Pp. 171-191 in *Urban Policy Analysis: Directions for Future Research. Urban Affairs Annual Reviews, Vol 21.* edited by T. N. Clark. Beverly Hills, CA: Sage.

Pfeffer, J. (1978). "The Micro Politics of Organizations." Pp. 29-50 in *Environments and Organizations.* edited by M. W. Meyer and Associates. San Francisco: Jossey-Bass.

Philpott, T. L. (1978). *The Slum and the Ghetto, Chicago 1880-1930.* New York: Oxford University Press.

Pittman-Munke, P. (1985). *Mary Richmond and the Wider Social Movement, Phildelphia 1900-1909.* Austin, TX: University of Texas at Austin Dissertation.

Pittman-Munke, P. (1986). "Catholic Social Work 1910-1925." *Charities USA,* 13 (9, 10):8-10, 25-30.

Piven, F. F. and Cloward, R. A. (1971). *Regulating the Poor: The Functions of Public Welfare.* New York: Random House.

Piven, F. F. and Cloward, R. A. (1982). *The New Class War.* New York: Pantheon Books.

Platt, A. M. (1969). *The Child Savers: The Invention of Delinquency.* Chicago: University of Chicago Press.

Plattner, M. F. (1979). "The Welfare State vs. the Redistributive State." *The Public Interest,* (55):28-48.

Poole, D. L. (1985). "The Future of Public-Private Sector Partnerships for the Provision of Human Services: Problems and Possibilities." *Journal of Applied Behavioral Science,* 21 (4):393-406.

Porter, D. O. and Warner, D. C. (1973). "How Effective are Grantor Controls: The Case of Federal Aid to Education." Pp. 276-302 in *Transfers in an Urbanized Economy.* edited by K. E. Boulding, M. Pfaff and A. Pfaff. Belmont, CA: Wadsworth Publishing.

Potuchek, J. L. (1986). "The Context of Social Service Funding: The Funding Relationship." *Social Service Review* 60 (3):421-436.

Powell, D. M. (1986). "Managing Organizational Problems in Alternative Service Organizations." *Administration in Social Work* 10 (3):57-70.

Powell, W. W. (1987). *The Nonprofit Sector: Research Handbook.* New Haven: Yale University Press.

Preston, S. H. (1984). "Children and the Elderly in the U.S." *Scientific American.* 251:44-49.

Rabinowitz, H. S., Simmeth, B. R. and Spero, J. R. (1979). "The Future of the United Way." *Social Service Review* 53 (2):275-284.

Rainey, H. G., Backoff, R. W., and Levine, C. H. (1976). "Comparing Public and Private Organizations." *Public Administration Review* 36 (2):233-244.

Rauch, J. (1975). "Women in Social Work: Friendly Visitors in Philadelphia, 1880." *Social Service Review.* 49 (2):241-259.

Rauschenbusch, W. (1907). *Christianity and the Social Crisis.* New York: The Macmillan Company.

Rawls, J. (1971). *A Theory of Justice.* Cambridge, MA: Harvard University Press.

Reich, R. B. (1983). *The Next American Frontier.* New York: Times Books.

Reichert, K. (1977). "The Drift Towards Entrepreneurialism in Health and Social Welfare: Implications for Social Work Education." *Administration in Social Work*, 1 (2):123-133.

Rein M. (1983a). "The Social Policy of the Firm." Pp. 3-22 in *From Policy to Practice*. edited by M. Rein. Armonk, NY: M. E. Sharpe.

Rein, M. (1983b). "Claims, Claiming, and Claim Structures." Pp. 23-39 in *From Policy to Practice*, edited by M. Rein. Armonk, NY: M. E. Sharpe.

Rein, M. and Rainwater, L. (eds.) (1986). *Public/Private Interplay in Social Protection*. Armonk, NY: M. E. Sharpe.

Reskin, B. J. (1984). *Sex Segregation in the Workplace: Trends, Explanations*. Washington, D.C.: National Academy Press.

Reznek, W. (1953). "Unemployment, Unrest and Relief in the United States During the Depression of 1893-1897." *Journal of Political Economy*, 61 (4):324-345.

Ricardo, D. (1971). *Principles of Political Economy and Taxation*. Harmondsworth: Penguin Books.

Richmond, M. E. (1897). "The Need of a Training School in Applied Philanthrophy." *Proceedings of the National Conference of Charities and Correction, 1897*. Boston: George H. Ellis.

Richmond, M. E. (1899). *Friendly Visiting Among the Poor: A Handbook for Charity Workers*. New York: The Macmillan Company.

Richmond M. E. (1930). "Motherhood and Pensions." Pp. 350-364 in *The Long View: Papers and Addresses of Mary E. Richmond*. edited by J. Colcord and R. Mann. New York: Russell Sage Foundation.

Robinson, V. (1930). *A Changing Psychology in Social Case Work*. Chapel Hill, N.C.: University of North Carolina Press.

Rochefort, D. A. (1981). "Progressive and Social Control Perspectives On Social Welfare." *Social Service Review*. 55 (4):568-592.

Rose, S. (1972). *The Betrayal of the Poor: The Transformation of Community Action*. Cambridge: Schenkmen Publishing.

Rose-Ackerman, S. (1986). *The Economics of Nonprofit Institutions*. New Haven: Yale University Press.

Rosenthal, M. G. (1986). "The Children's Bureau and the Juvenile Court: Delinquency Policy, 1912-1940." *Social Service Review*. 60 (2):303-318.

Rothman, D.J. (1971). *The Discovery of the Asylum: Social Order and Disorder in the New Republic*. Boston: Little, Brown and Company.

Rubinow, I. M. (1913). *Social Insurance*. New York: Henry Holt & Co.

Sabrosky, A. N., Thompson, J. C., and McPherson, K. A. (1983). "Organized Anarchies: Military Bureaucracy in the Future." Pp. 37-53 in *Bureaucracy As a Social Problem*, edited by W. B. Lithell, G. Sjoberg and L. A. Zurcher. Greenwich, CT: JAI Press.

Savas, E. S. (1982). *Privatizing the Public Sector*. Chatham, N.J.: Chatham House.

Schlesinger, A.M. (1957). *The Crisis of the Old Order*. Boston: Houghton Mifflin Company.

Schulter, D. B. (1979-80). "Economics and the Sociology of Consumption: Simon Patten and Early Academic Sociology in America, 1894-1904." *Journal of the History of Sociology* 2 (1):132-161.

Schuman, H., Steh, C., and Bobo, L. (1986). *Racial Attitudes in America: Trends and Interpretations*. Cambridge, MA: Harvard University Press.

Schwartz, J. E. (1983). *America's Hidden Success: A Reassessment of Twenty Years of Public Policy*. New York: W. W. Norton.

Scott, W. R. and Black, B. L. (1986). *The Organization of Mental Health Services: Societal and Community Systems*. Beverly Hills, CA: Sage.

Sennett, R. and Cobb, J. (1972). *Hidden Injuries of Class*. New York: Knopf.

Silberman, C. E. (1964). *Crisis in Black and White*. New York: Random House.

Simon, J. (1987). "The Tax Treatment of Nonprofit Organizations." Pp. 67-98 in *The Nonprofit Sector: A Research Handbook*. edited by W. W. Powell. New Haven: Yale University.

Smith, A. (1884). "Volunteer Visiting: The Organization Necessary to Make It Effective." *Proceedings, National Conference of Charities and Correction, 1884*.Boston: George H. Ellis.

Smith, A. (1937). *An Inquiry into the Nature and Causes of the Wealth of Nations*. New York: Modern Library.

Smith, P. (1966). *As a City Upon a Hill*. New York: Knopf.

Sowell, T. (1983). *Economics and the Politics of Race: An International Perspective*. New York: W. Morrow.

Spivey, W. A. (1985). "Problems and Paradoxes in Economic and Social Policies of Modern Welfare States." *Annuals of the American Academy of Political and Social Sciences*. 479:14-30.

Starr, P. (1985). "The Meaning of Privatization," in *Working Paper 6 - Privatization*. Washington, D.C.: National Conference on Social Welfare.

Steiner, G. V. (1966). *Social Insecurity: The Politics of Welfare*. Washington, D.C.: Brookings Institution.

Steiner, J. F. (1925). *Community Organization: A Study of Its Theory and Current Practice*. New York: The Century Co.

Stewart, W. R. (ed.) (1911). *The Philanthropic Work of Josephine Shaw Lowell*. New York: The Macmillan Company.

Stoesz, D. (1986). "Corporate Welfare: The Third Stage of Welfare in the United States." *Social Work* 31 (4):245-250.

Stone, D. A. (1984). *The Disabled State*. Philadelphia: Temple University Press.

Sullivan, W. M. (1982). *Reconstructing Public Philosophy*. Berkeley: University of California Press.

Taylor, J. B. (1983). "Bureaucratic Structure and Personality: The Merton Model Revisited." Pp. 151-171 in *Bureaucracy as a Social Problem*, edited by W.B. Litrell, G. Sjoberg and L.A. Zurcher. Greenwich CT: JAI Press.

Taylor-Gooby, P. and Dale, J. (1981). *Social Theory and Social Welfare*. London: Edward Arnold.

Taylor-Owen, S. J. (1986). *The History of the Profession of Social Work: A Second Look*. Waltham, MA: Brandeis University, Dissertation.

Theobold, R. (1986). *The Guaranteed Income: Next Step in Economic Evolution?* Garden City, NY: Doubleday.

Thompson, A. W. (1967). "American Socialism and the Russian Revolution of 1905-1906." Pp. 203-227 in *Freedom and Reform: Essays in Honor of Henry Steele Commager*, edited by H.M. Hyran and L.W. Levy. New York: Harper & Row.

Thurow, L. (1980). *The Zero-Sum Society: Distribution and the Possibilities for Economic Change*. New York: Basic Books.

Titmuss, R. M. (1970). *The Gift Relationship*. London: George Allen and Unwin.

Titmuss, R. (1975). *Social Policy*. New York: Pantheon.

Tobin, G. A. (ed.) (1985). *Social Planning and Human Service Delivery in the Voluntary Sector*. Westport, CT: Greenwood Press.

Tocqueville, A. de (1968). "Memoir on Pauperism" in Seymour, D. (trans. and ed.) *Tocqueville and Beaumont on Social Reform*. New York: Harper & Row.

Tolander, J. A. (1973). "The Response of Settlements to the Great Depression." *Social Work* 18 (5):92-103.

Trattner, W. I. (1979). *From Poor Law to Welfare State: A History of Social Welfare, Second Edition*. New York: Free Press.

Tullock, G. (1985). *The Politics of Bureaucracy*. Washington, D.C.: Public Affairs Press.

United Way of America (1976). *UWASIS II: A Taxonomy of Social Goals and Human Services.* Alexandria, VA: United Way of America.

Wade, L. C. (1964). *Graham Taylor, Pioneer for Justice, 1851-1938.* Chicago: University of Chicago Press.

Waite, F.T. (1960). *A Warm Friend for the Spirit.* Cleveland: Family Service Association.

Wald, L. D. (1895). "Nurses in 'Settlement Work'" *Proceedings, National Conference of Charities and Correction, 1895.* Pp. 264-267 Boston: George Ellis.

Walmsley, G. and Zald, M. N. (1973). *The Political Economy of Public Organizations.* Lexington, MA: D.C. Heath.

Warner, D. C. (ed.) (1977). *Towards new human rights: the social policies of the Kennedy and Johnson administrations.* Austin, TX: Lyndon B. Johnson School of Public Affairs, University of Texas at Austin.

Warren, R.L., Rose, S., and Burgunder, A. (1974). *The Structure of Urban Reform: Community Decision Organizations in Stability and Change.* Lexington, MA: Lexington Books.

Webb, S. and Webb, B. (1920). *A Constitution for the Socialist Commonwealth of Great Britain.* New York: Longmans, Green.

Weil, M. and Karls, J. M. (1985). *Case Management in Human Service Practice.* San Francisco: Jossey-Bass.

Weinstein, J. (1968). *The Corporate Ideal in the Liberal State, 1900-1918.* Boston: Beacon Press.

Weisbrod, B. A. (1977). *The Voluntary Nonprofit Sector.*Lexington, MA: D.C. Heath.

Weiss, N. J. (1974). *The National Urban League 1910-1940.* New York: Oxford University Press.

Westby, D. L. (1966). "The Civic Sphere in the American City." *Social Forces* 45 (2):161-169.

Wholey, J. S. (1983). *Evaluation and Effective Management.* Boston: Little, Brown and Company.

Wilensky H. and Lebeaux, C. (1965). *Industrial Society and Social Welfare, 2nd Edition.* New York: Free Press.

Williams, N., Sjoberg, G., and Sjoberg, A. F. (1983). "The Bureaucractic Personality: A Second Look." Pp. 173-189 in *Bureaucracy as a Social Problem*, edited by W.B. Litrell, W.B. Sjoberg and L.A. Zurcher. Greenwich, CT: JAI Press.

Williams, W. (1980). *The Implementation Perspective.* Berkeley, CA: University of California Press.

Wilson, E. O. (1978). "Altruism." *Harvard Magazine,* (Nov-Dec 1978): 23-28.

Wilson, W. J. (1985). "Cycle of Deprivation and the Underclass Debate." *Social Service Review.* 59 (4):541-559.

Withhorn, A. (1984). *Serving the People: Social Services and Social Change* New York: Columbia University Press.

Woods, E. M. (1929). *Robert A. Woods: Champion of Democracy.* Boston: Houghton Mifflin Co.

Zald, M. N. (1978). "On the Social Control of Industries." *Social Forces* 57:79-102.

Zurcher, L. and Snow, D. (1981). "Collective Behavior: Social Movements." Pp. 447-482 in *Social Psychology: Sociological Perspectives,* edited by M. Rosenberg. New York: Basic Books.

INDEX